# THE ECONOMICS OF JOHN RAE

John Rae wrote on a number of scientific subjects, but it is for his contribution to economics that he is best remembered. Although Rae was held in high esteem by some of the great names from the past who have openly acknowledged his originality and their indebtedness to him, he has not yet received all the attention he deserves. This collection of essays by respected economists redresses the general neglect of Rae as a classical economist, and examines his role as a political economist.

The contributions to the volume are presented in four sections:

- John Rae's life and works.
- Issues of methodology and history.
- Capital and related issues.
- Rae's contributions to the development of economic ideas in the history of economic thought.

They assess Rae's main contributions to economics in the areas of economic methodology, history of technology, conspicuous consumption, the theory of capital and technical change, the demand for and supply of capital, saving and interest in the theory of accumulation, monetary theory, international trade and public policy.

*The Economics of John Rae* is a much-needed evaluation of the work of an important economist, and will stimulate further study by historians of economic thought and methodology.

**O.F. Hamouda** is Professor of Economics at York University, Toronto, Ontario. **C. Lee** is Professor of Economics at the University of Aberdeen. **D. Mair** is Professor of Economics at Heriot-Watt University, Edinburgh.

# ROUTLEDGE STUDIES IN THE HISTORY OF ECONOMICS

1. ECONOMICS AS LITERATURE
*Willie Henderson*

2. SOCIALISM AND MARGINALISM IN ECONOMICS 1870–1930
*Edited by Ian Steedman*

3. HAYEK'S POLITICAL ECONOMY
The Socio-economics of Order
*Steve Fleetwood*

4. ON THE ORIGINS OF CLASSICAL ECONOMICS
Distribution and Value from William Petty to Adam Smith
*Tony Aspromourgos*

5. THE ECONOMICS OF JOAN ROBINSON
*Edited by Maria Cristina Marcuzzo, Luigi Pasinetti and Alesandro Roncaglia*

6. THE EVOLUTIONIST ECONOMICS OF LÉON WALRAS
*Albert Jolink*

7. KEYNES AND THE "CLASSICS"
A Study in Language, Epistemology and Mistaken Identities
*Michel Verdon*

8. THE HISTORY OF GAME THEORY, VOL. 1
From the Beginnings to 1945
*Robert W. and Mary Ann Dimand*

9. THE ECONOMICS OF W.S. JEVONS
*Sandra Peart*

10. GHANDI'S ECONOMIC THOUGHT
*Ajit K. Dasgupta*

11. EQUILIBRIUM AND ECONOMIC THEORY
*Edited by Giovanni Caravale*

12. AUSTRIAN ECONOMICS IN DEBATE
*Edited by Willem Keizer, Bert Tieben and Rudy van Zipj*

13. ANCIENT ECONOMIC THOUGHT
*B.B. Price*

14. THE POLITICAL ECONOMY OF SOCIAL CREDIT AND GUILD SOCIALISM
*Frances Hutchinson and Brian Burkitt*

15. ECONOMIC CAREERS
Economics and Economists in Britain 1930–1970
*Edited by Keith Tribe*

16. UNDERSTANDING "CLASSICAL" ECONOMICS
Studies in the long-period theory
*Heinz Kurz and Neri Salvadori*

17. HISTORY OF ENVIRONMENTAL ECONOMIC THOUGHT
*E. Kula*

18. ECONOMIC THOUGHT IN COMMUNIST AND POST-COMMUNIST EUROPE
*Hans Jurgen Wagener*

19. STUDIES IN THE HISTORY OF FRENCH POLITICAL ECONOMY
From Bodin to Walras
*Edited by Gilbert Faccarello*

20. THE ECONOMICS OF JOHN RAE
*Edited by O.F. Hamouda, C. Lee and D. Mair*

# THE ECONOMICS OF JOHN RAE

*Edited by O.F. Hamouda,*
*C. Lee and D. Mair*

ROUTLEDGE

London and New York

First published 1998
by Routledge
11 New Fetter Lane, London EC4P 4EE

Simultaneously published in the USA and Canada
by Routledge
29 West 35th Street, New York, NY 10001



Typeset in Garamond by
Florencetype Limited, Stoodleigh, Devon
Printed and bound in Great Britain by
TJ International Ltd, Padstow, Cornwall



*British Library Cataloguing in Publication Data*
A catalogue record for this book is available from the British Library

*Library of Congress Cataloguing in Publication Data*
A catalogue record for this book has been requested

ISBN 0–415–15867–2

DEDICATED TO R.W. JAMES

# CONTENTS

# CONTRIBUTORS

**Syed Ahmad** is Emeritus Professor of Economics at McMaster University, Hamilton, Ontario. His many publications include: *Capital in Economic Theory* (1991); "John Rae (1834), Schumpeter (1911) and Amsden (1989) on Technical Change and Economic Development" (1993); "Smith's Division of Labour and Rae's 'Invention'" (1996); and "On John Rae's Controversial Contributions to Economics" (1996).

**Anthony Brewer** is Professor of Economics at the University of Bristol in the United Kingdom. His many publications include the papers "John Rae's Theory of Capital and Economic Growth" (1990), and "Economic Growth and Technical Change: John Rae's Critique of Adam Smith" (1991).

**Robert W. Dimand** is Professor of Economics at Brock University, St. Catherines, Ontario. His many publications include: *The Origins of the Keynesian Revolution* (1988), "Political Protest and Political Arithmetic on the Niagara Frontier: Robert Gourlay's *Statistical Account of Upper Canada*" (1992), and "Ricardo and International Trade Theory" (1995).

**Alexander Dow** is Professor of Economics at Glasgow Caledonian University. With Sheila Dow, Alan Hutton, and Michael Keaney, he is a member of a working group dedicated to tracing the roots and legacy of a Scottish political economy tradition. The group has co-authored "Traditions in Economics: The Case of Scottish Political Economy" (1995).

**Sheila Dow** is Professor of Economics at the University of Stirling, Scotland. In addition to a large body of independent work, she is, together with Alexander Dow, Alan Hutton, and Michael Keaney, a member of the working group dedicated to tracing the roots and legacy of a Scottish political economy tradition.

**S.A. Drakopoulos** is associated to the department of Economics at the University of Aberdeen, Scotland, and to the Department of Philosophy and History of Science at the University of Athens, Greece. He is the author of *Values and Economic History* (1991).

**Michael J. Gootzeit** is Professor of Economics at the University of Memphis, Tennessee. His many publications include the paper "The Evolution of the Savings Concept" (1995), which is relevant to his contribution in this volume.

**O.F. Hamouda** is Professor of Economics at York University, Toronto, Ontario. He has published a number of works, and is co-author of *Verification in Economics and History* (Routledge, 1991), a study on the methodology of economics.

**Samuel Hollander** is Emeritus Professor of Economics at the University of Toronto, Ontario. His many publications include, *The Economics of Adam Smith* (1973), *The Economics of David Ricardo (1979)*, and *Classical Economics* (1987).

**Alan Hutton** is Lecturer in Economics at Glasgow Caledonian University, and, together with Alexander Dow, Sheila Dow, and Michael Keaney, a member of the working group dedicated to tracing the roots and legacy of a Scottish political economy tradition.

**R. Warren James**, who now lives in Ontario, is the distinguished biographer of John Rae, and was also responsible for the reissue in 1965 of Rae's *Statement of Some New Principles* and other works.

**Michael Keaney** is associated to the Department of Economics at Glasgow University, and, together with Alexander Dow, Sheila Dow, and Alan Hutton, is a member of the working group dedicated to tracing the roots and legacy of a Scottish political economy tradition.

**Anthony J. Laramie** is Professor of Economics at Merrimack College, Massachusetts. With Douglas Mair, he has co-authored several papers on a post-Keynesian Kaleckian theory of taxation and tax model, which they link with their study of John Rae in this volume.

**Clive Lee** is Professor of Economics at the University of Aberdeen. As a prominent local historian of Scotland, he has done much to promote John Rae as a "native son" of Aberdeen and to emphasize his place in the history of Marischal College and the University of Aberdeen.

**Douglas Mair** is Professor of Economics at Heriot-Watt University, Edinburgh. His keen desire to reawaken interest in John Rae is, in large part, the inspiration for this present volume. Among his published works is the paper "John Rae: Ugly Duckling or Black Swan?" (1990), and he was the editor of the volume, *The Scottish Contribution to Modern Economic Thought* (1990).

**Andrea Maneschi** is Professor of Economics at Vanderbilt University, Nashville, Tennessee. His many publications include the papers "John

Rae on Capital Theory, Inventions, Trade and Infant Industries" (1995), and "John Rae on Trade, Inventions, and Infant Industries: A Capital-Theoretic Perspective" (1998).

**Roger Mason** is Professor of Consumer Theory at the University of Salford in the United Kingdom. Among his many publications is *Conspicuous Consumption: A Study of Exceptional Consumer Behaviour* (1981).

**B.B. Price** is Visiting Professor at the Massachusetts Institute of Technology, Cambridge, Massachusetts, and Professor of History at York University, Toronto, Ontario. She has published several articles on the history of technology, and is co-author of *Verification in Economics and History* (Routledge, 1991).

**Thomas K. Rymes** is Professor of Economics at Carleton University, Ottawa, Ontario. His many publications include the paper "Technical Process, Research and Development" (1989), which is relevant to his contribution in this volume.

**Masazumi Wakatabe** is associated to the Department of Economics at the University of Toronto, Ontario, and to the Department of Economics at Waseda University, Japan. He is currently pursuing doctoral work dedicated to the study of the economics of John Rae.

# ACKNOWLEDGMENTS

The essays in this volume are the outcome of a conference that was part of the quincentenary celebration of the University of Aberdeen. The conference was held at the university on 27–29 March 1996 to mark the bicentenary of Rae's birth in Aberdeen on 1 June 1796 and to honour Rae as one of its distinguished alumni. Although the Aberdeen conference was an occasion for the group of international scholars gathered at King's College to celebrate Rae, it was also an opportunity to record appreciation of the work of R. Warren James (1965), Rae's biographer. Without James's devoted service to Rae's life and writings in Scotland and North America, Rae would not enjoy even his current rather limited recognition. Whatever the reason for the comparative neglect of Rae, James is wholly exonerated.

Rae has not yet received all the attention he deserves and a need was felt, from both the Scottish and the North American sides, to redress the general neglect of Rae as a classical economist and to access his role as a political economist. The aim in the present essays is thus to look afresh at Rae by assessing and discussing his main contributions to economics in the areas of economic methodology, history of technology, conspicuous consumption, the theory of capital and technical change, the demand for and supply of capital, saving and interest in the theory of accumulation, monetary theory, international trade, and public policy.

The editors acknowledge with gratitude financial assistance from the Scottish Economic Society towards the cost of the Rae conference. The Lord Provost and Council of the City of Aberdeen are thanked for their generous hospitality to all the conference participants in hosting a reception at the Town House. The editors also thank Alan Jarvis for his support, and his staff at Routledge and Grace Kim at MIT for editorial and production skills in bringing this collection of essays to publication.

# INTRODUCTION

To the extent Rae is known, it has been primarily for his *Statement of Some New Principles on the Subject of Political Economy Exposing the Fallacies of Free Trade and Some Other Doctrines Maintained in the "Wealth of Nations"* (1834) which contains, as well as an early strong critique of Smith's *Wealth of Nations*, the first systematic articulation of the infant industry argument for protection and a pioneering capital theory. Robbins (1968) in his *Theory of Economic Development* portrays Rae's "series of chapters on the theories of capital and invention [as] quite unique in the literature of their time, both for their originality and their insight". He describes Rae on the effects of invention and the growth of knowledge as "probably the most profound of all who have treated this subject" and on the articulation of the infant industry argument, "if we are looking for pure excellence of intellectual analysis, the palm must clearly go to John Rae" (Robbins 1968: 51, 89, 113).

John Rae was indeed a classic scholar, whose outstanding ideas earned him the praise of J.S. Mill, I. Fisher, E. Böhm-Bawerk and others. Rae's elaboration of a theory of capital was the precursor of much later theories, of Böhm-Bawerk and Fisher. Having heard about Rae's *New Principles* from Nassau Senior, John Stuart Mill read it and quoted from it at some length in his own *Principles of Political Economy* (1848). Mill compared Rae's analysis of the forces leading to the accumulation of capital with Malthus's work on population. Inspired further by Rae's carefully crafted justification of protection for infant industries and his effective rebuttal of Smith's critique of the argument, Mill also became convinced of its validity, and, through Mill's advocacy, Rae's argument entered the mainstream of economics.

Despite Mill's recognition, Rae's work was practically ignored by other classical economists and by the new generation of marginalists such as Jevons. Even the best-known pioneer of capital theory, Böhm-Bawerk, was aware of Rae only because of Mill's comments on his work, but those comments had not revealed to him that Rae's work centred on the theory of capital. When C.W. Mixter (1897: 190) pointed out that Rae "anticipated Böhm-Bawerk's theory of interest, in the substance of its leading features and in many of its details and even to a greater extent in the exact form of its expression," Böhm-Bawerk ([1884] 1900) very properly and magnanimously acknowledged his "belated recognition of Rae's highly original ideas". Irving Fisher was another latter-day admirer of Rae and dedicated his *Theory of Interest* (1930) "To the Memory of John Rae and of Eugen Von Böhm-Bawerk Who Laid the Foundations Upon Which I Have Endeavoured To Build," recognizing that "every essential part of [my own theory] was at least foreshadowed by John Rae in 1834."

Rae's influence on Schumpeter's early work is evident from *Theory of Economic Development* ([1911] 1934). The mature Schumpeter had lost none of his admiration for Rae, writing in *History of Economic Analysis* (1954: 468–9) "in vision and originality, Rae far surpassed the economists who were successful . . . For it is this that we must see in his work: another *Wealth of Nations* or, more correctly, something that with ten additional years of quiet work, graced by an adequate income, could have grown into another – and more profound – *Wealth of Nations*." The second book of Rae's *New Principles*, Schumpeter asserted, "may be called a theory of capital, conceived in unprecedented depth and breadth."

Lest it be thought that Rae's intellectual heritage is neoclassical or exclusively "Austrian," Mitchell (1934) regarded Rae as "the founding father of American institutionalism" due to his treatment of luxury expenditures and status-seeking ostentatious display. Rae made a significant contribution in this field which was to be overshadowed by Veblen's later explorations of pecuniary emulation and the formation of tastes. Veblen appears to have been rather noticeably sensitive to questions about his indebtedness to Rae.

It seems that Rae was held in high esteem by some of the great names from the past who have openly acknowledged his originality and their indebtedness to him. Yet his writings today are appreciated by only a coterie of cognoscenti. Despite James's best efforts at breathing life into Rae with his biography, and in editing and bringing to publication virtually all of his extant works, Rae's contribution has still failed to achieve the distinguished recognition which his contemporary readers felt it merits. Even in Scotland, Rae has been dismissed by Gray and Thompson (1980) as having at best offered some useful correctives to Smith's *Wealth of Nations* and having provided some ideas which were later picked up by Carey and Veblen. Macfie's (1955) much more sympathetic treatment of Rae surprisingly relegates him to the second division of Scottish political economists. Rae has not yet received all the attention he deserves.

Warren James has already done enormous research work on Rae's biography. Readers curious to learn more of the education and career of the fascinating man should turn to James (1951, 1965). Here we provide merely a brief sketch of Rae. At nineteen, he graduated with an MA from Marischal College in Aberdeen in 1815. As a student he displayed "remarkable inventive attitudes" and designed several ingenious pieces of scientific and engineering apparatus. From Aberdeen he went to Edinburgh University as a medical student and in his MD dissertation came to the conclusion that the physiological theories of his day were fundamentally false. After Edinburgh, Rae studied in Paris.

Family circumstances in Aberdeen forced Rae to emigrate with his wife from Scotland to Montreal in 1822. He shortly moved to Williamston and then later to Hamilton, in present-day Ontario, where he took up the post of village schoolmaster. He combined teaching with the practice of medicine and started to write articles on economic development for early Canadian learned journals. Rae was closely involved with the large Scottish community in Canada and was particularly associated with the Presbyterian Church of Scotland in its struggle with the Church of England to establish Scottish Presbyterian principles in education and religious practice. By the early 1830s, Rae had emerged as a leading spokesman for the Kirk and had also established a reputation as a serious thinker on the problems of economic development.

In Canada, Rae worked variously in the timber trade, as a schoolmaster and as a doctor. Later travels took him to Boston and New York as a teacher, to Central America as a doctor, to California in the 1848 Gold Rush as a teacher, to the Kingdom of Hawaii as a teacher, local judge, and medical officer, and finally back to the USA, where he died on Staten Island in 1872.

While in Canada, Rae became involved politically and aligned himself with a predominantly Scottish Presbyterian merchant faction, partly because he believed that the Presbyterian ethic had an important role to play in the development of a capital-hungry economy and partly because commercial links with Britain were of paramount importance to Canadian trade. Rae was already engaged in an extensive economic and statistical survey of Canada in the 1830s when he wrote his *New Principles*. This work was a by-product of his study of Canada and was conceived by Rae to provide a rationale for Canada's loyalty to the Crown and the Mother Country and its continuing colonial status. In 1834, Rae went to Boston to organize publication of his *New Principles*. There was in Boston at the time a vigorous protectionist lobby which was looking for an intellectual argument for protectionism as a counter to the laissez-faire liberalism of the *Wealth of Nations* which was very influential in North America. In the 1820s and 1830s, Lower Canada with its factions of French Canadians and Scottish merchants was caught up in this struggle of ideas abroad at the time in Europe and the USA. When Rae arrived from the antagonistic backwoods of Canada clutching a manuscript entitled *Statement of Some New Principles on the Subject of Political Economy Exposing the Fallacies of Free Trade and Some Other Doctrines Maintained in the "Wealth of Nations,"* he was welcomed by the protectionists with open arms.

All this can be learnt from James (1965a, vol. 1). Included in James's contribution to this collection, "Birthday Greetings to John Rae," are, however, some fascinating and hitherto unknown insights into Rae's character and personality. It seems that as a schoolmaster, Rae was held in much affection by his pupils. "He had a very loving disposition which endeared him to us all . . . he taught me rabbit, mink and muskrat trapping and other sports attractive to youth" (see p. 25). "In appearance he was tall, rather slender, and dignified" and was one of the most accomplished skaters in Hamilton whose "pupils labored diligently to master the long graceful stroke of the teacher" (Smith 1905: 14).

After being forced by religious politics to give up his career as a schoolteacher in Canada, Rae became in his own words "a wanderer and adventurer over the wide earth" (letter from Rae to H.B. Willson, December 27, 1849, quoted by James 1965a, 1: 101). At one stage, his travels took him to Hawaii where he was appalled by the efforts of the American missionaries to impose strict standards of Christian morality on the easy going sexual behaviour of the islanders. In his capacity as medical officer in Hawaii he strove manfully to control the spread of smallpox and sexual diseases, although by James's account, Rae's remedies appear to have been extremely primitive. Rae moved in the highest circles in Hawaii; on one occasion he tended the injuries from a horse-riding accident of a member of the entourage of King Kamehameha IV.

In later life, Rae's eyesight began to fail and in 1871 he accepted the invitation of his former student and benefactor, Sir Roderick Cameron, to live with him on his estate on Staten Island. Rae died there in 1872, and his gravesite on Staten Island is currently overgrown with weeds and bushes.

## The economics of John Rae

Undoubtedly Rae's approach to economics was influenced most prominently by his residence in Canada during the writing of his principal economic work, but there are three elements of that experience which seem to have had particular impact on the scope and content of his ideas:

1 the relative levels of economic development in Great Britain and Canada at the time of Rae's emigration;
2 the perspective on viewing the economic differences which Rae's Scottish education afforded him; and
3 the politically divisive context of Canadian life.

To each of these elements seem to be bound the stronger aspects of Rae's economic ideas. To Rae's highly educated perspective on the economic condition in general were connected his methodological approach to the exposition of economic ideas and counterideas and his sense of their place in a larger body of thought. To his awareness of the striking contrast in economic developments can be linked his economic theories per se on capital and its accumulation, money, technical change, production and consumption, and trade. To his experience of the political divisiveness of Canada is owed, at least in part, Rae's conviction in the necessity for public policies, whether legislated economic or morally persuasive ones. The first four chapters in the volume address issues of methodology and history.

## I

Rae emigrated to Canada at a prime age, already with a good, solid, versatile educational background obtained in both Aberdeen and Edinburgh. His knowledge of the classics and general philosophy led him to emphasize beginning any study, even political economics, by laying the foundation for its principles. He grounded his economics in particular in clearly distinguishing causes from effects and in devising an inductive method of inquiry into the sources of the wealth of a nation.

Much as the life of John Rae might be described as intriguing and dynamic, so too could his thought, especially as he exhibited such a clear general interest in methodologies. Hamouda in "On Rae's Methodology of Economics" argues that Rae believed in the possibility of knowing or at least of being exposed to knowledge and on the importance of the method of learning pursued. Rae felt that one kind of knowing could come easily to human beings – "popular," "explanatory," or "systematic" knowledge – but that only another, although more difficult to acquire, could, with its potential for more and surer conclusions, lead to truth and serve as judge – "inductive" or "scientific" knowledge. Rae highlighted two specific limitations to knowledge on the part of all human beings, our inability to forecast the future with precision and our partial perception, the latter fact being quite disturbing to him.

Rae took a very outspoken position on the appropriateness of one particular methodology, induction, esteeming it to be the most appropriate to acquiring and affirming knowledge, particularly as presented by the English philosopher Francis Bacon. Rae's advocacy of Bacon's method derived from six explicit reasons, among them its "paedagogical" applications, in its use of verifying tests, and ultimately, and most importantly, in its ability to select for erroneous common knowledge or other mistaken assertions. Rae uses his commitment to the inductive method of Bacon to two specific ends:

1 to show that induction is not the method used by Adam Smith in the construction of his arguments in the *Wealth of Nations*; and
2 to intimate that induction is the method by which one might refute the theses of Smith or at least be able to classify his affirmations as those of a special case.

Rae first established that "the object at which his [Smith's] philosophy aims" is the expression of "mere inventions of the imagination" or "an imaginary machine." None of his criticism of Smith's method ought to come as a surprise, however, Rae argued, for Smith himself did not intend for his work to be taken as an inductive study.

As for the methodology Rae actually employed in his own study of political economy, his critics found him hardly a purist, but from the combination of his adoption with Smith of a "common standard" for the scope of political economy and his residence in Canada during the time of his writing his economic work, he did develop a form of induction, and perhaps more importantly, an integrated hierarchical classification of all areas of human knowledge dependent upon empirical investigation as its foundation.

Another methodological aspect discussed by Rae is identified by Drakopoulos as "The Concept of Orders of Instruments and Goods." Given that with the marginalist revolution a significant shift in the classical framework has been observed, Drakopoulos sets out to illustrate, using Rae, and C. Menger, one of the first adherents of the marginalist school, how the word "order" conceptually changed in this shift. His examination focuses on Rae's application of "order" to "instruments" and Menger's, to "goods."

Rae's "instrument" is "any means for the attainment of some end," with the most basic "end" being the fulfilling of human wants. Rae provides examples of instruments, a field, wheat, flour, tools, machines, etc., and lists their three points in common:

1 they are formed by human labour;
2 they "produce events" for supplying human wants; and
3 between their formation and exhaustion, some time elapses.

Drakopoulos sees in the first point the classical theory of value, since labour is the common measurement of instruments' capacity.

Rae applies the concept of "order" to instruments. Despite few examples, Rae's rules for the placement of instruments into "orders" define them as ranks according to relative efficiency (in terms of time, capacity, and cost) of instruments' return. One might, according to Rae, posit an infinite number of orders, since both the length of time between an instrument's formation and its exhaustion (its lifespan), and the amount of capacity and the cost of its formation determine its order. For practical purposes, however, if an instrument has produced goods double in value to its original cost by the time of its exhaustion, for example, at the end of one year, it is of relative Order A. If after two years, it is of Order B, and so on.

Drakopoulos parallels Rae's establishing his theory of capital on time and cost of production with Menger's establishing his consumer theory of value on subjective satisfaction. Menger defines his four "orders" as "ranks of proximity to the satisfaction of human needs" and uses satisfaction for comparing "goods." His examples of goods are quite similar to Rae's instruments, but with first-order goods representing those which satisfy human needs directly (second-order goods, used for the production of the first-order goods, etc.), undeniably, the implication of the concept of "order" in Menger is radically different from that in Rae.

To complete the sophisticated methodological approach required for investigation of a theory of capital and technical change Rae studied extensively the history of technology. Technological change was an issue of extreme importance to John Rae. Price maintains in "Rae's Theory of the History of Technological Change" that lying inexplicitly behind Rae's route to a theory of technological change was his conviction in the value of history as a guide. In addition to providing the researcher with a rich data base, the historical perspective also contains both the dimension of time's passage, which Rae found particularly important in his conjoined investigation of technology and capital investment, and its course of changes, which, since it often cannot be predicted, exposes the limitations to obtaining theoretical conclusions from history. Rae acknowledged such limitations through three historical examples: the wedge, the plough, and the steam engine. These were examples Rae thought would prove problematic for the theorist of technological change, for only their histories could reveal the course of their evolution. Such technologies are "generally deriving their efficiency from principles, that have been the result of very extensive and accurate investigations of many series of events" (Rae 1834: 87).

Although Rae did not intend the whole of his *New Principles* as an examination of the history of technology even from a theoretical perspective, as Price discusses, he did, nonetheless, build a theory of the history of technological change, relying extensively on historical sources, as well as on his own interest in technology, his very personal experiences as inventor, and his own observations of technologies in actual use. Out of his combined historical information and theoretical ideas, Rae provided an explanation for how technological change *had taken place* in the past by means of what Price terms both a micro- and a macrotheory of the history of technological change, the former based upon his theory of the contributions of individual members to society at large, the latter upon his belief that at least 'the principle leading to the formation of instruments', the desire to accumulate, had to exist within a specific human culture for technological change to occur at all. Price highlights further Rae's reflections on the causes which determine the degree of 'technologization' of any society, i.e., the amount of its instruments, once the initial conditions for a technological presence exist. In the end, the legitimate question of the significance of Rae's theoretical ideas about history is posed to reveal a uniquely comprehensive relationship between, on the one hand, his history of technology, and capital theory and other divisions of natural history, and, on the other hand, his history of technology, and the theory of the history of technology and theories of fostering policies.

An example of Rae's use of both inductive analysis and historical behaviour is present in his perspective on luxury consumption. Although ostentatious economic display had already been recognized, John Rae's treatment of luxury consumption in *New Principles* added to a then meagre literature on the subject. Until Thorstein Veblen's classic 1899 treatise, *The Theory of the Leisure Class*, which owes much to Rae without acknowledgement, few economists had considered its significance, although after 1500, the case against luxury consumption had been extended beyond a claim for its being morally wrong to its being against commercial interest. Before Rae, Adam Smith, favourable successor to Mandeville's 1714 attack on the "virtues" of thrift and frugality, *The Fable of the Bees; or Private Vices, Public Benefits*, articulated that conspicuous consumption was and would be, a socially inspired part of the modern world, a functional motor of national economic effort.

Mason in "John Rae and Conspicious Consumption" has analyzed Rae's views, finding them largely influenced by two economists. Rae's ideas were at odds with his first influence, Adam Smith, for Rae saw conspicuous consumption as unnecessary, something to be resisted; it fed off vanity, especially that of the capitalist class, and had no redeeming features. He thought it possible that a balance of the social and benevolent affections and the intellectual powers of a society could work to ensure that conspicuous consumption would be kept to manageable levels, akin to Mandeville's descriptions of the seventeenth-century Dutch Republic whose ostentatious expenditure was made in articles of quality and permanence. When the specific forces which work against too great a level of conspicuous display, ethical community and individual values, are weakened and ineffective, long-term social and economic stability is threatened.

Rae believed that the conditions in "new" countries tended to lower the overall propensity to consume conspicuously, but conceded that vanity and conspicuous consumption can be found everywhere. Luxury goods, deriving their value from their relative scarcity secured by high prices and limited availability, represented, to Rae, a loss to society, in neither supplying real wants nor increasing overall well-being. He devised some policies and prescriptions, i.e., taxation and scarcity-reducing production, to ameliorate the threats of luxury production and conspicuous consumption, but also, and, positively reflecting his second major influence, Heinrich von Storch, he tackled the root cause of the problem, vanity itself, by advocating religious education, and the moral values it secured.

## II

When Rae left Scotland in 1822, the industrial revolution was at full steam. Textiles were already being produced in industrial proportions; the first train was about to roll from London to Glasgow; and the manufacturing sector was developing at an increasing scale. In Canada, except for the exploitation of some raw materials and primary products, the economy was largely undeveloped. The contrast was so striking that it provided Rae with the stimulus for many a question about the reasons for the contrast. Canada itself presented fertile ground for study.

Rae spent years collecting data about Canada's economy and probing for the causes of economic development, particularly putting to test Smith's famous inquiry into the wealth of a nation. Rae had come to North America with a copy of Smith in hand, and it undoubtedly served him as a guide to get his investigation started. His own observations led him, however, to develop an original theory of capital, technical change, and capital accumulation. Further, through the prism of the capital theory of his *New Principles,* which, as noted above, anticipated those of Böhm-Bawerk and Fisher, Rae's critique of Smith's *Wealth of Nations*, his pioneering analysis of the role of the inventive faculty and inventions and the growth of knowledge in economic development and foreign trade, and his related argument for infant-industry protection, can all be viewed. In the third section of this collection, six chapters deal with aspects of capital.

In his chapter on "Rae, Böhm-Bawerk, and Fisher on the Supply and Demand of Capital" Ahmad goes back farther than the recent appraisals of Dorfman (1993) and Samuelson (1994) to examine contributions to capital theory by John Rae (1834), and Böhm-Bawerk (1889) and Fisher (1907), through the study of all their texts on two major themes (considered by neoclassics in terms of supply and demand analysis): the determination of the rate of interest, or profit, and the rate of economic growth. Rae's capital theory argument and illustrations were of a richness to elicit the highest praise and citation by Mill (1848), and Ahmad's objectives are to assess what Böhm-Bawerk and Fisher borrowed from Rae, whether they made significant advances or developed original ideas, and whether Rae's presentation was not the clearest, most relevant of the three. He concludes that Rae's framework is the simplest, and Fisher's, the most general. Within the general equilibrium approach, Böhm-Bawerk and Fisher did make analytical advances over Rae, but neither made any significant addition to him on the relationship of capital to growth.

Rae gave much attention to "supply of capital," particularly to factors determining its magnitude, listing six in one summary passage. Although his views are much richer than Böhm-Bawerk's (1889) and Fisher's echo, among Böhm-Bawerk's famous "Reasons" for the existence of a positive rate of interest, of which the first two are treatable as influences on the supply of capital, lies Rae's one major omission. He did not reflect on "the pattern of the flow of income over time." Explanation may be due to differences in value theory: Rae's, a modified classical, the others', a neo-classical.

Rae also contributed to "demand for capital" theory, in the area of "ultimately diminishing marginal productivity of capital, with a given state of knowledge," and, most powerfully, in the area of "requisite needs for an increase in knowledge through invention." In discussing demand for capital, Rae defined "instruments," all goods and land, and "order," most easily understood in a point input-point output framework. Both Böhm-Bawerk and Fisher claimed outright originality in their analysis for "demand for capital" theory: Böhm-Bawerk through the "Third Reason," "the technical superiority of present good over the future good," in defining "capital intensity" in units of "time" in a flow input-point output framework, to yield an "average period of production," Fisher, in his formalization of "rate of return over cost," including reswitching.

John Rae's intention to refute Smith's *Causes of the Wealth of Nations* in his *New Principles* (1834) was carefully understated. His disagreement with Smith was not over the importance of capital accumulation, but its causes. It is Rae's focus on invention as the primary cause of growth and his argument based on three claims:

1 that invention has causes prior to the current saving;
2 that laissez-faire generates a suboptimal level of invention; and
3 that the state should intervene,

which has caught Brewer's attention in "Invention."

Rae did not define "invention" explicitly, but, going from music and poetry to import substitution, he suggested a concept much broader than, for example, Schumpeter's "innovation." Rae went to lengths both to emphasize the gap between the "inventor," the "man of genius," and the mass of mankind, and to dramatize the tribulations of the former and the costs of invention-stimulating social disruption on the latter. As he turned, however, to more directly economic cases and replaced the tortured genius by inventions proceeding logically and smoothly, with "full assurance" of success, the main line of the story is revealed: societies can only continue to accumulate for any length of time by adopting new methods of production, which themselves have to be invented. This seems, however, to pose a problem, for Rae argues that saving and thus capital accumulation depend on a willingness to wait for rewards, but that invention is needed to maintain the incentive to save. The solution for Rae lies in a case for state intervention for two explicit reasons: first, it can support invention (and inventive adaptation), for invention has causes which government policy can stimulate; and second, it can support infant industries.

There are parallels between Rae's ideas and those of Joseph Schumpeter: the pragmatic application of a new idea is followed by copying, and the total social benefit accruing from any innovation is only partly captured by the innovator. They held, however, conflicting views on the immediate consequences of innovation, with Schumpeter drawing sharply between invention and innovation and emphasizing the temporary lead and profit gain of the innovator over imitators, and Rae stressing instead the extra novelty cost incurred by the innovator. Technological import substitution thus provided the context for Rae's case for action by the "legislator." The state is needed to help set up production in new circumstances, for while emphasizing there are potential gains, Rae stressed the immediate start-up difficulties involved.

Rae began his critique of Smithian economics by arguing that Smith "in great measure misses that which is the real object at which his inquiry aims, the instigation of the true nature and causes of national wealth," and takes "what in truth are the results of general laws . . . for the laws themselves, and of so elevating effects into causes." Rae argues therefore that, since capital, or wealth, is the result of fundamental human activities, one should not study it as the cause, as he suggests Smith did, but rather those individual and collective activities which give rise to capital/wealth. In "John Rae: Capital and Growth Theory" Rymes advances that Rae was concerned especially with the individual and collective activity – individual, noting Smith's lack of distinction between individual and national wealth; collective, given his advocated role for the state in infant industry protection, and so on – of the effective desire of accumulation which directly codetermines rates of technical advance and rates of return to capital, which in turn codetermine rates of growth and capital accumulation. According to Rymes' analysis, Rae proceeded basically "in the neo-classical way," "aside from an Austrian sideslip."

Rae attributes wealth, or the stock of capital or instruments, in any society to four specific elements, of which two are the strength of the effective desire of accumulation and the progress of the inventive faculty. Rymes formulates equations to represent the relationship of these elements to wealth creation in Rae. For effective accumulation, since Rymes has only Rae's definition of the desire, or "the determination to sacrifice a certain amount of present good to obtain another greater amount at some future period," (or $\rho$, the rate of time preference) to go on, he turns to more current growth theories to determine that Rae means $n' = n'(R;\rho)$ dynamically, and, in steady state, $R = n' + \rho$, where $R$ is the real rate of return and $n'$, the Harrodian rate of technical progress: the higher $n'$, the higher $R$. He considers this reduction valid, for in a given state of knowledge, the greater the effective desire of accumulation, the lower would be the rate of time preference (and the greater the rate of saving); in a neoclassical endogenous-growth theoretical world in which diminishing returns to capital have been set aside, a lower rate of time preference (or a higher rate of saving) would also be associated with a higher rate of growth; and in the neo-Keynesian models, a higher rate of savings associated with a lower rate of time preference, leads, given $n'$, to a lower $R$ and hence, through $n' = n'(R)$, to a lower $n'$. For inventive activity, given Rae's declaration that it is invention which shows how profitable returns may be got from capital, Rymes gives $R = R(n')$.

In "Productive Savings, Invention, Investment Supply in Rae's Growth Theory," Gootzeit examines Rae's recommendation in the *New Principles* for rapid capital augmentation to increase per capita wealth nationally by analyzing Rae's appreciation of savings in relation to capital. He sees Rae downplaying personal savings to give more importance to the "productive" savings of the business sector. For Rae, personal savings lead to the formation of "personal instruments," or durable consumption goods, while business savings lead to the formation of "business instruments," or "capital." Rae saw the "augmentation" of capital stock by the business sector as a different process from the "accumulation" of durables by individuals, because, while individuals buy "the same old things" over and over, businesses purchase newly invented or adapted, technically improved capital goods for their potential to increase profits. Hence, the primary force of augmentation is technical improvement: after an invention takes place, businesses immediately desire to raise their rate of savings (*new instruments retained*) and invest, perhaps through direct lending from businesses one to another (*new instruments given on credit*).

Gootzeit illustrates in linear version an investment supply model he developed from Rae's *New Principles* in which $k$ is any positive parameter, and also in which, when $k = 1$, the simplification to the equation $(P_{RE} - i) = Wc$ of the equation $(P_{RE} - i) = GT(1 - k) + Wc$ is possible (where $P_{RE}$ = the expected general/average *profit rate* in the production of capital instruments, $Wc$ = the capitalist's *wage*, and $G$ = the average profitability of $T$, *technical improvement*). In this latter case, where $Wc$ is constant, the differential between $P_{RE}$ and $I$ remains constant when $T$ increases. If, however, $k > 1$, $(1 - k) < 0$, and when $T$ increases, $(P_{RE} - i)$ falls toward zero as $I$ increases faster that $P_{RE}$.

Gootzeit ends discussion of the model and his chapter on the possible implication of a short-run direct relation between invention and the rate of interest which Böhm-Bawerk, Mixter and Fisher criticized as a part of Rae's theory: invention would cause the interest rate to rise. Considering Rae misunderstood, Gootzeit asserts that the only theoretical mechanism left to Rae for making the attributed prediction was that invention caused the expected profit rate to rise and that this somehow contributed to the interest increase. Inversely, however, he notes, rapid increase in market interest rate would cause a reduction in the volume of credit through a breakdown in the credit allocation, when otherwise investment would expand smoothly as technology improves.

The subtitle of John Rae's *New Principles* proclaimed its "Exposing the Fallacies of the System of FREE TRADE, and of Some Other Doctrines Maintained in the *Wealth of Nations*." Although, not surprisingly, Rae's book was construed as a polemic against Adam Smith, Dimand observes that Rae's analysis of international trade is linked in spirit to the *Wealth of Nations*, Book 1, where Smith discussed the division of labour and made a case for free trade's offering greater market extension. It is instead Rae's rejection of Smith's "identification" of saving rather than invention as the mainspring of economic development that Dimand sees as the root of the polemics in "Rae and International Trade." His rejection primarily of Smith's claim, that, if the state were not to promote the establishment of new industry using imported technology, the nation's capital would be just as profitably employed, is thus the focus of Dimand's chapter, "Rae and International Trade."

By March 1825 Rae had formulated his basic infant industry argument for government protection and international trade, along with a sketchy anticipation of his later analysis of invention as augmentor of capital stock. Rae used the establishment of England's woollen manufacture to advance his test for government encouragement: although an industry might not be privately profitable at first, given factor prices, is there the promise of future successful competition? Rae first illustrated his claim with industries using domestic raw materials, but extended it to the use of imported inputs in the case where the classical assumption of full employment of resources fails to hold. Rae endorsed government support for the invention of machines to facilitate and abridge labor in granting patents or in paying compensation for an invention made freely available. In contrast to the mercantile system denounced by Adam Smith, government intervention was for Rae to be temporary.

In response to Smith's classical case for free trade, the crucial innovation of Rae's analysis of gains from trade was his consideration that the opportunity to make beneficial international exchanges was equivalent to invention in stimulating economic growth. It allowed increased consumption from the same resources by raising the internal rate of return, by carrying capital goods more quickly through the period in which their issue is double the labour expended in forming them, and by thus creating an incentive, and hence a desire, to increase capital stock and productive capacity.

Maneschi in his chapter "John Rae and the Promotion of Infant Industries" emphasizes yet further the connection between Rae's capital theory and his trade policies, specifically with respect to infant industries. As noted above, Rae made two fundamental contributions which came to the attention of John Stuart Mill through Nassau Senior: his argument in favor of the promotion of infant industries and his pioneering capital theory. The circumstances surrounding infant industries are mainly analyzed in Book I of the *New Principles,* devoted to a critique of Adam Smith's *Wealth of Nations*, while his capital theory was formulated in Book II. Related policy implications for the transfer of technology from abroad are outlined in Book III, which, according to Maneschi, would have been the logical place to combine the advocacy of infant promotion of Book I with the capital-theoretic framework of Book II, particularly since Rae's position on the former pertains to capital theory, rather than trade theory. Instead Rae decided to devote the last book to the policy implications for legislators.

Although his powerful advocacy of the promotion of infant industries, and the full title of his book, might suggest that Rae was opposed to free trade, Maneschi asserts, like Hollander to follow, that he was not, and examines the question of whether it was consistent of Rae simultaneously to support free trade and the promotion of infant industries by various means, including duties. Maneschi reminds his readers that, although according to mainstream international-trade theory, free trade is optimal if certain static assumptions are satisfied – for example, a given technology, given factors of production and a frictionless and timeless movement along a given production possibility surface – these assumptions are not relevant to an analysis of infant industries, which focuses on the introduction of a new technology and the accompanying benefits and costs. At the same time as criticizing Smith, especially Book 4 of the *Wealth of Nations* which contains the principal elements of his foreign trade theory, Rae, in proposing what came to be known as the "Mill test," "the commodity, the product of the art in question, comes to be made at the same cost in the country to which its manufacture is transferred, as in that from which it comes, or at less cost than there" (Rae 1834: 364), was establishing his own criterion for a successful infant industry and a policy of raising a society's profit rate. Rae, like Hamilton, advocated caution in recommending candidates for promotion as infant industries, but felt the successes, just like free trade, would improve the world allocation of resources.

## III

The last four chapters of the present volume are devoted to Rae's contributions to the development of economic ideas in the history of economic thought. In terms of his intellectual heritage, Rae is in general representative of the Scottish tradition of political economy, which both Macfie (1955) and Dow (1987) have identified, but he is also unrepresentative in some key respects. For example, Macfie (1955) sees Rae as only a "considerable satellite," in the same category as Lauderdale, Hutcheson and McCulloch.

It is argued that it is the Scottish context of Rae's upbringing which allows for any expectation that Rae might represent the Scottish tradition. Rae's education was indeed in Scotland as well as in Paris (the Auld Alliance and all that), and his formative years as an economist in Canada were spent in a milieu which was seeking to preserve traditional Scottish values in religion and education. Some of Rae's ideas might well thus by reason of his education be encompassed within the larger idea of a Scottish political economy tradition whose influence has survived to some degree in Scotland and elsewhere, and even manifests some strength in the Scottish economics profession in the 1790s.

In making the case further that Rae is representative of the Scottish tradition, it is found useful to focus on a comparison of him with Smith. *New Principles* is best understood as setting out a system of economic development based on the principle of innovation; *Wealth of Nations* is best seen as a system of economic development based on the principle of the division of labour. Rae criticized Smith for confusing effects with causes, arguing that Smith essentially engages in "explanation" rather than in induction. Whereas Smith saw the "division of labour" as the cause of economic development, Rae saw it as the effect. Smith, according to Rae, was guilty of relying too heavily on surface differences and of not trying hard enough to develop understanding of the underlying system. There is, however, scope for a fusion of Smith and Rae in terms of their respective consideration of the context of invention, and in general, from a certain perspective, their differences might be treated as differences in theoretical content rather than in methodology, given that Rae was essentially criticizing Smith for not taking his methodology far enough.

In "John Rae and Adam Smith" Hollander establishes the broad lines of Rae's critique of Smith as maintaining an unconditional laissez-faire stance on economic development in the *Wealth of Nations*, including the methodological charge against him of ruinous logical and model-building inconsistencies, by considering, first, Smith's recognition of foreign sources of new technology, and even, of government intervention, and second, Smith's own case against luxury consumption. What emerges is that the contrast between Rae and Smith on the role of government in development is greatly exaggerated by Rae, especially considering Rae's extreme caution in practice based on spillover effects and Smith's selective allowances for a degree of legitimate intervention.

It is true, however, that while the risk and acquisition of skill attached to new ventures, and the positive social waste of some purely speculative ventures and "prodigal" uses justified for Smith some role for government, he was subdued and unexpansive about his cases for intervention, affording Rae thereby the misleading impression of his uncompromising hostility towards infant-industry protection and his neglect to denigrate excessive consumption and advocate commodity cost-raising measures at the expense of luxury. Thus consideration of the legitimacy of Rae's methodological complaints against Smith arises. Rae accused Smith of faulty and self-contradictory procedures and of irresponsible model building in his use of the deductive adoption of axioms and the carrying out of them to "their extreme consequences" (the "Ricardian Vice"). Smith's apparent inconsistency reflects, Hollander surmises, both evaluations based on specific empirical circumstances and his alternative views of human behaviour and its relation to the institutional environment. Thus Smith is rightly understood to be defending both "the competence of an authority to direct the investor" and more strongly the rule "that government officials have no role to play in the direction of private resources." Nonetheless, Rae could not condone that, despite Smith's recognition that his axioms were wanting empirically and required creating "exceptional" outcomes, he failed to modify or strengthen the axiomatic foundation of his general models. Hollander observes, however, that Rae's own focus was almost exclusively on generalizations, and that where the axioms of the model on which Smith based his case, as, for example, for a freely operating development process or regarding the strong savings propensity, were not satisfied, to his credit Smith did not blindly apply, but counterbalanced the results of the "universalist" general model.

Rae's capital theory has been recognized as his highest achievement, but, in seeking the basis of Rae's monetary ideas, Wakatabe notes in "Rae, Monetary Economist: Another Scottish Tradition in a Canadian Setting," that his whole system is a theory of economic development, composed of a theory of technological change and one of capital accumulation. Both are based on "microfoundations," an "accumulative principle," and an "inventive principle" respectively; together, emphasizing uncertainty and its effect on capital accumulation, these constitute the basis of his monetary thought.

In *New Principles*, like Smith, Rae first explains the origin and use of money, arguing, that as the social division of labour extends, men begin exchanging for some required goods instead of making them. Then relying on the Smithian butcher–baker exchange example, Rae distinguishes cash- or monetary systems and credit- or banking- systems. He considers money a medium of exchange and commodity money only a theoretical base for a monetary economy. In reality, most transactions occur by credit, however flawed, as it depends on the interdependence of contracts and has the liability of parties' potential failure.

The greater attention than Smith which Rae gave to time in connection with economic theory enabled him to point to an uncertainty element in exchange and demand for money and arrive at a precautionary version of demand for money. Rae's demand theory led to the conclusion that three conditions may cause scarce money: an accumulation principle too weak or one too short-acting to carry instruments to the more slowly returning orders, or such a superabundance of materials, that instruments are of very quickly returning orders.

Recent tensions over interpreting Rae's thought in relation to Smith's could resound on analysis of their banking theories. Both Rae and Smith were great proponents of banking and, basing their theories on the current systems, Scottish and/or Canadian, discussed its disadvantages and benefits. Rae's distinct purpose, however, was to show how the introduction of a credit system, however inherently unstable and vulnerable to a deficiency of real principle as a circulation base and to exogenous panics or "distress," was still beneficial in reducing uncertainty, transaction costs, deficiency in the circulating medium, and agent's need for idle cash holding.

The contribution "Rae and the Tradition of Scottish Political Economy" by Dow et al. is part of a larger project which aims to specify more fully the idea of a Scottish political economy tradition, to assess the degree to which its influence has survived in Scotland and elsewhere, and to assess its strength in the Scottish economics profession in the 1990s. The key characteristics of the Scottish political economy tradition have been identified by the project as:

1 a concern with practical issues;
2 a consequent preference for an understanding in breadth of the background to these issues, over in depth of isolated aspects of the same issues;
3 a preference for drawing on several disciplines in an integrated manner to provide that breadth;
4 a preference for arguing from first principles;
5 a preference for approaching a subject's first principles by discussing their historical development;
6 a specification of first principles in terms of a non-individualistic representation of human nature, with a consequent emphasis on social or conventional behaviour;
7 an acceptance of the limitations of theory; and
8 a recognition of the sociological and psychological aspects of theory appraisal.

It is the purpose of Dow et al. to argue that Rae is, in general, representative of the Scottish tradition of political economy, but is unrepresentative in some key respects. It is argued that it is the Scottish context of Rae's upbringing which allows for any expectation that Rae might represent the Scottish tradition, and that the effect of his education in the tradition is evident from his concern with practical issues, his capacity to apply himself constructively to a range of fields, and his concern with education. In making the case further that Rae is representative of the Scottish tradition, it is found useful to focus on a comparison of him with Smith. In this context, the last two features of the tradition pose the greatest difficulty vis-à-vis Rae, for Rae critiqued Smith's philosophy of science, at the level of content (notably with respect to the distinction between individual and national wealth), but also at the level of methodology. The first sense in which Rae's philosophy of science is at odds with the Scottish tradition is his rhetorical adoption of a dualistic view of science as falling either into deduction or induction, but since neither Rae nor Smith conformed to Rae's characterization of himself as inductivist nor Smith as "deductivist," in traditional fashion, both extensively employed empirical evidence in conjunction with a conceptual framework which transcended observation. As regards the last feature, there is also scope for a fusion of Smith and Rae in terms of their respective consideration of the context of invention. In general, from a certain perspective, their differences might be treated as differences in theoretical content, rather than in methodology, given that Rae was essentially criticizing Smith for not taking his methodology far enough.

Finally, in the last chapter, "John Rae: an early post-Keynesian," Mair and Laramie argue that it is quite legitimate to identify the method and content of modern post-Keynesian economics with the Scottish political economy tradition – of which Rae was undoubtedly a member. Although Rae's analysis of taxation was only incidental to his view that the State had a legitimate role to play in curbing the excesses of luxurious consumption, it is his emphasis on the dynamic effects of the revenues raised from the taxation of luxury goods that finds its parallel in present day post-Keynesian thinking. By comparison with the comparative statics of much of modern public finance theory, Rae's perception of the importance of fiscal dynamics was remarkably advanced.

## IV

Even among those who have studied John Rae as intensely as the above discussion reflects, there is no single opinion as to the value of his overall contribution to economics. Nonetheless, there is a general sense that his disagreement with Smith should not be exaggerated nor his criticism of Smith inflated, especially in the field of international trade. On the one hand, some of Rae's explicit attacks were not directed at Smith himself, but rather at some of his followers. On the other hand, Rae's argument for protectionism was not a universal position: it pertained only to an underdeveloped economy such as the Canadian one of his day.

It seems that there is no doubt that in some specific areas of economics Rae has left his own mark. For example, in the field of capital theory, Rae was the forefather of the theories which were developed by Böhm-Bawerk who was drawn to acknowledge Rae's contribution only later, and Fisher who acknowledged Rae at the outset. In the case of conspicuous consumption, there too Rae was ahead of his time in predating Veblen, who, although he never acknowledged his indebtedness to Rae, had him undoubtedly as one source of his ideas. There is further the area of methodology in which Rae's independent ideas were noteworthy and continue to be relevant to today's disciplinary discussions. Rae's emphasis both on disentangling the causes and effects of the creation of the wealth of a nation and on advocating a method of investigation which should rely on observation, induction, could have a sustained impact. It is thus certainly worthwhile to devote further attention to Rae, and it is hoped that the current state of examination of his ideas might stimulate further study by historians of economic thought and methodology.

# Part I

# JOHN RAE'S LIFE AND WORKS

# 1

# BIRTHDAY GREETINGS TO JOHN RAE

*R. Warren James*

## I

Although both literature and history have been enriched by some of the great diarists and correspondents it was not unusual years ago for men of prominence to destroy their personal papers before they died. Whatever their reasons, they caused their future biographers frustration and endless trouble. In the case of John Rae, there is no evidence that his letters or other personal papers were intentionally destroyed. They were simply dissipated in the course of his wanderings and when he died he left for posterity a collection of scientific papers, mainly about geology, badly disorganized, and almost nothing of a personal nature. There was a handwritten note on the back page of a child's exercise book: "Never have advocated any measure but from a settled conviction of its justice a profound feeling of its righteousness." On the same page is another note, "Feby 20 1855. One cow sent to Pasture."

There are large gaps in Rae's life. Little is known about his childhood. In one brief autobiographical note he indicated that his youthful plans were to pursue a scholarly career in Europe to be supported by an expected generous patrimony. His father's bankruptcy upset his plans. He explained, "a sudden and unexpected change took place in my circumstances, and I exchanged the literary leisure of Europe for the solitude and labours of the Canadian backwoods."[1] Nothing survives about his marriage except the date of his wife's death in Hamilton as a result of cholera. What is known is that his life was marred by controversy. From the time he was a medical student he took on the established powers, not the least of which was Adam Smith, with penetrating intelligence and literary skill. He had useful allies at different times but basically his efforts were in vain, except once. This was when he published his *Statement of Some New Principles on the Subject of Political Economy* in 1834 and left an enduring monument.

The 1965 reissue of this book did attract some attention in the economic journals and some of the reviews were kind, others not quite so kind. My impression was that it made barely a ripple in Canadian academic circles.

Apart from a few acknowledgments of presentation copies I did not receive a letter from anyone in the academy. I put Rae aside and turned to other things which occupied me fully for the next twenty-five years. As a result, I was startled to receive a letter from Professor Douglas Mair in Edinburgh in 1989 that accompanied a draft article on Rae which he proposed to publish. He asked for my comments but I begged off and turned his paper over to someone else for assessment. My excuse was that I had not looked at Rae for many years nor had I followed the recent literature. It was quite impractical for me to make any useful suggestions on the substantive aspects of Rae's work. On the other hand, Rae had an interesting life and career and this creates a hazard for biographers: the smallest detail of the subject's life becomes important and anything that throws light on character, temperament, or lifestyle assumes exaggerated importance. Perhaps this is based on the hope that some minor incident will generate some afflatus of major consequence.

The reprinting of Rae's book together with a volume devoted to his life and miscellaneous writings had a wearisome gestation period. One of the complications was that there was an early announcement of the project followed by a very long delay. The obstacles are of minor interest. Sometime in the mid-1950s I learned through Professor Joseph Dorfman of Colombia that Kelly & Millman of New York, a firm specializing in photographic reprints of economic classics, were proposing to reissue Rae's book. I immediately wrote to them offering to contribute a preface if the project proceeded. Millman wrote back that I was premature, but if they decided to go ahead they would get in touch with me. They did not do this and in 1965 reprinted Rae's book without any reference to me. This obviously hurt the sales of the University of Toronto reprint.

Detailed records of the sales by the University of Toronto Press are buried in their archives and not easily available. However, by reconstructing royalty statements it can be estimated that the sales were about 600–800 copies. The retail price was $22.50 Canadian which now seems a bargain, but in 1965 that price was high. Initially there was no promotion campaign worth mentioning, but when it became evident that there was a surplus some offerings were made at fire-sale prices and, in a short time, the 1965 edition by the University of Toronto Press was out of print and again scarce. That is enough of the grubby commercial details!

## II

Some years ago Jacob Viner warned me of the perils of biographers. They usually end up by falling in love with their subjects or disliking them to the point of contempt. Despite this caution and the virtues of dispassionate appraisal I admit freely that my admiration for John Rae grew as I learned more about him. I willingly accept the charge of hagiolatry.

At least twice I was deeply moved by events in his life. The first was when he was in California. He was walking along a lonely path, probably in 1849 or 1850, sick with malaria and with no money, obviously in great distress, when he found a five-dollar gold piece on the path. I rejoiced at his good fortune. The second event occurred late in his life. He wrote to the Board of Health in Hawaii advising that he had vaccinated a number of native children against smallpox. He explained that the arrangement was that he would be paid twenty-five cents for each vaccination and asked if he should send the names of the children. The Board of Health replied that this would not be necessary. This exchange occurred when Rae was 73 or 74.

Rae's character and personality remain ill-defined. Some fragmentary details have survived that throw some light on his nature. In one letter he speaks of himself, but his meaning is far from clear. He writes: "of my peculiar organization . . . of cruel mental suffering in early youth, the fruits, the avengers perhaps, of a momentary yielding to violent passions."[2]

One anecdote of his behavior as a schoolteacher is recorded, although it is probably apocryphal. The story is that in the classroom Rae habitually tilted his chair back and rested his head against the wall. Some mischievous boys rubbed some cobbler's wax on the wall and when Rae next leaned forward his wig stuck to the wax. The general resultant merriment was so loud that the assistant master, Dr Tassie, later famous as the headmaster of the grammar school in Galt, came running in to investigate the unseemly uproar.

Rae was apparently regarded with affection by his pupils. In 1938, a group of his students in Hamilton presented him with an inkstand, penknife and silver pencil case. Years later, a number of tributes were paid to him by his former pupils. One of them referred to him as "dear Dr. Rae" and said that he "had a very loving disposition that endeared him to us all" (Stephen J. Jones). Another wrote that, "He entered into all their sports and amusements, often bringing his chemical knowledge into play" (John Robert Martin). One of his pupils said, "Rae was a charming companion for young and old. He taught me rabbit, mink and muskrat trapping and other sports attractive to youth" (R.W. Cameron). "He was undoubtedly a man of deep learning and research, and made a powerful impression on all who knew him. He was amiable and thoughtful of others" (George H. Mills).[3] These testimonials show that Rae had a kind and affectionate temperament.

It is curious that Rae was sometimes overshadowed by his assistant Dr Tassie. In a small volume celebrating the fiftieth anniversary of the Ontario Educational Association published in 1911 there are some reminiscences by the Lieutenant Governor of Ontario, Sir John Morison Gibson:

> I wandered to the city of Hamilton and became a "Tassie boy." . . . The words "Tassie boy" have a very distinct and well understood meaning. Though he left Hamilton very soon after I became

> one of his pupils, it has always been somewhat pleasant to include myself in the very numerous list of prominent men in the Province who call themselves old "Tassie boys."[4]

Perhaps the reason for the omission of any reference to Rae was that Gibson was in the primary grades, the responsibility of Tassie. Gibson's further explanation was erroneous. He said, in referring to Tassie: "A very short time after he left Hamilton that city closed its Grammar School. The city was financially embarrassed and could not afford to maintain it."[5] In fact, the grammar schools were financed by the province and the embarrassment of the city was not financial. It might be appropriate to erect a plaque "John Rae taught here," but the school has long been demolished.

No portrait of Rae has come to light. There was a picture of him taken in Montreal in 1834 but it is now lost. Perhaps this is the likeness of Rae that once hung in the home of Sir Roderick Cameron, Rae's pupil, lifelong friend, and benefactor. Cameron had become extremely wealthy and had a summer place of 300 acres on Staten Island. There are scattered comments about Rae's physique in letters, one of which states in part, "When he walked abroad [in Maui] his tall spare form was seen always accompanied by two large dogs."[6] In his younger days and in a colder climate, a local historian wrote about him: "In appearance he was tall, rather slender and dignified. People looked on him as one of the most graceful skaters in the city, and many of his pupils labored diligently to master the long graceful strokes of the teacher."[7]

Some of the gaps in Rae's life arise because of the complete lack of correspondence between Rae and his family. No letter to his parents, siblings, or wife has survived. Perhaps there was ill will, although Rae remained on amiable terms with his sister Ann Cuthbert Fleming, the wife of James Fleming, a Montreal merchant. The reference library of Metropolitan Toronto has an autographed copy of Rae's book inscribed, "To my friend James Fleming," and it is known that Ann Cuthbert experimented for a short time with the teaching of grammar to Rae's students in Hamilton.

There were episodes in Rae's life of disappointment and frustration and yet, as far as one can tell, he preserved an equable temperament and an optimistic outlook. One example will suffice. In 1851, Rae wrote to Cameron in Hamilton telling him that he had given a series of lectures on geology in Honolulu to the Royal Hawaiian Agricultural Society. In the letter he said, "Probably, in the course of a year or so I shall be appointed Geologist for the Hawaiian Kingdom."[8]

## III

There is another aspect of Rae's character, in addition to his relations with his pupils and other individuals. This is his feelings about native or primitive people. Unfortunately, no information is available about his relations with native peoples in Canada. He has left no record of his views on his *métis* students or their parents or Indians in general. It was not until he was established in Maui that he began to record his assessment of the natives and, in so doing, he revealed quite a lot about himself. Again in a letter to Cameron he wrote:

> I like the people, thoughtlessness, idleness and extreme license of life are the great defects, and I fear will make them melt away from the earth; It is a pity for they are able, kind-hearted and really an intelligent race.[9]

There was trouble in paradise. About 1820 the American Board of Commissioners for Foreign Missions in New England became aware of the existence of the heathen in Hawaii and grasped the chance to pluck some brands from the burning. They dispatched a band of Congregationalist missionaries to carry the banner. Even Rae admitted that the sexual mores of the islanders were comparable to the imaginative antics of Greece and Rome. Of course, the natives confined their favors to their friends, but they had no known enemies. The missionaries responded like a bear after honey. The main obstacle they encountered was that the natives had no sense of sin, a lack which the missionaries set about to remedy. They forced the women into absurd Mother Hubbards and forecast the tortures of eternal hellfire for unrepentant sinners. The political power of the missionaries was sufficient to convert sins into crimes. Those convicted of sexual misdemeanors were often sentenced to build roads, a punishment for men and women alike. The road to Hana on Maui was built by convict labor, something which Rae must have found abhorrent. Richard Henry Dana, the author of *Two Years Before the Mast*, in a letter to the *New York Tribune* in 1860 outlined the achievements of the missionaries:

> They found these islanders a nation of half-naked savages, living in the surf and on the sand, eating raw fish, fighting among themselves, tyrannized over by feudal chiefs, and abandoned to sensuality; they now see them decently clothed, recognizing the law of marriage, knowing something of account, going to school and public worship with more regularity than the people do at home.[10]

To Rae, the missionaries were completely wrong. He wrote in a series of articles in the *Polynesian* in 1861:

> I believe it will be found that all attempts to amend the morality of any nation by legislative enactments and government action, have ever proved worse than useless. Human nature somehow rises

> up in arms against any force from without that would compel it to be good or righteous after any particular fashion, and, in the tumult of the rebellion thus excited treads down and stifles those inward monitors to which the soul would otherwise have been inclined to listen. The thing has often been tried and always with bad success.[11]

Rae's attacks on the missionaries are an eloquent appeal for the humane and understanding treatment of the natives and for tolerance of their exotic attitude to life. He made his sympathetic views abundantly plain. While his nature and his attitude to people begin to emerge there are other parts of Rae's life that are initially far from obvious.

## IV

One of the unexplained aspects of Rae's career was how he became a schoolteacher in Williamstown, Glengarry County as a young man in his mid-twenties. To throw some light on this it is necessary to sketch briefly the organization of the fur trade in Canada. The Hudson's Bay Company, founded in 1670, was able to persuade the Indians to bring their furs to the posts on the shores of Hudson Bay. In contrast, the North West Company, its powerful rival with headquarters in Montreal, sent its pedlars by canoe to trade with the Indians at various posts in the interior of the continent and return to Montreal with freight canoes loaded with the year's harvest. The North West Company was a type of syndicate, or association of partnerships. The traders who stayed in the interior through the winter were known as "wintering partners." There was, naturally, bitter rivalry between the two great fur companies to the point where there was armed conflict and bloodshed.

The wintering partners of the North West Company were "The Lords of the Lakes and the Forests," virile and rich, and it was natural that they should form liaisons with the native aristocracy. The unions were usually with daughters or close relatives of Indian Chiefs, persons of high social standing among the Indians. For example, Amelia, Lady Douglas, the wife of the Governor of British Colombia was the granddaughter of a Cree chief. The marriages were usually informal and not blessed by traditional church rituals although sometimes the unions were recognized in native ceremonies. If the couples settled down in the western territories, there were no social problems, but difficulties could be anticipated if the couples moved to urban centers such as Montreal. For one thing, it would not be easy for native wives to adapt to city life. This explains why, if the couple stayed together and moved to the east when the man retired they tended to hive off to smaller communities in such places as Glengarry County and the Eastern Townships of Quebec. One notable example is David Thompson, famous as an explorer and cartographer, who settled in Williamstown after he left the North West Company. In other examples, the wife stayed in the west and the children were brought to Montreal to be educated. Many of these children moved west to rejoin their tribes after their exposure to city life.

Local records show that there were at least six Indian wives living in Williamstown or nearby, although one of the unions broke up, and in other cases the wives rejected life in Glengarry County and returned to their tribes in the west. There were numerous children in some of the families or attached to the men of the North West Company. One student of the area records that one Cree woman left three sons and a daughter fathered by one of the Nor'Westers in the care of Isabella, daughter of the Hon. Neil McLean of Cornwall. Isabella became formally the second wife of the fur trader.[12]

Hugh McGillis and his Indian wife had seven children. The records of the Revd. John Bethune, the earliest Presbyterian minister in Williamstown indicate that there were numerous *métis* children baptized in the early years of the nineteenth century.

It has become plain that Rae was employed as a teacher for the children of the wintering partners and their Indian wives. Rae announced by an advertisement in the Montreal *Herald* on May 4, 1822 that he had been appointed master of the school at Williamstown. How Rae was selected for this position is not known but possibly it was through his sister Ann Cuthbert whose marriage had brought her into contact with influential Nor'Westers in Montreal. Rae gave as references the Revd. John Mackenzie, Bethune's successor as Presbyterian minister in Williamstown, Alexander Skakel, headmaster of the Royal Grammar School in Montreal, and the Revd. Henry Esson, a Presbyterian minister and also a schoolteacher in Montreal who had been a fellow student of Rae at Marischal College. In addition to the usual branches, Rae announced that he would provide private lessons in the Greek and French languages, elocution, English composition, and drawing. The mind reels as the prospect of young *métis* being tutored in Greek and drawing.

But that does not explain how there happened to be an enclave of retired Nor'Westers in Williamstown and environs. The decade 1810–20 produced some bizarre climatic variations whose effects were felt in North America and in other parts of the northern hemisphere. There was an anomalous spell of cold weather culminating in the years 1816 and 1817. This period was marked by persistent blasts of Arctic winds with resultant poor harvests, starvation, and misery. Frost and snow were recorded in the St. Lawrence Valley in June 1816. The underlying disruption of normal weather patterns was complicated by the catastrophic eruption of the Mount Tambora volcano on the island of Sumbawa in Indonesia in 1815.[13] It was the largest volcanic eruption in the previous 20,000 years, significantly greater than the Krakatau eruption of 1883. The Mount Tambora volcano spewed out material probably in excess of 80 $km^3$. The corresponding estimate for Krakatau is 17 $km^3$. Before long the volcanic dust veil from Mount Tambora extended in the upper atmosphere around the world. The extraordinary weather may have resulted from a combination of the dust veil from the Mount Tambora eruption, some unusual sunspot activity and from some anomalous atmospheric phenomenon. Apart from these factors, there was a serious drought throughout central North America. The low water levels in the rivers used for transport disrupted normal methods of travel by canoe and forced the use of carts for hauling freight. In addition, the fur-bearing animals were badly stressed, often by the late thawing of the rivers. In addition to the malevolent natural phenomena there were overriding economic influences at work, and at the end of the day, the North West Company was absorbed by the Hudson's Bay Company in 1821 just as John Rae was arriving in Canada.

These assorted events were to signal the end of the North West Company and new beginnings for Williamstown and John Rae. An appreciable number of the wintering partners of the North West Company withdrew from the company and moved to Williamstown or nearby areas. Generally speaking, these Nor'Westers were wealthy men and established themselves on large farms. They were no city dwellers and chose this area instead of Montreal, about fifty miles west of the city.

An idea of their ethnic background can be gathered from a sample of their names: John McGillivray, Archibald McLellan, Big John (*le borgne*) MacDonald, Finnan "The Buffalo" McDonald (so-called because he survived an encounter with a wounded bull buffalo), Angus McGillis, Hugh McGillis, Angus Bethune, David Thompson, Paul Fraser and Duncan Cameron. There were many others in the area. One bond in the community was the prevalence of Gaelic. Two sermons were preached by the Revd. John Bethune on Sunday, one in English and the other in Gaelic.

Records of Rae's school in Williamstown do not exist. It was a private boarding school, although he may have had some day pupils, and quite different from the common schools that dotted upper Canada. Rae continued with his school for nearly ten years and then there is a hiatus of several years when there is some uncertainty about his activities. When he next appeared he was the author of his book on political economy published in Boston in 1834. By the end of that year he was headmaster of the Gore District Grammar School in Hamilton, Upper Canada. Probably his book was originally intended as a preface or introduction to a major study of the current conditions and resources of the province, but the manuscript for this work was lost in the mail.

The period of Rae's life devoted to schoolteaching in Canada is fairly well known, but the next phase of his career transforms his life and interests. He says in a letter to a friend, "in beginning old age [I] have become a wanderer and adventurer over the wide earth." He was 54 at the time.

In the immediate future he was to devote himself to the observation of medical matters and the practice of medicine.

## V

Quite recently, my attention was called to a letter by Rae published in the June 1856 issue of *The Medical Chronicle or Montreal Monthly Journal of Medicine.*[14] The title of the two-part letter was "Diseases peculiar to the Sandwich Islands" and the author was described as John Rae, M.D., Kaoli, Hana, Mani [sic], S.I. He had made his way to California by the way of Panama and writes. "I embarked at Panama as surgeon in the ship *Brutus* in the end of February '49." This is puzzling because his wife died in August, 1849 according to an obituary notice in the *Montreal Gazette*, August 28, 1849. When Rae embarked on his travels his wife remained in Hamilton. There is nothing to indicate that he left because of marital discord since Rae referred to the loss of his wife as a "great and soul penetrating sorrow."[15]

Rae's account of medical conditions among the Hawaiian natives is interesting and repellent at the same time. There was a lively commerce between the mainland and the islands and, as might be anticipated, the natives were decimated by a variety of European ailments, the most devastating being smallpox. A severe outbreak in 1853, especially on the main island, led to an urgent campaign of vaccination. Rae wrote a letter to the *Polynesian* on September 24, 1853, urging the passage of adequate health laws and regulations to provide direct aid to the natives in districts affected by the smallpox epidemic. According to Rae, the population fell from 80,000 in 1849 to 70,000 in 1854, mainly because of this pestilence.

In the great metropolitan centers medical knowledge was primitive in the mid-nineteenth century and even more rudimentary in such isolated places as Hawaii. Rae had not been seriously exposed to medical advances since his days as a student in Edinburgh around 1820 and he was still influenced by the fashion for violent purges and miasmic theories of disease transmission. Oddly enough, he spoke highly of a native healer who had devised a method of sweating his patients over a heated bed of stimulant native herbs.

One of the most serious health problems was the spread of sexually transmitted diseases. The sailors, arriving on the islands after months at sea, must have thought they had landed in Heaven. Unhappily, they left a legacy of social diseases which overpowered the crude remedies of the doctors. Rae skated over the problem of sexually transmitted disease and was optimistic about the prospects of cure. He wrote:

> Deep seated, and very malignant ulcers of the throat, and other parts, with total derangement of the system have carried off, and still carry off, many. But I believe there are few of these latter

> cases that would not yield to the persevering use of the appropriate remedies.[16]

Measles and influenza were scourges, as well as poorly identified fevers. For them, Rae dispensed quinine with regularity. He also mentions prescribing "a combination of Dover's Powders, acet. of lead, and calomel with occasional doses of castor oil, or rhubarb and magnesia."[17] Dover's Powder consists of ipecacuanha root, powdered opium, and sulphate of potash. It was contraindicated when the brain was out of order. However, it was recommended for the relief of heartburn. The so-called "blue pill" was a standby. It appeared to be a standard remedy as a purgative. It consisted of two parts of metallic mercury rubbed together with three parts of conserve of roses. Although not widely used today, it can be given as a laxative for dogs. One of the other standards was James's Powder. It consisted of antimony trioxide and calcium phosphate. Its therapeutic properties are dubious, but it could serve as an emetic or a purgative, whichever seemed called for.

Rae seemed unfamiliar with influenza and it was first known as Lahaina fever or Bolo fever. An epidemic spread gradually through the islands and Rae treated it with James's Powder, slight doses of mercurial and saline purgatives, quinine, and finally opium. In spite of this drastic régime many recovered in a short time.

The natives were convinced of the curative powers of bleeding and Rae himself was an advocate. He reproached himself for the scanty use of bleeding when surgeon on the *Brutus*, and said that those who had not been bled showed symptoms of some visceral obstruction. However, his report stated, "None died,"[18] perhaps because the weather improved as they approached San Francisco.

Rae gives the impression that he was called on to deal with broken bones and similar trauma. He refers to one episode when the king (Kamehameha IV) was travelling on horseback on Maui and a young woman with the group fell from her horse and broke her collar bone and dislocated her arm. Rae was able to patch her up, but went on to say that the accident was discussed the next morning when he was breakfasting with King Kamehameha and Prince Lot. Rae must have been a person of some standing in the community to be breakfasting with royalty.

How Rae lived as he grew older is obscure, but it is certain that with the death in 1865 of R.C. Wyllie, the Minister of Foreign Relations and member of the House of Nobles, Rae lost an influential friend and supporter. He continued his connection with the Board of Health and there is a record in the minutes of a payment of $118 for successful vaccinations in 1868. At this time Rae was 73 and it is possible that his fees for vaccination were his only income. The same minutes record that Dr Rae had reported three lepers living at Hana and he should make arrangements to send them to Honolulu for examination.[19] In his medical article in the Montreal journal it is curious that he emphasized the prevalence of cutaneous ailments, but did not mention leprosy. By this time his stay in Maui was nearly over, and it is appropriate to look ahead for nearly thirty years to the happy chance that he came to the attention of Frank W. Taussig and Charles Whitney Mixter.

## VI

Towards the end of the nineteenth century Rae became closely associated with Charles Whitney Mixter, then a graduate student in economics at Harvard. Mixter's academic credentials were impressive. He was born in 1867 in Massachusetts and graduated from Johns Hopkins in 1892. He then spent a couple of years in Berlin and Göttingen after which he enrolled in economics at Harvard. Naturally, he studied under Frank W. Taussig. He took his doctor's degree at Harvard in 1897 and spent several years as an instructor there.[20] Sometime in the 1890s Taussig called Mixter's attention to the resemblance between the work of John Rae and Eugen von Böhm-Bawerk. This prompted Mixter to write an article "A Forerunner of Böhm-Bawerk," published in the *Quarterly Journal of Economics* in 1897. This excited Böhm-Bawerk's interest and in the second edition of his *History and Critique of Interest Theories* published in 1900 he devoted a whole chapter of fifty-three pages to Rae, part of which was devoted to exploding Mixter's thesis. Böhm-Bawerk explained that he had not dealt with Rae in the first edition of his history because of the scarcity of Rae's book, but he had been able to borrow a copy from Menger. I have composed an inelegant clerihew on this mix-up:

Charles Whitney Mixter
Conceived an incorrect picture
Of Rae and the classical work
Of Eugen von Böhm-Bawerk

There were various recantations and rejoinders but the flurry of interest led Mixter to reissue Rae's work in 1905. For unknown reasons Mixter decided that Rae could be improved by rearrangement and editing. Mixter has been scolded enough for his bad judgment on this score but rather then dwell on his aberration I want to express gratitude to him for his painstaking and irreplaceable work on Rae's life. He collected and assembled the essential facts about Rae, without which Rae would have remained a shadowy figure. Gaps remain, since Mixter, with his New England background, was not well equipped to explain the complexities of Rae's involvement in a variety of civil and religious controversies in Canada. He did, nevertheless, piece together a mine of information that is essential to anyone attempting to understand the many aspects of Rae's life.

Despite Mixter's misinterpretation of Rae, he became interested in his background and this led to Sir Roderick Cameron. Cameron was helpful to Mixter, giving him all of Rae's papers that remained at his death. Cameron himself died in 1900. Mixter lost a valuable source of information about Rae and was forced to look elsewhere for the outlines of Rae's biography.

Acting on a suggestion from a student from McGill, Mixter wrote from Cambridge to the editor of the "Notes and Queries" column of the *Montreal Daily Star* on February 25, 1889 asking for information about Rae and referring to him as "this distinguished Canadian." The response was surprisingly good. The *Star* printed two of the replies. One was from Henry J. Morgan, a well-known antiquarian and scholar and author of *Bibliotheca Canadensis* (1867) who outlined the main features of Rae's life in Canada and corrected the confusion with Dr John Rae, the Hudson's Bay Company factor and Arctic explorer. The other printed reply was from Robert Skakel Knight,[21] Rae's great-nephew in which he gave an account of the Rae family in Canada, with emphasis on their literary activities. The final paragraph of Knight's letter was revealing:

> Dr. Rae was a remarkable man. An Englishman who knew him in the Sandwich islands told me that he could only compare him to some of the grand old Scotch gentlemen in Sir Walter Scott's novels. But he said that he was quite incapable of taking care of money, so that other people had to look out for him all the time. Literary work was all that he cared for.[22]

There were still over forty letters from which Mixter drew his biographical sketch which prefaced the 1905 edition of Rae's book, now entitled *The Sociology of Capital*.

The bulk of the material given to Mixter by Cameron consisted of Rae's extensive writings on geology. Even as a young man Rae was interested in geology, and this interest was stimulated by his life in Hawaii, since Maui and the other islands were ideal for the study of tides, volcanoes, lava, and like matters. Mixter lacked the expertise to assess the validity of Rae's theories, so about 1904 he appealed to one of his friends at Harvard, Dr T.A. Jaggar, who was working as a geologist in Hawaii, and sent him the manuscripts for review. There the papers rested for about fifty years until by good fortune Miss Elizabeth B. Barrett, the secretary of Dr Jaggar noticed a reference to these papers in a Canadian journal article. Dr Jaggar, in the meantime, had become a distinguished volcanologist at the university of Hawaii. Dr Jaggar and the University of Hawaii, especially Miss Janet Bell, kindly provided microfilm copies of all these documents. God is sometimes good to His children! Unfortunately, a lot of Rae's essays were written in pencil on blue paper and were not easy to reproduce by microfilm. Much of the material was badly disorganized and some of the *bonnes bouches* such as Rae's essay on the geology of Canada in 1821 were missing. In any case I owe a special debt of gratitude to Dr Jaggar, Miss Barrett and their colleagues for their sharp eyes and generous spirit.

## VII

The next development was more tantalizing. In 1989 I happened to be in the National Library in Ottawa and by chance noticed a bound volume *The National Union Catalog of Manuscript Collections*. There was a reference to John Rae in the index, something which always piques my interest, and I was surprised to find an entry which read in part:

> Rae, John 1796–1872
>
> Economist, geologist, educator and judge, of Hawaii and Canada. Letters, notes and notebooks (1849–71) dealing mostly with geology, the Hawaiian Islands and the Hawaiian people, a paper entitled a trip around East Maui; and 43 letters about Rae written to Charles Whitney Mixter during the period 1899–1904 by various persons.

These were in the possession of the University of Hawaii. It was noted that the collection was in part a gift from Thomas A. Jaggar in 1952 and in part a purchase from Mrs. Joseph McCord in 1959. How the Mixter letters found their way to Hawaii is not known.

An immediate appeal was sent to the University of Hawaii seeking access to these letters, but the reply was that they had been misplaced. A series of further appeals have been sent to the library since 1989 but the answer remains the same, though perhaps a little testier as the appeals multiply. The letters remain in the maw of the archives of the University of Hawaii and whether they will ever by uncovered, only God knows.

## VIII

In his declining years Rae's eyesight began to fail, and he finally yielded to the urgings of Sir Roderick Cameron to leave Maui in the summer of 1871 to stay at Cameron's place on Staten Island. He was able to survive only one winter and died on July 12, 1872 in his seventy-seventh year.

In the mid-1950s I visited John Rae's grave in Woodland Cemetery, Staten Island. I have forgotten the precise date, but the tariff on the ferry was five cents, so it was in another age. The caretaker of the cemetery was obliging, although the records were in error. They showed that R.W. Cameron had been buried in Plot no. 718 on July 16, 1872. A clerical error had been made at some stage, resulting in confusion between the owner of the plot and the occupant. Mixter must be considered authoritative on this point since he obviously discussed the question with Cameron. Mixter writes: "He was buried in Woodland Cemetery, Staten Island, in a lot purchased by Sir Roderick, 'in which two others, one a faithful servant and the other a distant relative are buried'."[23] In any case, Cameron is buried in an elaborate tomb in Williamstown.

Rae's grave is in an old section of the cemetery and, when last seen, was overgrown with weeds and bushes. An effort has been made recently to have this grave site tidied up, preferably before the bicentennial of his birth. However, telephone calls and correspondence with the current caretaker have had no result. There was some hope that the New York State Division of Cemeteries would help, but the director was dismissed and the agency eliminated because of the change in state administration in 1995. Further appeals may result in a more encouraging outcome. Rae, from whatever vantage point he has, would be pleased at a small material token of respect and even more pleased that small groups of sympathetic and learned people are celebrating his birthday.

## Notes

1 C.W. Mixter, *John Rae: The Sociological Theory of Capital* (New York: Macmillan, 1905), p. iv.
2 Ibid., p. xli.
3 All quotation from pupils are from ibid., pp. xxiii–xxiv.
4 Ontario Educational Association, *Jubilee Banquet April 18 1911* (Toronto: University of Toronto, 1911), p. 15.
5 Ibid.
6 Mixter, *Sociological Theory*, p. xxvii.
7 J.H. Smith, *The Central High School Jubilee Re-union, August 1903* (Hamilton, 1905), p. 14.
8 *Hamilton Gazette*, January 19, 1852.
9 Ibid.
10 Manley Hopkins, *Hawaii: The Past, Present and Future of its Island Kingdom* (London: Longman, Green, Longman and Roberts, 1866), 2nd edn. p. 380.
11 R.W. James, *John Rae: Political Economist* (Toronto: University of Toronto Press, 1965), i. 329.
12 David G. Anderson, "Indian Wives of the Glengarry Nor'Westers," *Glengarry Life*, no. 36, Glengarry Historical Society, 1993. I am greatly indebted to David Anderson for information about the early development of Williamstown and its connection with the North West Company.
13 C.R. Harington (ed.), *The Year without A Summer? World Climate in 1816*, (Ottawa: Canadian Museum of Nature, 1992), passim.
14 *The Medical Chronicle or Montreal Monthly Journal of Medicine*, vol. 4 (1856), ed. William Wright M.D. and D.C. MacCallum, M.N.
15 Mixter, *Sociological Theory*, p. xxv.
16 *The Medical Chronicle* op. cit., vol. 4, p. 7.

17 Ibid. 55.
18 Ibid. 53.
19 Board of Health Minutes, 14th Folder (1) 1868–9, November 12, 1869.
20 He later became a professor of economics at the University of Vermont and then joined the faculty of Clark University. His academic work was interrupted on two occasions by ventures in the business world. Finally, he ended his career in the 1920s and 1930s as a staff economist for the United States Tariff Commission. Whether Mixter's employment was related to the fact that Taussig was the first chairman of the commission from 1917 to 1919 is pure surmise.
21 Robert Skakel Knight was the grandson of Ann Cuthbert by her first marriage to Robert Knight.
22 *Montreal Daily Star*, March 10, 1899.
23 Mixter, *Sociological Theory*, p. xxviii. Mixter does not identify the source of the excerpt in quotation marks.

# Part II

# ISSUES OF METHODOLOGY AND HISTORY

2

# ON RAE'S METHODOLOGY OF ECONOMICS

*O.F. Hamouda*

Much as the life of John Rae might be described as intriguing and dynamic, so too could his thought. Although I had not at first envisaged that this topic would necessitate an overview of virtually all of Rae's intellectual contribution, I now believe that it does, at least briefly. Therefore I begin with the broadest notions involved in any discussion of a methodology, that it can be useful to the absorption and transmission of knowledge to discuss Rae's commitment to learning, his position on the limitations on knowledge, and his rhetoric for a most appropriate methodology for any subject. As a second part of the chapter I shall examine the methodologies Rae actually employed in his study of political economy from three points of view: that of his critics, his own opinion, and finally my own from my reading of his work containing economic ideas. Some closing remarks will reflect on the importance and relevance of Rae's methodology for economics today.

## Rae's espoused methodologies

Rae was clearly generally interested in methodologies. References to approaches to the possible absorption and transmission of knowledge are scattered throughout his writing. He was obviously committed, both pragmatically as a teacher and abstractly as a thinker, to the possibility of learning. At the same time, he drew attention to certain limitations on knowledge of which, he felt, everyone ought to be aware. The clearest indication of his concern with methodology lies, however, in his discussion of the philosophy and methodology of Francis Bacon within his only major surviving work, *Statement of Some New Principles on the Subject of Political Economy Exposing the Fallacies of the System of Free Trade, and of Some Doctrines Maintained in the "Wealth of Nations"* (1834).

### *Rae's Belief in Knowledge*

Rae believed in the possibility of knowing or at least of being exposed to knowledge and in the importance of the method of learning pursued. What humans come to know depends, he felt, in large part on the way they come to know it. "Where the principles of investigation are different, the conclusions arrived at can hardly agree."

He felt that a certain kind of knowing could come easily to human beings. Most people are "practical observers" of the events they encounter in their daily life. They extend that modest pool of experiences, about which they are knowledgeable, to produce broad opinions about the rest of the world. Citing Francis Bacon ([1620] 1813), Rae characterized the most common process of the individual's learning as a reasoning process, from familiar notions which are "products of the imagination," based on a few particular experienced instances "of familiar occurrence," and perhaps some generally admitted maxims, to the formulation of very general conclusions (Bacon, L. I, cxxv, cited by Rae 1834: 338; Bacon, Preface, and L. I, xviii & xix, cited by Rae 1834: 333–34; Bacon, L. I, xxviii, cited by Rae 1834: 334). "[T]he philosophy of system takes things which, because familiar, are admitted as obvious, as the media for explaining all other things" (Rae 1834: 330).

This type of knowledge Rae refers to variably as "popular", "explanatory", or "systematic." Although he denigrates it throughout chapter 15 of Book II of his *Principles*, he concludes that it does have a place in the world of ideas, "to explain plausibly" (Rae 1834: 331):

> A clear, orderly and extensive view is given of a vast number of interesting and important facts, connected by a few familiar principles. *A great body of knowledge is thus brought before the mind in a shape which it can readily grasp, and easily command.* The object being not to discover, but to arrange and methodize, all the subordinate principles of the system are artfully bent so as to embrace the phenomena, and care is taken that the imagination be not shocked by a view of matters that shall seem irreconcilable to the aspect of affairs which the contemplation of the world of life itself presents. Nor is it to be disputed that a general system of the sort, besides the pleasure and the advantage derived from it, is likely to be nearer the truth than speculations of the same nature, confined to particular parts. [emphasis added]
>
> (Rae 1834: 351)

His objection to this type of common knowledge was its assumed status as "fixed and immutable truth" and its extension to "judging all other particulars" (see Bacon, L. I, cxxv, cited by Rae 1834: 338). "It is evident," wrote Rae, "that however it might systemize and explain facts already known, it could not conduct to new truths" (Rae 1834: 331).

Only another form of knowledge could to Rae's mind lead to truth and serve as judge: inductive or scientific knowledge. He describes its process as one of "collecting, comparing, and arranging" phenomena, as it "rises gradually and slowly from fact to fact and only at last arrives at the most general conclusions . . . real laws of nature" (Rae 1834: 342 and 333–34). It finds "its materials in things very various in themselves, and gathered together from different quarters, cannot make a forcible impression on the mind, and must necessarily appear to it as something harsh, unusual, and mysterious" (Bacon, L. I, xxviii, cited by Rae 1834: 334). Nonetheless,

> the experience of what true science is, has accustomed us to expect that in this, as in other branches of inquiry, the farther we advance the larger and larger a compass of undeniable facts should present themselves, that we should be able more and more evidently to connect phenomena, that seemed at first disjointed and isolated, and that, the indistinctness of distance being removed, truth should stand clearly before us
>
> (Rae 1834: 348)

Along with its potential for more and surer conclusions, scientific knowledge was the more difficult to acquire. Rae seemed to believe that while potentially accessible to anyone, it was "confined to the few, its spirit being difficult to seize" (Rae 1834: 329). It required certain "intellectual powers . . . in the minds of members of society" (Rae 1834: 124) and was therefore "above the grasp of the commonality, and only to be comprehended by them in its effects" (Rae 1834: 329).

One last point about Rae's belief in and commitment to the human potential to learn. He had great faith in human retention of what is known, and in the improvement of human action based upon that knowledge. The "power" for change which applied knowledge afforded was in fact the main catalyst to Rae's desire to foster intellectual inquiries. His very definition of "instruments," "any means for the attainment of some end . . . as owe their chief efficacy to what are called the mechanic powers," refers to this belief (Rae 1834: 86). From knowledgeable human beings, instruments derive their "power" of supplying humans' future wants, by virtue of both human reason guiding their labour and human "knowledge of the course of events," their employ (Rae 1834: 87). Human beings themselves acquire the "power" to determine the course of events at large from knowledge:

> [T]he result of a successful inquiry into the nature of wealth, would terminate in affording the means of exposing the errors that legislators had committed from not attending to all the circumstances

> connected with the growth of that wealth, whose progress it had been their aim to advance, and would so teach them, not that they ought to remain inactive, but how they may act safely, and advantageously; and that thus, it would maintain the analogy running through the whole of man's connexion with the trains of events going on around him, the course of which he governs by ascertaining exactly what it is. That here, as elsewhere, his *advance in knowledge would show him his power*, not his impotence. [emphasis added]
>
> (Rae 1834: 361–2)

## Rae on the limitations to knowledge

Rae acknowledged two specific limitations to knowledge on the part of all human beings: our inability to forecast the future with precision, and our partial perception. Sounding almost biblical, Rae observed, "life, and the power to enjoy it, are the most uncertain of all things, and we are not guided altogether by reason. We know not the period when death may come upon us, . . . life, too, is of uncertain duration and the time that death comes between us and all our possessions [is] unknown." He did not think that this uncertainty left human beings completely in the dark, however, for, since the natural world follows laws of cause and effect, both the inevitability of some ends, or effects, and the evidence for change toward those ends can guide human ignorance: "we know that it [death] may come in a few days, and must come in a few years" and "the approaches of old age are at least certain, and are dulling, day by day, the relish of every pleasure" (Rae 1834: 119–20).

The limitations of partial perception appear to have been to Rae more disturbing than lack of foreknowledge:[1] "there is nothing more apt to mislead us, when investigating the causes determining the motions of any great system, than to take our station at some particular point in it." The danger is that "examining the appearances there presented to us" at both a specific time and place, we might "suppose that they must be precisely similar through the whole sphere of action." Rae offers the example of using the case of human beings in the Great Britain of his day whose "regard to mere self interest, may now prompt to a course of action leading to making a large provision for the wants of others and in every place." One would be quite in error to assume that in any society at any time such self-interest would have the same effect. Taking the case of the ancient Romans, he argues that, as they themselves recognized, self-interested pursuit of wealth "commonly generated evil," not altruism. The partial perception which examination of only one culture at only one point in time affords might lead, Rae warned, to the limited knowledge and unwarranted conclusion that communities "must therefore do thus always and in every place" (Rae 1834: 124–5).

## Rae's espousal of the inductive method

In addition to Rae's general commitment to learning and his position on the limitations on knowledge, he took a very outspoken position on the appropriateness of one particular methodology, induction, as presented by the English philosopher Francis Bacon. Rae was committed to the inductive method of Bacon from at least three perspectives: epistemological, ontological, and paedagogical. Rae espoused the method in chapter 15 of Book Two of his *Principles*, "Of the *Wealth of Nations* as a branch of the Philosophy of Induction," quoting throughout from his own translation of the Latin of Bacon's *Novum Organum*. He represented the method he advanced as Bacon's and any deviation from his inspiring source is minor. The point here is not to discuss Rae's indebtedness to Bacon, which he openly acknowledged, but rather to extrapolate from his exposition of Bacon which components of Bacon's inductive method were most significant to Rae. The reason for this emphasis will be discussed in turn.

Rae esteemed induction to be the most appropriate method for acquiring and affirming knowledge for at least six reasons. The first two were epistemological. Bacon's form of induction was for Rae, and many other intellectuals of the nineteenth century, the route to the "scientific knowledge" described above. It set out the way of studying and learning about phenomena, as to (1) their occurrence (place, time, frequency, etc.) and (2) their cause or effect, and both, through observation. Through induction, "complicated series of phenomena, connected with sensible motions of all sorts" could become the object of scientific study (Rae 1834: 330). Since, according to the inductive method, "wherever a scientific cause, or law, or principle operated, there the thing itself, of which it is said to be the cause, is necessarily produced," observation of a thing can lead to learning of its cause (Rae 1834: 343, citing Bacon, L. II, iv), and seeing it as the effect.

Two other of Rae's reasons were ontological. Rae saw in Bacon's inductive method the possibility of (3) affirming laws or principles about the existence and occurrence of phenomena, and (4) determining, "what is a principle by pointing out what it is not," that is by "*negative instances*" (Rae 1834: 344). Induction "seeks for laws regulating the general system," "the real principles governing nature" (Rae 1834: 331, and 342). Following Bacon, Rae asserted that "the whole inductive philosophy may, indeed, be said to rest on the impossibility of the occurrence of exceptions to real laws." The principles themselves "never vary," so that "nothing is to be received for the true scientific cause, unless the thing of which it is the cause," exists "along with it" (Rae 1834: 343).

The fifth and six reasons for Rae's advocacy of Bacon's inductive method derived from his conviction in its "paedagogical" application, namely (5) in its use for verifying tests, and ultimately, and most importantly, (6) in its ability to select for erroneous common knowledge or other mistaken assertions. Rae seems to relish the inductive method as glorying in "remote and heterogeneous examples," for they are the ones which can test the constancy of "real principles" (Rae 1834: 344–45). Apparent outliers are all the more important, since in the scientific method, "one observation or experiment concerning a real principle, if there be no inaccurcacy in it, has always in science been esteemed as good as a thousand" (Rae 1834: 344). As for ability of the inductive method to teach, we turn to comment on a passage cited earlier: "the result of *a successful inquiry* into the nature of wealth [read, one conducted according to the inductive method] . . . *would so teach them* [the legislators], not that they ought to remain inactive [as asserted by Smith], but *how they may act safely, and advantageously*" (emphasis added) (Rae 1834: 361).

Rae uses his commitment to the inductive method of Bacon to two specific ends:

1 To show that induction is not the method used by Adam Smith in the construction of his arguments in his work *An Inquiry into the Nature and Causes of the Wealth of Nations* (1776).
2 To intimate that induction is the method by which one might refute the theses of Smith or at least be able to classify his affirmations as those of a special case.

Rae asserted that Smith's "speculations are not to be considered as inductive investigations and expositions" for three reasons: "1st. from the object at which his philosophy aims: 2d. from the methods which he adopts to attain it: 3d. from the consequences which have resulted from his labors" (Rae 1834: 331–2). He pursued a discussion of each of these reasons and, in so doing, carried out an "inductive" method of evaluating the exposition of another writer. He uses the "phenomena" of Smith's own words, albeit some from "The Principles which lead and direct Philosophical Inquiries, illustrated by the History of Astronomy, of Ancient Physics, Logic and Metaphysics," and his analysis of Smith's form of argumentation in the *Wealth of Nations*.

Rae first established that "the object at which his philosophy aims" is the expression of "mere inventions of the imagination" or "an imaginary machine" (Rae 1834: 332). Smith's method, Rae induced, employs the use of the principles of sympathy, as evidenced this time in the *Theory of Moral Sentiments*, or antipathy, from "his fragments of the imitative arts" (Rae 1834: 335–6). Rae was apparently guided by the assumption that sympathy (or antipathy), as the principle than which "there is perhaps no one . . . more capable of serving as a familiar bond of connexion between the phenomena of the moral world," is what Smith would use to search "for some common and familiar observation" and make it "serve as the means of connecting any series of interesting events" (ibid. 335 and 333). Rae's general comments about the consequences which resulted from Smith's labors appear to be the weakest part of his analysis.[2] Rae spoke of Smith's stretching "any common measure of faith in such abstractions," of his doctrines having "something in them so strange, so contrary to experience, . . . so paradoxical, that they have in most people rather the effect of exciting surprise, than producing belief," and of his instances seeming "contrary to the usual progress of real knowledge" (ibid. 346, 347 and 348). They belie, however, a very serious examination of the faulty relationship of Smith's examples to his conclusions regarding capital, and even introduce instances in which, his followers, reasoning from his principles, "have arrived at conclusions differing considerably from his" own (ibid. 348–9).

None of his criticism of Smith's method ought to come as a surprise, Rae would, however, argue, for Smith himself did not, as Rae asserted, intend for his work to be taken as an inductive study. Thus, despite its focus on Smith's exposition, Rae's vigorous critique of the method of Smith is targeted not on Smith himself, but on his "disciples and followers" who "in claiming for the speculations contained in the Wealth of Nations, and for the doctrines they have founded on them, the rank of an experimental science, the conclusions of which are entitled to the same credence with other experimental sciences, act injudiciously, and . . . injure the cause of that philosopher and conceal his real merits" (Rae 1834: 350). It is these disciples whom Rae would blame for his need to assail Smith's work, for they alone had elevated it to that level of credence from which it had to be removed. To discredit Smith's attributed methodology was the first of two ends to which Rae apparently intended to use the inductive method. Rae seems also to have seen induction as the route by which he could refute the theses of Adam Smith, which brings us to the discussion of the methodology John Rae actually did employ in his thought and writing on political economy.

## Rae's methodologies for political economy

In the second part of this chapter I shall examine the methodologies Rae actually employed in his study of political economy. The first perspective on his methods will be that presented by the critics of his economic writing. Next, his own opinion of his methodologies will be discussed. Finally, from my reading of his work, particularly his texts containing economic ideas, I shall present my impression of Rae's methodology for political economy.

### *Rae's critics on his methodology for political economy*

As we have just recounted, Rae espoused the inductive methodology of Francis Bacon in his *New Principles on the Subject of Political Economy*. Nonetheless, from the very first assessments of his published work, it was clear that reviewers did not categorize, nor even identify, Rae as an inductivist. First, it would appear that to his contemporaries, methodology was far from the most striking aspect of this writing. Many reviewers were struck by Rae's literary style. The reviewer in the Boston *Daily Advertizer* noted the "intelligible language" (cited by James (1965a, 1: 163) from the *Montreal Gazette*, August 26, 1834). Francesco Ferrara favoured his "clear and forthright way" of expounding theory (*Biblioteca dell' economista* (first series), XI, xxv, cited by James (1965a, 1:170) in R.W.J.'s translation). Alexander Hill Everett, editor of the *North American Review*, wrote in his journal that the author "exhibited great ingenuity, extensive reading, and a *remarkable power of style*" (emphasis added) (January 1835, 129, cited by James 1965a 1:165).

Second, even when addressing something akin to political economic methodology, Rae's critics found him hardly a purist. Without referring to any specific methodology, Everett wrote of Rae's "excessive refinement and abstraction." (*North American Review*, January 1835, 129, cited in James 1965a, 1: 165). From the reviewer in the Boston *Daily Advertizer* again, Rae's illustrations showed an author of both "great acuteness of *observation, and* a mind stored with the treasures of *classical learning*" (emphasis added) (cited by James (1965a, 1: 163) from the *Montreal Gazette*, August 26, 1834). John Stuart Mill wrote of Rae's *Principles*, "In no other book known to me is so much light thrown, both from *principle and history*, on the causes which determine the accumulation of capital" (emphasis added) (Mill [1848] 1927: 165, cited in James, 1965a, 1:168).

### *Rae's own reflections on his methodology of political economy*

Rae did not frequently cast himself as a character in his work on political economy. In addition to biographical references in the *Principles'* short preface and postscript, there are, however, a few passages in his other extant writings which give added insight into how he perceived his approach to scholarly investigation generally. Rae saw two sources to scholarship, neither of which he felt he had ever had the full liberty to enjoy:

> Fortune has not permitted me to be the student I would have desired. The study of such a one is in *the spacious library* where undisturbed and uncontrolled he can roam over the thoughts and read the souls of men of all times and countries; or else *the wide world itself*, with all conveniences to explore it and examine the various aspects of nature and of man which it exhibits – *or better still, each alternately*. [emphasis added]
>
> (Letter of 1849, cited in James 1965a, 1: 101)

With his emigration to Canada in 1822, Rae never again knew the spacious libraries of his student days in Aberdeen and spoke regretfully at the opening of his *Principles* of "the field of my inquiries being much contracted." He does nonetheless seem to have felt some degree of satisfaction in having been a student for some time in "the wide world itself." "Geology has ever been with me a favourite study," he wrote in a letter in 1849 (cited in James 1965a, 1: 101). Of all his scholarly investigations, he is the most explicit about his methodology for pursuing geology:

> These two things[,] the actual present condition and the previous changes and revolutions[,] are conjoined because as the one has produced the other *we are thus enabled reasoning upward to deduce the cause from the effect; and again downward, the effect from the cause*[,] each mutually assisting in ascertaining and elucidating the other. Thus has the science [of geology] advanced to important conclusions. [emphasis added]
>
> (Rae, Lectures before the Royal Hawaiian Agricultural Society (after 1851), cited in James 1965a, 1: 117)

Insight into his own ideas on his methodology for political economy can, however, also be found. When pursuing issues of political economy, Rae was vaguely aware of his methodological originality. "Now as concerns Canadian independence, or annexation, . . . I had become accustomed to *view it from a point and in a light different* from that in which politicians of the hour necessarily regard it" (emphasis added) (Letter of 1849, cited in James, 1965a, 1: 101). He explained that he had first perceived history alone to be the foundation for addressing political economic questions. "When one commences the study of history, it is generally under the apprehension that this study will serve as a *master key* to the problems of the day, and will enable him not only to form just conclusions concerning them, but, if so prompted, to address his contemporaries with authority and power" (emphasis added) (ibid.). Then, however, as he pursued further his study of history, he found, in order to render it meaningful, he had to combine it with "the philosophical spirit of investigating it which has begun to give its proper life to the inquiries of the age." Having combined history with "philosophy," Rae saw his thinking conducted "to a far higher elevation whence it takes in a great reach of the whole tide of humanity lying beneath" (ibid.).

It is difficult to find Rae speaking more explicitly about his methodology for political economy. He seems to have considered it transparent enough to render such analysis unnecessary:

> It will be perceived that there is an essential difference between the modes of investigation which I have followed in the preceeding pages, and those guiding the speculations of the celebrated philosoper, from whose opinions I venture to dissent. . . . It so happens, however, that *concerning the principles of investigation*

> *themselves, there is a common standard* to which the disciples of Adam Smith refer, and on the rules drawn from which, I also conceive, the determination of the questions debated must ultimately rest. [emphasis added]
>
> (Rae 1834: 328)

He implied that the most basic element of the "common standard" is that political economy be undertaken as "a science of experiment, a branch of the inductive philosophy" whose methodology as described by Francis Bacon is subsequently cited extensively by Rae (1834: 328 ff.).

Before the important issue of Rae's concern that political economy be studied as an inductive science is discussed, other elements of the "common standard" should also be noted, first among them being perhaps the accepted subject of political economy. "It is the [true] nature of wealth in the general, and the laws regulating its increase and diminution, that can alone, as I conceive, form the proper subject of philosophical investigation. These being determined, from them may be deduced the manner in which particular societies, or particular individuals, come to possess this or that amount of wealth" (Rae 1834: 1). More specifically, political economy investigates the nature and causes of all the circumstances whose general tendency it is to "advance the wealth of society, [i.e.,] the capital and stock of communities" (ibid. 265). At the opening of his *Principles*, Rae proposed "partially to attempt" an investigation of this subject (ibid. 5).

I would argue that the "common standard" of Smith's approach to political economy offered him the "method" for how to address but a part of the vast subject, whose scope included for Smith, at least, "value, riches, stock, capital, wealth, profit, self-interest, the desire of bettering one's condition" (Rae 1834: 336).

> His theory pretends to show, that the source of the wealth of nations, the abundance, that is, of all the materials of comfort and enjoyment, the necessaries, the conveniences, the amusements of life which men possess, is to be found in the gradual accumulation of capital by the undisturbed industry and economy of individuals, continually, through the division of labour, introducing improvements in the modes in which this labor operates with that capital, and, consequently, increasing with the greatest possible rapidity the returns from them. His doctrine is, that the accumulation of capital by individuals, being thus the only thing required to produce that abundance with the greatest possible rapidity, ought never to be interfered with by the legislature; and that, if he does so, it must necessarily be to the detriment of the society for which he legislates. If, therefore, even according to him, there are other sources, than the mere accumulation of capital, and consequent

> division of labor, on which nations are dependent for turning their labor and capital to the best account, and thus drawing from their resources the most abundant returns of necessaries, conveniences, and amusements, that is of wealth; in so far, his theory would seem imperfect, and his doctrine inapplicable.
>
> (Rae 1834: 42)

Thus Rae saw in Smith's standard the methodological possibility for investigating, not all causes, but which of many possible causes and/or whether any one particular causative source exists for the advancement of a nation's wealth. Under scrutiny thus might come the choices of such causes as division of labor or ingenuity and education, free trade or protectionism, greed and selfishness or altruism and benevolence, conspicious consumption or moderation, individual interest or communal concern, laissez-faire or government intervention, and so on.

Rae himself turned "to the part of the system with which we are specifically interested," capital, especially in the form of invention. Should capital alone affect the augmentation of a nation's wealth, he stated boldly, "disputes concerning its [wealth's] manner of existence, its increase and decrease will terminate" (Rae 1834: 5). Too experienced a scholar, however, to display such unqualfied optimism in the acceptance of his ideas, he added that if the mere developed affirmation of another position were insufficient for its adoption, instead of a disagreement "hinging on plausible arguments," it might "be settled by a reference to ascertainable facts" (ibid.). Common standard alone would oblige the inquiry into observations (ibid. 336), and that any position taken should be internally consistent according to both logic and "admitted facts" (ibid. 407). According to Rae, these criteria could also be applied to existing theories, as he applied them to Smith's:

> we find, in reality, that as far as it is concerned, the theory is thus inconsistent with events admitted by its author, that hence this portion of it is contradictory to itself, and to admitted phenomena, and that consequently the doctrine drawn from it cannot here be maintained.
>
> (Rae 1834: 42)

### *Our perspective on Rae's methodology for political economy*

Neither Rae's own espousal of the appropriate methodology of the study of political economy nor his extant writings on political economy alone express clearly his actual relationship of induction and political economy. With the aid of three "case studies" of how Rae actually presented his own arguments in political economy, their relationship in his methodology might be more easily deciphered. His perspectives both on the issues of causality, simplification, and agglomeration, and on the empirical basis of induction will also serve as guides. Citing Greek philosophy, Rae wrote of causality: "*Ex nihilo nihil fit.* Nothing can spring out of nothing. Everything must have a cause" (Rae 1834: 12). The key to carrying out the study of political economy was, for Rae, discovering those causes which conduce material means to the prosperity of the individual and the community and, in so doing, distinguish the causes from the effects of that prosperity. He decried Smith's followers' "uniform tendency to hold that up as an explanation of other things [i.e., as a cause], which in reality, is the very thing itself to be explained [i.e., the effect]" (Rae 1834: 1). The most significant example of this confusion turned for Rae on the issue of trading policy; specifically, the holding up of free trade as a primary cause of a nation's wealth. From his earliest extant writing on political economy, "Sketches of the Origin and Progress of Manufactures and of the Policy Which Has Regulated Their Legislative Encouragement in Great Britain and in Other Countries" (Rae 1825), to his most developed positions on national prosperity, Rae maintained that free trade could only be seen as the effect of a nation's prosperity, for only when a nation had achieved the military security, competitive advantage, a high level of employment, a standing in international trade, sophisticated integration, and development of technology could it continue to prosper without the protectionist policies not available under free trade.

Accepting the intellectual duty of distinguishing the causes of prosperity from its effect was for Rae first and foremost in the political economist's calling. He refined that calling somewhat by suggesting that a single cause may be "discovered sufficient to account for the phenomena." The test for "sufficiency" would be that even the "smallest sensible" change would not be possible without its "aid." From the outset of the *New Principles*, Rae asserted that the essential cause of human economic progress is "invention," for "to every great advance which nations make in the acquisition of wealth, *it is necessary* that invention leading to improvement should lend its aid" (emphasis added) (Rae 1834: 24). Thus with his logical conviction in unique sufficient causes, Rae methodologically both advocates that "we should confine ourselves to it [invention]" in our study of political economy and echoes the falsificationist position of his "common standard" discussion.

Before introducing three "case studies" of how Rae actually presented his own arguments in political economy, a few introductory comments on the techniques of simplification and agglomeration will be added. Partly because of the questions which a probing for the root cause evokes and partly due to his desire for clarity of commmunication, Rae used the device of defining as a methodological tool. For example, "What is it, in the nature of man or matter that makes anything constitute a capital, or yield a profit?" (Rae 1834: 342) elicits the answer, "Man as a reasoning animal is rather to be considered as an instrument in her [Nature's] hands, through which she effects much of that change in the order of events, and consequent progress from good to better" (ibid. 361). Defining alone, however, does not eliminate the issue of how to deal with the defined entities in political economy, as representative singulars or as singular composites. In most instances, Rae opts for the latter. In the case of "man" he rationalizes, "man hardly exists but in the social state," therefore man, human being, "community, society, nation, state, or people, [are] terms which, as far as our subject is concerned, may be considered synonymous" (ibid. 95).

Rae's other formalizing conventions are relatively easy to observe in connection with his capital theory. In one instance Rae acknowledges proceeding hypothetically, although the emphasis ought really be drawn to his "hypothesis" as a mode of simplification:

> [T]his mode of determining the capacity of similar instruments, is, in many cases incorrect, and that the instances are very numerous, where the relative capacities of the instruments of the same sort, *depend on other causes than their mere physical properties*. The assumption, therefore, that they may be so determined, is to be considered as hypothetical, and to be tolerated from the difficulty of otherwise treating the subject; in the same manner as the hypothetic existence, of strictly mathematical lines, and the absence of friction and of the resistence of the air, is excused, in reasonings concerning the mechanical properties of matter. [emphasis added]
>
> (Rae 1834: 94)[3]

James (1965a, 1: 148) observed that in addition to conceiving of "cost of production of instruments . . . measured solely in terms of labour," Rae "suggests as a further measure of simplification that the contribution of these co-operating instruments can be measured by an equivalent amount of labour. All this amounts to adopting a standardized and abstract daily wage as a *numeraire*." As for wages of labor, Rae conceived that he could disregard a supposed vibration above and below, a fixed standard toward which their amount always tends, and consider the subject "under the most simple conditions possible." Although this did not eliminate all difficulties, Rae felt this form of simplification, "the most simple assumption and that the errors arising from which may be supposed to balance each other," presented itself as the methodological option for two reasons. He intended at that point neither "to enter into any investigation of the principles determining the amount of the wages of labor in all societies, and at all times, nor to discuss the somewhat contradictory doctrines that have been maintained on this subject" (Rae 1834: 97).

Averages are a frequently incorporated device: "Rae formulates quite clearly the notion of an average period of production and an average period of exhaustion." Nonetheless, considered to have "no economic significance" attached to them, they have been brushed aside (James 1965a, 1: 149). They hold some interest, however, in this discussion, for, since Rae applied the notion of a representative average when assessing circumstances in many different social scientific areas, they point to some possible universality in his methodology:

> It is also assumed that the average character of the members of different portions of the same community is similar, so that, were a considerable number of inhabitants of any particular state, taken from one part of its territories, they would closely resemble an equal number, taken from any other part.
>
> (Rae 1834: 96)

There are at least three texts which offer great insight into Rae's pursuit of political economy: his unsigned "Sketches of the Origin and Progress of Manufactures and of the Policy Which Has Regulated Their Legislative Encouragement in Great Britain and in Other Countries" published in March, 1825,[4] his prospectus of "Outlines of the Natural History and Statistics of Canada," dated July 1840,[5] and, of course, his *Statement of Some New Principles on the Subject of Political Economy Exposing the Fallacies of the System of Free Trade, and of Some Doctrines Maintained in the "Wealth of Nations,"* published in 1834. Each one seems to exemplify, however, a somewhat different methodological approach. There are two particular elements to look for: one is Rae's perspective on the issue of causality; the other is his emphasis on the empirical basis of induction. Taking these two together, one can begin to establish the place he dedicated to political economy within the larger issue of how the world is studied.

"Sketches of the Origin and Progress of Manufactures" begins with a story-like scenario of the steps of economic "advancement of society" from its purely agricultural beginnings to its involvement in foreign exchange. From this point of extended development, the single sketch biforcates to depict one society engaged in "passive commerce" and another in "active commerce." Until the lines of "advancement" diverge Rae presents no substantiating evidence for his hypothetical[6] course of events. Even subsequently, his characterization of the "passive economy" is reinforced with only the following: "we, at an early period of their history find such manufactures as the following dispersed in different quarters: coarse woollens and linens; provisions and liquors; hides and leather; vegetable and fish oils.""This progress has been particularly observable in the United States of North America" alone supports his depiction of the "active economy."

When, however, Rae reaches the second section of his article, "the circumstances and political principles which appear to have regulated the legislative encouragement of manufactures in European countries," he claims to have derived his ideas empirically from having kept "in view the progress of events and of commercial legislation in Great Britain." Once the seven target conditions (secure national independence, exploited benefits of competitive advantage, general employment, exploited foreign/colonial commerce, reigning international peace, genius, talent and industry turned to devising the substitution of machinery for human labor), which he presents as extrapolations from observation, are met, Rae concludes that then "the patronage of the government may be no longer necessary." Further, "*{F}rom this review of the progress of Great Britain*, we may venture to draw the following *inference* of general utility, namely . . . the progress of manufacturing industry may be left to the sagacious superintendence of private industry" (emphasis added) (Rae, "Sketches," in James 1965a, 1: 200).

By the third section, Rae's observations are put to yet further use: "We shall now consider various methods of encouraging the establishment and progress of manufactures, directing our view to the practice of the free instead of the despotic governments of Europe." Rae isolates seven different spheres in which encouragement might be undertaken: capital, materials, workmen, implements and machines, subsistance, abundance of fuel and facility of transportation, education of the people, or a general diffusion of elementary knowledge, and customers or a market. For each, he draws on his observation of the impact of government economic intervention in France, England, Holland, Scotland, Ireland, and the English colonies of North America. Without doubt he rests his case for advocating many diverse types of policies on the lessons afforded by observation of past experience in democratic countries. In this particular work, therefore, Rae moves from dynamic model building with the mere hint of an inductive foundation, to theory building based on the historical experience of Great Britain, to prescriptive recommendations formed again from past empirical reference points.

In the second example here of Rae's writing, his prospectus of "Outlines of the Natural History and Statistics of Canada," the use of induction is far more pervasive. Rae describes the whole of his proposed work on Canada as one designed to trace "the great natural causes, the operation of which has given to the country those distinctive features that both characterize it as a whole, and discriminate one portion of it from the other." (Rae, "Prospectus" in James 1965a, 1: 70). His method for "tracing causes" was primarily empirical observation. First of all, he had traversed the whole of the terrain whereof he wrote:

> For the eighteen years that the author has lived in Canada, he has had this object continually in view, and been collecting materials for it. He has resided in various parts of the country, and traversed all the surveyed parts of it in every direction, from 50 miles below Quebec to Lake St. Clair.
>
> (Rae, "Prospectus" in James 1965a, 1: 71)

Rae considered himself, undoubtedly rightly, unique in having done so:

> It is believed that no work approaching in plan to the present, has been *published by anyone personally acquainted with the country*, . . . Dr Rolph's production . . . laboured under the disadvantage of its author being at the time himself only personally acquainted with a small portion of the Upper Province.
>
> (Rae, "Prospectus" in James 1965a, 1: 71)

Secondly, Rae had engaged in the "collecting,[7] comparing, and arranging" of his observed facts. His work would contain all the pertinent current observations,

> [by] *enumerating* its [the land's] artificial divisions, *tracing* the natural regions, or regions to which they respectively belong; *stating* the progress of agriculture, commerce and population in each, the facilities of communication, either natural or artificial which it enjoys, its particular products and other statistical details.
>
> (Rae, "Prospectus" in James 1965a, 1: 71)

and include some historical details: "proceeding to detail the progress of settlement in it, and the extent to which its vast resources have hitherto been developed" (Rae, "Prospectus" in James 1965a, 1: 71).

While the empirical steps in his work evoke Rae's earlier description of the scientific method, Rae recognized the more logical ones as the being far more off-puttingly "scientific." He intended in his "Outline" to establish two interrelated sets of causalities. One set would reveal the cause of the present characteristics of Canada, which Rae admitted to having learned more easily than anticipated. He writes of the author, himself, that

> as he proceeded with it, he had the gratification of finding, that those causes, to the agency of which may be traced the characteristics of Canada, are not numerous in themselves, and that their operations are very clearly and strikingly marked.
>
> (Rae, "Prospectus" in James 1965a, 1: 70)

The other set would expose the causes of the "capabilities of the country" and "make the Book a practically useful and popular work." Investigation of both sets, Rae felt, required working from the particular, "the peculiarities of the various sections of Canada" to the general, as from particular raw materials to general applications. "A knowledge of all these particulars [climate, flora, fauna, soil, etc.] would seem to furnish a sufficient ground work for comprehending [both] the real nature and capabilities of the country" (Rae, "Prospectus" in James 1965a, 1: 71). He attempted to deflate his readers anxieties, however, by adding that:

> Science will only therefore be called in, when it clearly explains facts and phenomena of general interest, and care will be taken that all scientific principles introduced, be brought forward in a way that may make them perfectly intelligible to the general reader.
> (Rae, "Prospectus" in James 1965a, 1: 71)

With all the emphasis on induction and causal argumentation, it would nonetheless be legitimate to note that the "Outline" was not intended to be a pure work on political economy. The political economics, strickly speaking, was to have appeared in an appendix in the form of "some general notices on the effects of the prices of land, wages of labour, and profits of stock, as modifying the operations of the exports, imports, revenues and all other information that can thus be most conveniently embodied" (Rae, "Prospectus" in James 1965a, 1: 71). Two comments are thus in order. First, the work was clearly intended to have political economic overtones, as manifest in Rae's disclaimer to the readership:

> Though specifically designed for the British public, it is hoped that the work will be of interest to the Canadian reader, by making him well acquainted with the peculiarities of the various sections of *this important dependency of the Empire which he inhabits*, and perhaps by calling attention to interesting phenomena, which he had not previously remarked. [emphasis added]
> (Rae, "Prospectus" in James 1965a, 1: 71)

Second, the fact that political economic data and presumably some conclusions derived from them figure within Rae's predominantly natural historical work is very significant. Just as his pan-application of "averages" across the social sciences bespeaks an integrative methodological approach, his interweaving of inductive facts here gives a similar effect.

One might now add a few more observations about the third text of Rae, his magnum opus, published in 1834, chronologically between the two works already discussed. Despite Rae's rhetorical infatuation with Smith's methodological "errors," his work is primarily an argument for government intervention in the economic sphere, of course another position which Rae felt put him at odds with Smith. Rae's principal purpose was to analyze the factors which determine accumulation of capital. However, unlike his later "Outline," *New Principles* was conceived neither by Rae nor his readers as a textbook. This meant that, in some sense, Rae had liberated himself from the rigors of the paedagogical elements of Baconian methodology, namely, its application as test verifier and eliminator of erroneous common knowledge or other mistaken assertions, and could focus on "ascertaining exactly what it is" (Rae 1834: 361): setting out the occurrence (place, time, frequency, etc.), and cause and effect of phenomena, and establishing laws or principles about that occurrence. From this perspective, Book Two is a lengthy "inductive" exposition of the existence of instruments and the wealth they generate, when, how and why they come to generate that wealth.

Rae's *Principles* also contains a third book, however, and were Rae to have completed the inductive exercise, one would expect it to have contained the last steps of verifying and weeding out errors. Instead, Rae pursues the perspective noted above, but rather than having eliminated the "paedagogical" steps entirely, it would appear that he used Book Three to shift the focus of verifying, not backward on his own theory, but outward to the institution responsible for policy:

> *the result of a successful inquiry into the nature of wealth, would terminate in affording the means of exposing the errors that legislators had committed from not attending to all the circumstances connected with the growth of that wealth*, whose progress it had been their aim to advance, . . . [emphasis added]
>
> (Rae 1834: 361–62)

The quotation continues:

> and would so teach them, not that they ought to remain *inactive*, but how they may act safely, and advantageously; and that thus, it would maintain the analogy running through the whole of man's connexion with the trains of events going on around him, the course of which he governs by *ascertaining exactly what it is*.
>
> (ibid.)

The dichotomy Rae sets out between "ascertaining exactly what it is" via Baconian induction and "inventing with the imagination" in Smithian style is perhaps not the most revealing of his methodological convictions. The distinction between "passive" and "active" postures in every aspect of living, including thinking, was far more important and telling for Rae. He used the distinction often, always loading the notion of "activity" with positive connotations, and "passivity," sometimes with negative ones. Rae frequently, however, tempered the counterpart to "activity" to mean a more low-keyed complementary posture. Examples abound in Rae: from his uses in the quote above from the *Principles* where he opposes the "inactive" or passive posture of the legislator, "passitivity" connoting a "laissez-faire," non-interventionist position, to those in his "Sketches" text, where "active commerce" entails one country's exchange with one or more other countries, and "passive commerce," exchange in which production is "chiefly regulated by internal demand" (Rae, "Sketches" in James 1965a, 1: 196, n. (a)).

Most significant, however, is that Rae's active–passive duality seems to provide the methodological link for his entire approach to all learning and to be the key to his classification of knowledge. To help envisage the way Rae saw this relationship, a diagram is presented here, depicting the place of political economy within the larger context of Rae's intellectual world. The placement of Rae's political economy in the central plane, below the "active" inductive and the complementarily "passive" reflective studies, and above the "active" pursuit of appropriate policies, represents Rae's own perspective in the following way.

Taking political economy as the focal study and defining it, as Rae does, as the study of how material means can conduce to the prosperity of the individual and the community and assuming, again as Rae, that these "common standards" are accepted:

1 that the subject of political economy is the causes of the wealth of a nation,
2 that the method of political economy is induction, and
3 that the possibility exists for investigating, not all causes, but that one which is the sufficient one for the advancement of a nation's wealth,

the key to carrying out the study of political economy was for Rae discovering one or more causes which conduce material means to the prosperity of the individual and the community. Crucial to the study is the distinguishing of the causes from the effects of that prosperity. According to Rae, Smith fell into grave error on this. By a quick falsification method, Rae questioned whether division of labour is a cause and not an effect of technological invention, whether free trade is a cause or an outcome of economic development, whether greed and selfishness have causative potential to lead to a nation's prosperity, or whether they are only the effect of when a nation is already rich.

On what basis, however, does one decide what information or reasonings can be entered as the causal premises of political economic theory? Rae believed that its causes ought to be established both through inductive investigation and by means of "past knowledge, accumulated in books, in libraries" about natural and human phenomena.

> Political Economy . . . is to be considered but as *a branch of a larger science*, having for its object, to trace the laws to which man is subject as a moral and intellectual animal, *acted on by the system of things existing in the world, and acting, in turn on them*, to explain from those laws the events which his past history, as far as is known, exhibits and to collect the means of ascertaining what will be the future course of it. [emphasis added]
>
> (Rae 1934: 78)

For Rae, the study of political economy found thus its place within the hierarchy of studies, dependent upon the conclusions of "a larger science," one which first of all encompasses all the laws affecting human beings, both in terms of their capacity to think and to act, which secondly recounts the effects of those laws in the past, and which thirdly can "collect the means of ascertaining what will be the future course" of human events. In other words, all the conclusions of the empirical natural sciences (or the study of natural histories), of the empirical social sciences (or human histories), and presumably of any other reasonable means of anticipating the future from the past (the "thoughts and readings of the souls of men", perhaps philosophical and literary works) are prerequistes for the study of political economy.

Alas, Rae wrote all too little on the prerequisite divisions of human learning, and of what he did write far too little has survived. Included in Figure 2.1 are, however, only those subjects to which he alludes. Rae's first application of the inductive method was to natural history. There it is an appropriate method because of the numerous observables. Rae notes three natural historical studies: Geology – the history of the earth, or the observation of natural resources; Geography – the study of the way the earth is laid out, or the observation of topography and climate; and Flora and Fauna – the study of things naturally existing before man arrives in any region, comprising observation of local plants and animals. Rae anticipated the transformation of any study's inductive data into useful information, in these cases, about material means. In Geology, natural resources are seen as raw materials for human production; in Geography, topographical configurations are seen as possible routes of communication (rivers, seas, mountain passes, etc.); in both Geography and in the study of Flora and Fauna, climate is seen as conducive to habitation of specific flora and fauna – and to man – and to the production of food resources, in the form of plants and animals

Rae also applied the method of induction to human history and its subdivisions: Anthropology – the study of human life, in the observation of human settlement and activity; History of Technology – the historical study of ingenuity, in the observation of inventions; Political History – the study of human political organization, in the observation of past political organizations; and Philology – the study of language and communication, in the observation of language and other means of communicating behaviour. From these four, again Rae foresaw the derivation of useful information: from Anthropology – information about human welfare (Are humans well adapted to their environment?); from History of Technology – information about technological progress and education (To what end is human ingenuity applied? How is human ingenuity transferred from generation to generation, or from country to country?); from Political History – information about government and government policies (Which forms of policy

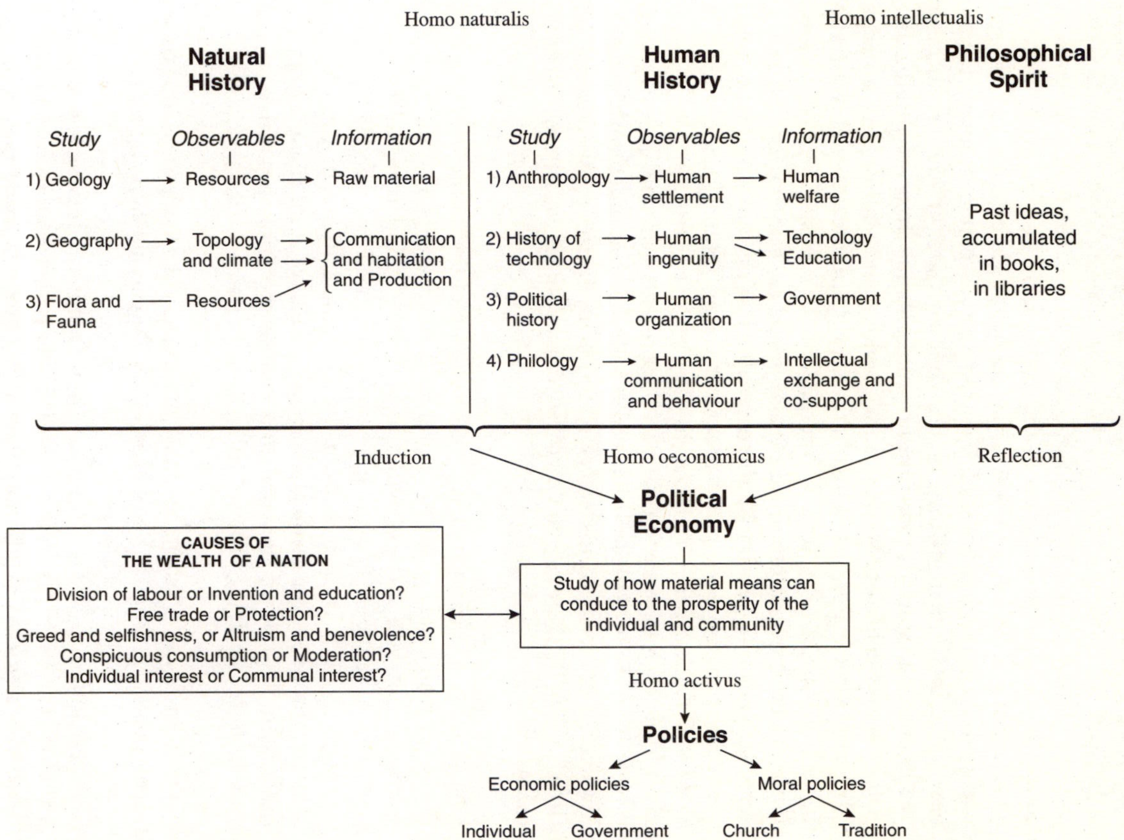


*Figure 2.1* Rae's methodology of economics

work best?); and from Philology – information about intellectual exchange and support of each other (How can humans communicate constructively and help meet each other's needs?).

Natural history and human history are then the inductive source of information for how best the material means for the perpetuation of a human social life can be fostered. Rae felt, however, that in order to make the most beneficial use of the information, about the places which are potential locations for human habitation and about past human experience in living in certain locations and ways, the inductive data has to be infused or conjoined with another body of knowledge: that part of human history not observable in "human history" – past human thought, the products of the "Philosophical Spirit". One might think about these as intellectual reflections in the fields of: Metaphysics/Theology and Philosophy, perhaps even literary works. Rae attributed advances in numerous fields to the fruitful combination of "active" methods and "passive" philosophical reasoning, observing "philosophical reasoning and experimenting having led to great and positive results & these results having in turn given fresh impetus to a spirit of sober rational & persevering inquiry" (Rae, letter to Dr Archibald Hall, April 15, 1852, in James 1965a, 1: 420).

This survey of Rae's prerequisite studies reveals why his investigation into virtually every accessible intellectual realm in the nineteenth century is reknown. In addition to his travel testimonials in the prospectus to the "Outline" of 1840, there are his own reflections on his variety of pursuits. For example:

> I have, however, lately written an article unfolding some views in Geology, which are, I believe, novel, and even to myself somewhat startling, but yet, I think will ultimately be found true. Certain phenomena in these [Hawaiian] islands, and on this ocean, led me to them. . . . I have also written, for a medical friend in Canada, some observations on medical matters . . . I have, too, made some progress in a work on the condition and prospects of these islands.
> (Rae, letter to John Stuart Mill, 1853, in James 1965a, 1: 109)

There are even traces of their reputed quality, as for example, John Stuart Mill's comments on one of Rae's articles on Polynesian languages: it

> will, I think, place Dr. Rae very high among ethnologists and philologists. . . . If his hypothesis [regarding the manner in which the most primitive words may have originated] is made out, it is the keystone of the science of philology, it is *a priori* extremely probable, and the facts he brings forward establish a strong case of verification *a posteriori*.
>
> (James 1965a, 1: 119)

The two methodological sources, induction and reflection, are thus the foundation of Rae's political economic theory and the source of his premises, that is his theoretical causes. Once his prerequiste studies' conclusions are established, they become premises for political economy. More than a methodological affinity for Rae made political science, among the other studies, supremely important to Rae. Indeed, it presented the ideal combination of prerequisite studies for his desired mode of pursuing any study, through "active" induction and "passive" reflection, as noted earlier,

> The study of such a one is in *the spacious library* where undisturbed and uncontrolled he can roam over the thoughts and read the souls of men of all times and countries; or else *the wide world itself*, with all conveniences to explore it and examine the various aspects of nature and of man which it exhibits – *or better still, each alternately*. [emphasis added]
>
> (Letter of 1849, cited by James 1965a, 1: 101).

But further still, it had a purpose. The issues of political economy deeply concerned Rae. Once provided with a foundation, he could establish a political economic theory to reach his conclusions, that is, his theoretical causes of the prosperity of a nation. From the inductive and reflective premises, building an economic theory was a reasonably straightforward matter of leading logical and consistent arguments to their conclusions. Just as in the case of the purely inductive studies, Rae looked forward to the use to which those conclusions could and ought to be put: policies.

The conclusions of political economics, Rae wrote, can take the form of rules or reasoned guidelines according to which both appropriate policy decisions can be made: "the investigation of the political economist, would seem to be confined to the tracing out, from the principles of his science, *rules determining when the passage of any art is practicable, and when the benefits deriving from it will exceed, or fall short of the necessary expense of effecting the passage*" [emphasis added] (Rae, 1834: 364), and inappropriate decisions can be detected:

> [T]he result of a successful inquiry into the nature of wealth, would terminate in affording *the means of exposing the errors* that legislators had committed from not attending to all the circumstances connected with the growth of that wealth, whose progress it had been their aim to advance. [emphasis added]
>
> (ibid. 361)

The policies emanating from (the conclusions of) political economics can be of two types: economic policies, to be implemented either by individuals or government legislators, or ethical "policies," to be "implemented" by either the church or local tradition (the two being frequently mutually exclusive!). Although Rae does allude to ethical policies in the need to rectify the ill-treatment of the maverick genius in society and the erosion of social traditions which maintain appropriate prosperity-inducing behaviour, in his *Principles*, Rae focused almost exclusively on the policy actions of the legislators, as to "how they may act safely, and advantageously" for the economic good of their community. Rae's advocacy position is clear: legislators must become "actively" interventionary, as opposed to holding the "passive" posture of Smithian laissez-faire economics, in especially two circumstances which political economic theory can demonstrate to exist: first, "*when the passage of any art is practicable*," that is, when the transfer of a technology from one region or country to another could be effected given the natural and human resources of the receiving locale; and second, "*when the benefits deriving from it will exceed, or fall short of the necessary expense of effecting the passage*," that is, when the economic return from the expense of the transfer will ultimately surpass the initial cost involved (Rae 1834: 364).

For Rae, the role of the legislator was to implement "actively" appropriate policy, the role of the political economist to teach of that role: "the result of a successful inquiry into the nature of wealth . . . would so teach them [legislators], not that they ought to remain inactive, but how they may act safely, and advantageously" (Rae 1834: 361–62). Rae's professional commitment to teaching was alluded to earlier, as was his faith in its value. He retained an optimism in the results of the endeavor throughout his life and nearing the end of his days, expressed the extent to which he felt its purpose ought to be honed: "the best education is undoubtedly that which most conduces to the prosperity and happiness of the individual, and of the community of which he or she is to be a member" ("Thoughts on the System of Legislation . . . in the Hawaiian Islands," *Polynesian*, March 16, 1861, cited in James 1965a, 1: 351).

In being paedagogically transmitted, according to Rae, political economics would nonetheless fulfil the much broader purpose of unifying human beings, intellectually and pragmatically, with their natural world:

> it would maintain the analogy running through the whole of man's connection with the trains of events going on around him, the course of which he governs by ascertaining exactly what it is. That here, as elsewhere, his advance in knowledge would show him his power, not his impotence.
>
> (Rae 1834: 361–62)

## Conclusion

Three quick points might be made by way of a conclusion to this look at Rae's methodology. It is complex and highly integrated. It cannot be taken at face value. Rae was certainly not explicit about the actual methods he employed or about the weight he gave to their importance. Lastly, induction, for Rae, had the specific meaning of empirical observation, whereby premises for subalternated theories could be derived from the conclusions of empirical studies. One cannot take his anti-Smithian rhetoric about Baconian induction at face value because even as he embraces in words Bacon's induction as the answer, he does not play out his admiration as a strict adherent. That is, however, when his methodological complexity becomes most evident, for only when the study of political economy is placed within the whole of human intellectual endeavour can Rae's own appreciation for an inductive methodology become evident.

## Notes

1 Rae does, however, note that concern for a lack of foreknowledge may in certain "savage" societies affect "development of the accumlative principle." In the case of the life of the American Indian hunter, for example, "man may be said to be necessarily improvident, and regardless of futurity, because, in it, the future presents nothing, which can be with certainty either foreseen, or governed" (Rae 1834: 131).

2 Rae's observations regarding the impact of Smith's conclusions on his readers' expectations or beliefs are considered weak arguments for objection, because Rae described the very same reactions in his *Principles* (1834: 334) as being part of the usual impact of scientific knowledge on its recipients.

3 Rae addresses his notion, of physical properties or qualities being the main source of an instrument's capacity, in several passages: identifying them, for example, specifically as the root source of all effects (Rae 1834: 97).

4 See James (1965a, 1: 195–206) for its reprint and *op. cit.*, 19, n. 21, for comments on its attribution.

5 See James (1965a, 1: 70–72 for its reprint.

6 Only one instance of Rae's acknowledged use of hypothesis has been detected. See Rae 1834: 94 and discussion above.

7 It might also be interesting to note here the frequency with which Rae uses the idea of collecting. In his article, "Sketches" (discussed above), in the context of his policy suggestions regarding "workmen, implements and machines," Rae advocates establishing Chambers of Commerce to collect information on crops and stocks and regarding "subsistence," again, to study and collect information on the localized fertility of the soil and the weather.

3

# THE CONCEPT OF ORDERS OF INSTRUMENTS AND GOODS IN RAE AND MENGER

*S.A. Drakopoulos*[1]

## Introduction

Many works have pointed out the shift in conceptual framework that took place with the marginalist revolution. The emergence of marginalism represented a theoretical shift of major importance with two main characteristics: the change of emphasis to questions of allocation and a movement away from a supply-based explanation of value and prices to a demand-based explanation. A number of historians of economics have characterized this change as an example of scientific revolution in the sense of modern philosophies of science like Kuhn's and Lakatos' (e.g., Coats 1969; Bronfenbrenner 1971; Blaug 1976; Deane 1978).[2] If one accepts the general logic of paradigms or research programs, one is ready to accept the fundamental change in the ways of formulating, and analyzing facts and concepts and in general, the change in conceptual framework.

One can discern an example of the above fundamental change in a critical comparison of a particular aspect of the work of the classical economist J. Rae and of one of the first adherents of the marginalist school, C. Menger. This aspect is the idea of orders. In particular, both economists had as a basis a similar view that objects can be classified in terms of orders. However, they developed a completely different theory which was driven by their respective conceptual framework.

The purpose of this chapter is therefore to illustrate by using the case of Rae and Menger, how the same idea can lead to completely different approaches depending on the conceptual framework. Thus the chapter starts with a brief section on Rae and Menger in historical perspective. In the next section I shall discuss and compare the concept of orders of instruments which can be found in Rae with the orders of goods which is in Menger's work.

## Rae and Menger in historical perspective

Rae (1796–1872) can be classified as belonging to the classical school. Emerging from the Universities of Aberdeen and Edinburgh, he published one main work in Boston, entitled *The Statement of Some New Principles on the Subject of Political Economy, Exposing the Fallacies of the System of Free Trade and of Some other Doctrines Maintained in the "Wealth of Nations."* The book was published in 1834 and, as the title indicates, it was targeted against some of Adam Smith's views. More specifically, he attacked the role of the free-trade and the anti-state views of Smith (Schumpeter 1954: 468–9 and Roll 1973: 418). Apart from his attack on Smith, Rae developed a thorough theory of capital which, as we shall see, had as a starting point the idea of orders of instruments.

Although J.S. Mill had quoted the book, it did not make considerable impact among his contemporaries. Some of his ideas resurface almost 50 years later, in Böhm-Bawerk's theory of capital. Initially, he learned of Rae's ideas through Mill, but later he cited from Rae's book itself (see Mixter 1897, 1902). After a few years, there was a new rearranged edition of his book by C. Mixter (1905) under the title *Sociological Theory of Capital*, through which Rae's ideas started to be re-introduced in the history of economic thought. It has to be pointed out, though, that for the majority of historians, he still remains one of the lesser figures.

On the other hand, Menger (1840–1921) is thought to be a member of the marginalist trinity, although an increasing number of historians of economic thought have promoted the view that Menger cannot be categorized in the same school as Jevons and Walras (see, e.g., Jaffe 1976; Loasby 1976; Alter 1982, 1990; Staley 1989). Menger's ideas were much more influential in terms of subsequent influence than Rae. He was the founder of the Austrian school which can still be discerned as one of the non-orthodox approaches. Menger, for instance influenced the economic thought of E. von Böhm-Bawerk and through him Hayek (Backhouse 1985: 93). The uses of the concept of margin in his economic analysis, his subjective theory of value, and his emphasis upon competitive markets are the main elements which justify his position in the development of marginalist thought (Drakopoulos 1991: 74). The main body of his work is to be found in his first book which has been translated into English as *Principles of Economics* ([1871] 1950). His well-known methodological anti-historicist position can be found in his second book translated as *Problems of Economics and Sociology* (1883).

## Wants, instruments, and goods

For Rae, human wants is the basic concept. "The end [for man] is a supply for future wants" (Rae 1834: 83). On this concept he builds the notion of instrument, which is central in his analysis: "The term instrument is, in general, properly enough employed, to denote any means for the attainment of some end" (Rae, 1834: 86). Combining the above with his definition of end, it is clear, that instruments are the means for the attainment of human wants. The more detailed definition that Rae gives is the following:

> In general then, all those changes which man makes, in the form of arrangements of the parts of material objects, for the purpose of supplying his future wants, and which derive their power of doing this from his knowledge of the course of events, and the changes which his labor, guided by his reason, is hence enabled to make in the issue of these events, may be termed instruments.
>
> (Rae 1834: 87)

Almost forty years later, Menger's definition of the good is conducted in very similar terms. According to Menger, a thing can become a good when the four following conditions are present:

> 1) A human need, 2) Such properties as render the thing capable of being brought into a causal connection with the satisfaction of this need, 3) Human knowledge of this causal connection, 4) Command of the thing sufficient to direct it to the satisfaction of the need.
>
> (Menger [1871] 1950: 52)

It is clear that the two definitions are extremely similar.

Rae goes on to give a number of examples of instruments. For him, a field and the wheat grown on this field are instruments. The want that the wheat satisfies is nourishment (Rae 1834: 88). Further examples are the flour, all tools and machines, houses, ships, cattle, gardens, stores (ibid. 88–9). Menger also gives examples of goods which are more or less similar to the ones we saw in Rae (Menger [1871] 1950: 57). Thus up to this point, one can observe that both authors have extremely similar ideas.

Rae proceeds to list the common points to all instruments:

> 1. They are all either *directly* formed by human labor, or *indirectly* through the aid of other instruments . . .
> 2. All instruments . . . either produce, or contribute to the production, of events supplying some of our wants. Their power to produce such events, or the amount of them that they do produce, may be termed their *capacity*. . . .
> 3. Between the formation and exhaustion of instruments a space of time intervenes.
>
> (Rae 1834: 91–3)

The first point gives the first hint for a classical theory of value. Rae's theory of value is not entirely clear as Böhm-Bawerk ([1889] 1959: 237) had also pointed out. However, one can argue that he held a classical theory in a wider sense (see Ahmad in this volume, p. 115; Maneschi (forthcoming)). As far as the second point is concerned, Rae explicitly states that the measure with which capacities are measured is labour. Again this reinforces the move towards a classical-oriented theory of value. Furthermore, the term "exhaustion" is defined as the passage of things from the class of instruments, into things which are not instruments (Rae 1834: 93).

It is clear that up to now, Rae only talks about instruments, without any reference to the concept of good. For Rae goods are just a special category of instruments. Their distinguishing characteristic is that they can be exchanged:

> Some instruments are easily moved from place to place, and, on this account, they are peculiar facilities, in exchanging them with others. This seems to be the character distinguishing what are called goods, or commodities, from other instruments.
>
> (Rae 1834: 94)

The common measure of instruments is labor. As Rae states: "a day's labor as the unit, serving as the base of calculations, concerning the formation and exhaustion of the capacity of instruments" (ibid. 98). On the other hand, Menger uses satisfaction as the key concept with which different goods are compared. In particular, in the table that he constructs, he compares the magnitudes of satisfaction of different goods by using a scale of satisfactions (Menger [1871] 1950: 127).

Thus one can observe the point of departure here for the two authors. Rae uses labor as the key for comparing instruments and goods, while Menger adopts the concept of satisfaction.

## Orders of instruments and goods

The next concept that Rae builds is the idea of orders of instruments. The basic element which determines the order is time:

> Every instrument would find a place, in some part of a series, of which the orders were determined by the period of time at which instruments placed in them, issue, or would issue, if not before exhausted, in events equivalent to double the labor expended in forming them.
>
> (Rae 1834: 100)

According to Rae, theoretically it is possible to have an infinite number of orders, since the time period determines the order. The definition of instruments which belong to Order A is the following: "They in one year issue in events equivalent to double the labor expended on their formation" (ibid. 101).

By the same reasoning, the definition for Order B is in the same lines, the only difference being that instead of one year, we have two years. The same holds for all other orders. Rae realizes it is possible that many instruments might not be exhausted in an exact number of years or that the capacities might not double the cost of formation. However, it would be possible to "reduce the instruments to some order that may be interposed between two proximate orders" (Rae 1834: 102). One can observe that Rae had a cardinal approach.

Menger, on the other hand, defines orders purely in terms of their proximity to the satisfaction of human needs. More specifically, Menger proceeds to separate goods into four orders. The goods of the first order are those that directly satisfy human needs and therefore acquire value. The second-order goods are those used for the production of the first-order goods, and it is only through this relationship that they acquire their goods character (Menger [1871] 1950: 57). By the same principle, the third-order goods are those that are used for the production of the second-order goods. Finally, the fourth-order goods are those that are used for the production of the third-order goods (ibid.). Thus one can note that only first-order goods which directly satisfy needs have direct value. Values of higher-order goods are imputed (Drakopoulos 1991). Furthermore, Menger's schema is characterized by an ordinal dimension.

Given the above, Menger provides some examples of orders of goods. According to Menger, bread, beverages, clothes are examples of first-order goods since they directly satisfy human needs. The labor service of a journeyman baker and ordinary flour are examples of second-order goods. Grain mills, wheat, rye, and the labour services applied to the production of flour are examples of third-order goods because they are used in the production of the second-order goods. Finally, the fields for the cultivation of wheat and rye, instruments and appliances necessary for their cultivation, and the specific labor services of farmers are examples of fourth-order goods (Merger [1871] 1950: 57).

Rae, based on the definition of orders of instruments, gives two general rules for the placement of instruments into orders. The first rule is as follows: "the shorter the space of time between the period of its formation, and that of its exhaustion, the nearer will any instrument be placed to the order A, that is, towards the more quickly returning orders" (Rae 1834: 108). The second rule relates the capacity and the cost of formation: "the greater the capacity, and the less the cost of its formation, the nearer will any instrument be to the order A; the less the capacity, the greater the cost of formation, the further will it be from A" (ibid.).

The summary of the above is that the proximity of instruments to A is inversely as the cost and the time, and directly as the capacity (Rae 1834: 108). As a final point here, Rae accepts that it is possible to place an instrument further from order A: "the procedure of adding to the durability, by adding equally to the expense of formation, will have greater effect in placing an instrument further from A, the more it is subjected to its operation" (ibid. 111).

Rae gives virtually no specific examples of instruments belonging to orders. However, it is not very difficult to place instruments to orders based on his general definition. It might be interesting to see where the examples that Menger supplies would be placed in Rae's schema. Bread and beverages are first order goods in Menger's system but similarly, they are close to the A orders of instruments in Rae's schema since the period between their formation and exhaustion is short and also because of the relatively low cost of formation. By the same reasoning, grain mills, an example of a third-order good according to Menger, must be further away from the order A since the use time period and the cost are higher than the previous two. The fields for the cultivation of wheat and rye and the instruments necessary for their cultivation, which are all fourth-order goods in Menger's approach, are again even farther away from order A since their cost of formation and the use time are even higher. Thus one can observe that there is a general agreement between the two authors concerning the placement of goods in lower and higher orders. This can be seen as an additional indication that, in the long run, classical and marginal value theories converge.

However, it should be pointed out that the general implications of the concept of order in Menger are radically different from those of Rae. In particular, in Menger's system, capital goods are placed in the category of higher-order goods since they are indirectly linked to human needs. This means that the idea of capital goods or means of production becomes a special category of incomplete consumable goods. The consequence of this is that it "extends the range of the principle of marginal utility over the whole area of production and distribution" (Schumpeter 1954: 913). In general, cost phenomena are explained by the principle of marginal utility.

On the other hand, Rae's approach enables him to set the basis of a theory of capital which is founded upon the concepts of time and cost of production. It is indicative that subsequent historians of economic thought gave Rae the highest credit for his idea that the lengthening of the process of production will in most cases increase the physical amount of the final product (e.g., Schumpeter 1954: 469).

It is possible to think of other similar examples in the history of economic thought where an apparently similar concept or an idea acquires different role and meaning in a new conceptual framework. The example of the concept of utility can be mentioned here. More specifically, it is not unknown that many classical economists such as Ricardo and Mill used the utility approach even in some connection to the theory of value. For instance, Ricardo thought that commodities possess utility and that utility is absolutely essential to exchangeable value (Ricardo [1817] 1978: 5). Furthermore, Mill, in the process of defining wealth explicitly accepts that utilities are embodied in material objects (Mill [1848] 1909: 46–8). However, utility was never employed to build an entirely subjective theory of value as was the case with the marginalist school.

## Concluding comments

The basic idea of this chapter was to examine the concept of orders of instruments in the thought of Rae and the concept of orders of goods in Menger. It was seen that both writers had an exceptionally similar definition of instruments and goods based on the idea of human needs. Subsequently, they both devised the concept of order which categorizes instruments and goods. For Rae, the basic criterion for the placement of instruments to orders is time and the cost of formation. These ideas were the building blocks for a classical theory of capital, technology, and accumulation. For Menger, the placement of goods in orders depends on how directly they satisfy human needs. Reflecting the marginalist perspective, Menger's wider aim was the construction of a theory of consumer. The two criteria also indicate the difference between a classical theory of value that Rae had and the subjective theory of value that was followed by Menger. In spite of this however, the paper showed that there is a general agreement between the two authors concerning the placement of goods in lower and higher orders. Given the different theories of value on which they are based, this point is of particular importance. It was then argued that the case of orders in Rae and Menger is a good example of how the same idea can lead to completely different approaches depending on the conceptual framework: Rae's thought is closer to the traditional themes of the classicals, while Menger's ideas reflect the shift of emphasis to demand-based theories. A similar example might be the concept of embodied utility which was employed by classical economists, but it never led to a utility-based theory of value. Thus the findings of this chapter might be seen as reinforcing the belief that the role of conceptual framework, or paradigm if one wants to follow a Kuhnian approach, is important in understanding the development of economic thought.

## Notes

1 Department of Economics, University of Aberdeen, Aberdeen AB9 2TY, U.K. and Department of Philosophy and History of Science, University of Athens, 37 J. Kennedy Str. 161 21, Athens, Greece. Acknowledgments are due to the

participants of the John Rae Bicentenary Conference held at the University of Aberdeen in March 1996. I am especially indebted to Professors S. Hollander and S. Ahmad. The usual disclaimer applies.

2 It has to be noted though that not all historians of economics accept the idea of scientific revolutions especially with reference to the classical and the marginalist schools (e.g., Hollander 1979).

# 4

# RAE'S THEORY OF THE HISTORY OF TECHNOLOGICAL CHANGE

*B.B. Price*

In Rae's *New Principles*, technological change was an issue of extreme importance. Rae had become quickly aware that technology is the root cause of economic prosperity and social benefit. As in all of his intellectual inquiries he set about researching it from many different perspectives. His investigations into the histories of various technologies evolved in several directions. One was his pursuit of detailed accounts of the stages in the historical development of certain technologies. Another was his relatively pure political economic route, examining, through capital theory, the general economic causes and results of technological change. In this chapter, Rae's theory of the history of technology is addressed; it is in some respects his combination of both history and political economy, yielding a theoretical inquiry into the reasons for technological change in the past.

## Rae's history in light of theory

Rae's conviction in the value of history as a guide to theoretical investigation lies inexplicitly behind his idea that history specifically provides the route to understanding and developing a theory of technological change. An initial reasoning was a quite general one, applicable to virtually any theoretical investigation:

> [T]here is nothing more apt to mislead us, when investigating the causes determining the motions of any great system, than to take our station at some particular point in it, and examining the appearances there presented to us, to suppose that they must be precisely similar through the whole sphere of action.
>
> (Rae 1834: 125)

To Rae's mind a historical perspective could guide one away from narrow and erroneous conclusions, by presenting the investigator with a much greater wealth of examples that otherwise his mere experience or that of his immediate contemporaries might afford. "[I]f we confine our attention to the present times, and to some particular parts of the globe" we may find ourselves drawing completely unwarranted generalizations, Rae asserted, pointing the finger thereby at Adam Smith's claims for the "universally" beneficial value of self-interest (ibid.).

In addition to providing the researcher with a richer data base, however, the historical perspective also contains imbedded within it the dimension of time's passage, which Rae found particularly important in his investigation of technologies. He conceived all technological change within the context of time. Not only did Rae note quite generally that "all events take place in time," but that because this is the case time has elapsed between when a piece of technology comes into use and when it ceases to be useful: between the "formation and exhaustion of instruments" a space of time exists (Rae 1834: 100).

Rae did not, however, intend the whole of his *Statement of Some New Principles on the Subject of Political Economy, Exposing the Fallacies of the System of Free Trade, and of Some Doctrines Maintained in the* "Wealth of Nations" to be an examination of the history of technology even from a theoretical perspective. Nonetheless, its consideration does play a significant part in his thought, and specifically here, it is important to note that Rae wanted his reader to believe that he had gleaned many of his theoretical assertions about technological change from the historically known course of such changes. In an extremely concentrated discussion (Rae 1834: 224–53), he presented some half a dozen histories, a few with his sources for the historical detail duely noted.[1] He introduced and identified the various histories as examples or instances,[2] announcing generally:

> The limited objects of the present inquiry, however, forbid our entering into the lengthened train of speculation, that would be necessary fully *to establish these conclusions by an adequate investigation of the progress of inventions. I shall content myself with adducing a sufficient number of instances*. [emphasis added]
>
> (Rae 1834: 225)

In some passages Rae actually acknowledged limitations to his primary desire to obtain theoretical conclusions from the history of technological change. He seems to have had relatively little patience with detail, and frequently pushed on to conclusions while acknowledging an insufficiency of facts (e.g., Rae 1834: 225, 226). In many cases a course of events' being probable as recounted was adequate grounds for his assuming it had occurred thus, particularly if its "probable-ness" was reinforced by observations of corroborating practices "in more recent times."[3] Nonetheless, Rae was very respectful of the great range of experiences usually required to arrive at the greatest efficacy of a technology and therefore of the long, and perhaps unpredicatably circuitous, series of changes which might make up its history. To Rae, the physical qualities of any technologcal device posed difficulty in assessing *a priori* its most proper application.

He offered three examples which derive from his historical investigations: the simple instrument of the wedge, the somewhat more complex instrument of the plough, and the much more complicated machines of the steam engine and cotton mill. First, the wedge:

> A wedge operates in many ways, besides those that may be considered to be derived from mathematical principles; as for instance in the percussion, which it received and communicates, and through means of which, if skillfully applied, the most solid rocks may be rent.
>
> (Rae 1834: 87)

The many possible ways of its operation pose therefore a potential problem to any theorist in assuming the course of the use of the wedge in, for example, man's desire to build sacred architecture out of stone. From Figure 4.1 derived from Rae, it can be seen that historically he attributes to the Egyptians the first use of the wedge, as chisel, for sacred architecture. The wedge figures in his history as the first application of "invention" to religious stone architecture, used, "slowly, by dint of strokes intermitted not for generations," to excavate or cut rock, an art he notes as already perfected by the "ancient Troglodytes" (Rae 1834: 231, 234). The actual forming of the wedge in terms of its own weight and material and the means of communicating its percussive power is unmentioned by Rae, although he acknowledges that therein lies its own history.

The example of the plough is even more problematic for Rae the theorist:

> The farther we recede from such simple instruments, the more extensive do we find the action of properties, which could only be ascertained by a long series of observations. It would be impossible, for instance, to give any *a priori* rules for the construction of that most useful instrument the plough. It is, no doubt, a wedge, but the particular form giving the greatest efficacy to it, is a point of very difficult determination, not yet, perhaps, fully ascertained. It is accurate observation that has guided the construction of it, to its present efficiency, and which may be expected to render it still more perfect.
>
> (Rae 1834: 87)

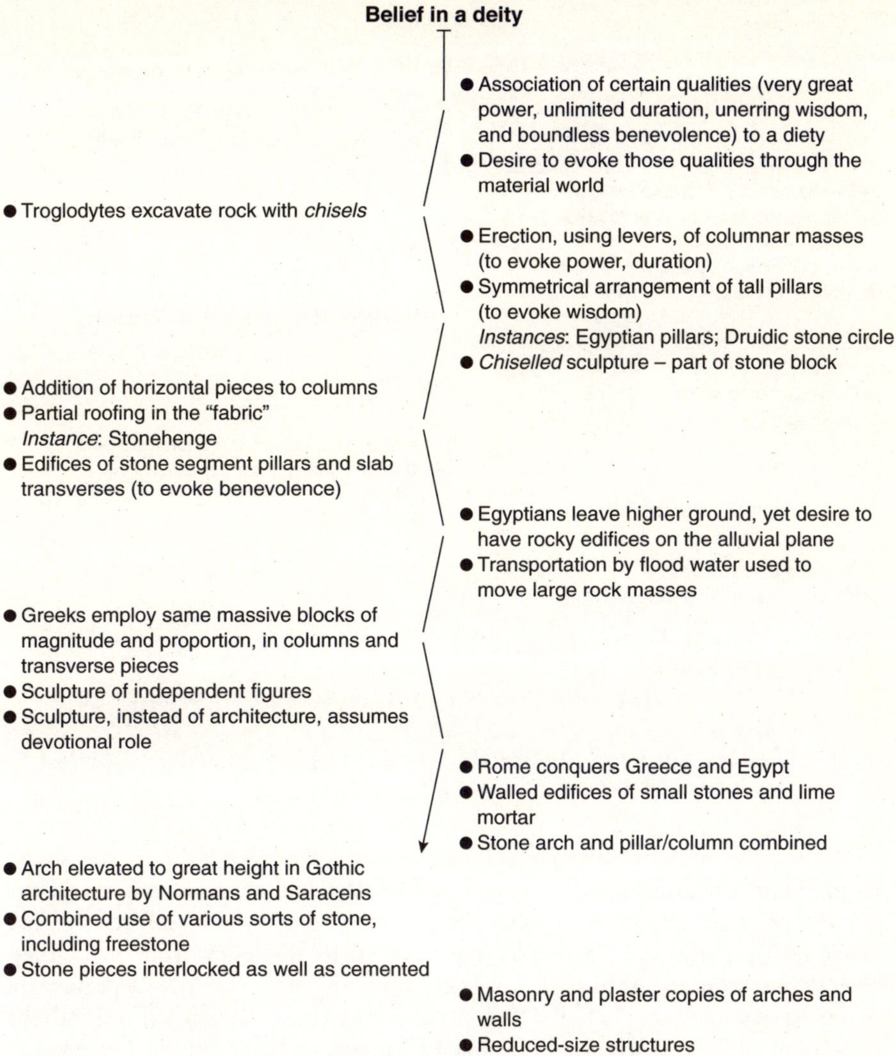


*Figure 4.1* Rae's history of sacred architecture

The course of that "accurate observation" which has guided construction and undoubtedly also use of the plough was traced directly by Rae the historian (see Figure 4.2). Despite his use of "probable-ness" to fill gaps in his history, his inclusion of the plough in his collection of technological histories might have been one of his most revealing statements about the difficulty of theorizing *a priori* steps in technological change without a detailed record.

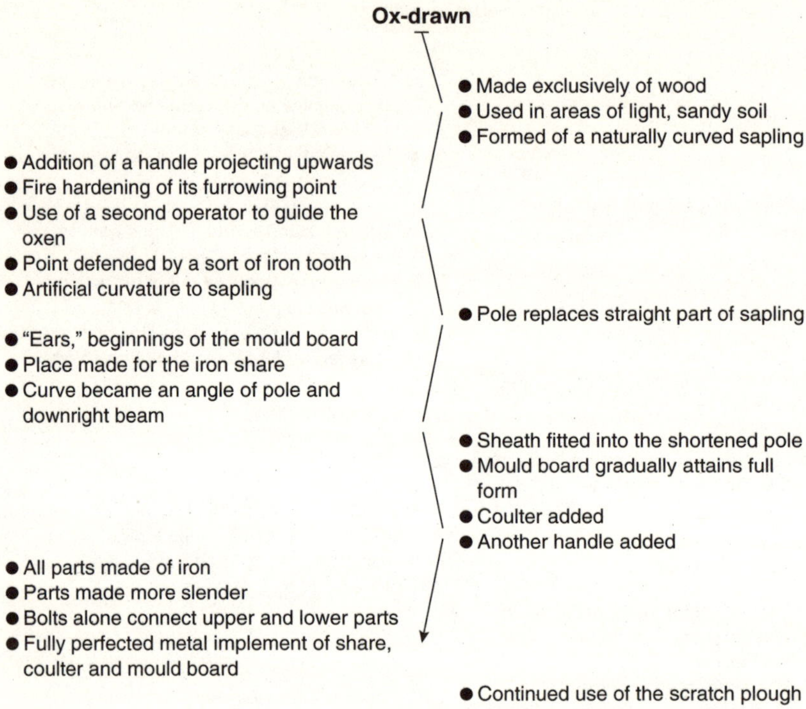


*Figure 4.2* Rae's history of the plough

As for the most highly complicated machines known to Rae, the steam engine and the cotton mill, the observation that only history can reveal the course of their evolution applies, Rae says, "with double force," because such technologies are "generally deriving their efficiency from principles, that have been the result of very extensive and accurate investigations of many series of events" (Rae 1834: 87). Again those investigations and the results of those investigations cannot be known and charted *a priori*. Hence, again, similar to the case of the plough, Rae tellingly offers a history, rather than a theory, of the steps toward the technological change which brought the steam engine about (see Figure 4.3). (Unfortunately Rae did not provide his own history of the cotton mill.)

As shall be discussed below, Rae did, nonetheless, build a theory of the history of technological change and to do so relied extensively on ahistorical sources: his own interest in technology and his very personal experiences as inventor, as well as his own observations of technologies in actual use. As the organization of his major work reflects, to his theoretical discussion of historical change in chapter 10 he seems to have already methodically

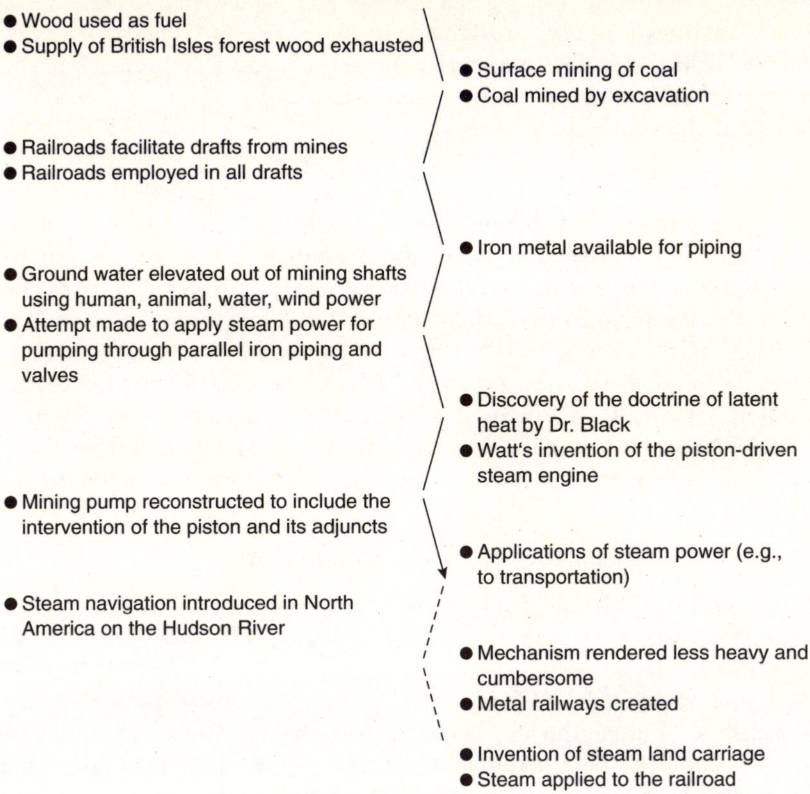


*Figure 4.3* Rae's history of steam power

brought both his impressionistic ideas on invention (presented earlier in the same chapter) and current cultural observations (esp. chapter 7). Rae's coalescing theory on technological change appears to some extent to have in fact provided for him a strongly "extra-historical perspective" for the observation and theoretical explanation of technological patterns in history. Even as applicable to history, Rae's initial perspective was comprised of numerous elements. To note especially would be his abstract capital theory model for analyzing the use of instruments, his general propositions from many sources (such as the epistemological "Men first see in the concrete, afterwards in the abstract" (Rae 1834: 239) ) and his knowledge of scientific principles (e.g., of "the expanse and collapse of a vapor" (246) ).

The sense that theory dominated Rae's historical examination is reinforced by the fact that theoretical terms, such as "instrument," "power," etc. critical to his historical examples, follow from preceeding theoretical discussions.

> The term instrument is, in general, properly enough employed, to denote any means for the attainment of some end. In common use, however, and as applied to material things, it seems to be restricted to such arrangements of matter as owe their chief efficacy to what are called the mechanic powers.
>
> (Rae 1834: 86)

By "mechanic powers" Rae seems to have meant two types of an instrument's functioning. On the one hand, the operation of instruments can be chiefly analyzed along mathematical or mechanical principles. Rae cites the examples of a lever, considered according to "the properties of a mathematical line," and wedge, as well as that of a spade, "which is a combination of the two." "In all these cases, however," Rae wrote, "other principles than those which are merely mathematical must enter our calculations." Thus, on the other hand, instruments are also instruments by virtue of the action of their physical properties, such as according to their weight or substance.

## Rae's theory in light of history

Out of his combined historical information and theoretical ideas, what then was Rae's explanation for how technological change *had taken place* in the past? Rae had what might be termed a micro- and a macrotheory of the history of technological change. In the context of his *Statement* they appear as an individual theory and a societal theory. Rae's derivation of each theory from the past activity of specific sectors and the sources for each of Rae's theories will be discussed in the context of a micro/macro division.

### *Rae's microtheory*

Rae's microtheory of past technological change is based upon his theory of the contributions of individual members to society at large. In the context of technological change, the members which interest him most are those who have been considered to have novel or new ideas that can be turned into technological inventions. Their main contribution to technological change is to propose new instruments and thereby to initiate realizations of new technologies.

Inventions "generally take their rise in this way," says Rae. The first step is the occurance of the idea. "Some idea new, or conceived to be new, flits by chance across the brain of a man unaccustomed to new ideas." The next immediate step is the contemplation of that idea by the one who conceived it: "The novelty of the thing, and still more so the novelty of its occurring to himself, sets it in a point of view that puts out of sight all other conceptions and magnifies itself so prodigiously that he can see nothing else." These two phases, while critical, are perhaps the least publicized of the theoretical process, for, Rae believed, "nine out of ten of all mechanical schemes are abortive" (Rae, draft of a letter to Hugh Bowlby Wilson, *c.*1850–65, in James 1965a, 1: 112). In other words, most of Rae's history of inventions is nonhistory!

Although the source of Rae's statistical evidence is unknown, he seems to have derived some of his theory of invention from historical examples, as well as from his own experience. He mentions only the fewest of inventors throughout history. Quite obviously, the historical names "that now pass current" are rarely those of the unrecognized inventors (Rae 1834: 215). Galileo is noted as an almost casualty, as one having "experienced at first either comparative neglect, or partial, or general opposition" (ibid. 215). Watt (ibid. 248),[4] and Guttenburg, Peter Schoeffer, and Fust (ibid. 250) represent success stories.

From his own past, Rae derived the data that inventors' brainstorms are most frequently not perceived as feasible. He had himself designed a device for determining sea-current rates and direction:

> I was then [*c.*1811–14] under a very eminent professor of mathematics in the Marischal College, Aberdeen, the late Dr. [Robert] Hamilton, and showed it him. He allowed it sound in theory and ingenious, but smiled it down as impracticable. . . . Dr. Hamilton's objection to my scheme was that it was very good on paper. . . . *I cannot but think, however, that the temper of mind which led him to object was one with which all inventions are commonly, one might almost say reasonably, met.* [emphasis added]
>
> (Rae, draft of a letter to Hugh Bowlby Wilson, *c.*1850–65, in James 1965a, 1: 112)[5]

As, however, Rae insisted regarding his own project, if inventions derive from a fertile combination of reason and observation, however inexperienced the inventor in inventing, the ideas often can be realized.[6] In fact, he argued that this inspirational combination was the source of any and all realizable technologies.

> It is true, that, in most instances, men simply copy the proceeding of others, and think not of the principles on which they conduct their operations, nor of the observations from which these must originally have been deduced. But, *though the knowledge thus acquired from this storing of observations, and deduction of principles from them, is not the mode in which individual men operate, it is the mode in which the operations they carry on must have been first brought into practice, and on which they are all founded.* [emphasis added]
>
> (Rae 1834: 83–4)

Rae cites both textual and observational evidence for his claim. He is so sure of the textual evidence that he asserts that were his claim not true this would be reflected in "any complete treatise on any art." The full historical record of any technology, in some sense, according to Rae, affirms that "on examining it, we would invariably find it to contain a set of observations, the result of [past] experience, and of reasonings, and rules, drawn from these observations" (ibid. 86).

In effect, any realized individual contribution to technology is, for Rae, the result of a series of theoretically derivable steps, all of which depend upon observation and reason. In most respects, realizing an invention is not a fundamentally different activity from any other. According to Rae, human beings undertake to make technological changes for the same reasons and by the same general means they "proceed" to do anything: "The proceedings of man are every where similar. He has always an end in view, he employs means to effect this end, and there is a manner through which he effects it" (ibid. 83). What separates the realizing of an invention from other activities is, however, its novelty, its being the *very first time* a "proceeding" has either had that certain end in view, has met that end in that specific way, or has gone about meeting an end in a certain way.

Thus how "the vast number of qualities and powers, and of new practical combinations of them . . . [that] have been discovered and applied to use" had indeed come about, interested Rae, especially as he noted both that for much of human history there had not been much realization of inventions and that in many as-it-were potential instances this was with good reason. For much of human history and still in his day, Rae observed that most individuals concerned themselves so with "the busy circle of actual life and occupations" that they simply have not "turned their eyes" toward inventing (Rae 1834: 254). Among those that have, however, most presented such impractical ideas as inventions that it was "reasonable" to object to their realization (Rae, draft of a letter to Hugh Bowlby Wilson, *c.*1850–65, in James 1965a, 1: 112). So what then was the key to successfully inventing a realizable technological device? Rae set out a theoretical answer.

The process of devising a realizable invention, which Rae connects directly to his observation of Native Americans, has four steps:

1 The individual starts by taking advantage of his knowledge of the nature of things around him.
2 He finds himself specifically instructed, by observing succeeding trains of events forming phenomena, or by perceiving laws which regulate specific motions, to be able to direct them himself, at least conceptually.
3 His knowledge of the materials around him enables him actually to form the device he wants.

4 His knowledge of the manner in which natural change occurs enables him to place that device within the natural world and occasion it to produce what he will desire later.

Rae elaborated briefly on each step. By virtue of the first step, once human beings know the nature of things around them, they realize that at that time not every thing they have is abundant enough, or satisfying enough to them in other ways. In addition, they project to the future. Since, first, the known present conditions are presumed not to be "improving" without human intervention, and second, current wants and desires will be similar in the future, they assume that the present lack will also be felt in the future. The inventor, according to Rae, would not concern himself with thinking about how to secure or enhance the supply of things which already exist in abundance relative to his wants and desires (Rae 1834: 83). Those individuals, however, who profoundly desire to change a present dearth of certain things for the future, move on to the next step.

In the second step, the individual develops his "capacity for perceiving, and retaining in his mind, the course of events and the connexion of one with another" (Rae 1834: 81). That capacity affords him a twofold knowledge: "of the qualities with which nature has endowned the materials within his reach" and "of the series of events in consequence arising among them." With that knowledge he can determine what the materials and the course of events unmodified would cause to bring about in the future and how he might change them to provide for his wants (ibid. 83). "This provident forethought distinguishes him from the inferiour animals, and the degree in which he possesses it marks his rank in the scale of civilization" (ibid. 81).

The invention is realized in the third step through material changes. This is where the astuteness of the combination of the would-be inventor's "faculties of observation and reason" is tested.[7] As an inventor who has progressed through steps one and two, he ought to have, through the application of his knowledge, "the power of effecting" the material changes he has thus far only thought possible, "for these objects of his desires are mere arrangements of matter" (Rae 1834: 81). Rae sees the realizer's task as changing one particular arrangement of matter to produce, "through his corporeal powers" (as distinct from his previously most active cerebral powers), a new arrangement (ibid. 83). Thus, for example, the inventor-farmer devised and made "an iron hook having a form and edge which experience had ascertained to be best adapted for this purpose," cutting down the perceptably ripe grain (ibid. 84).

By the fourth step, to Rae's mind, the inventor-realizer is aware of having so altered "the trains of events" proceeding from things that he may expect results in the future which differ from those that the nature of things in the past has brought about. The new relationship of material things, by virtue of their including the invention, "may either form, or cause to be formed, or put in his possession, objects fitted to supply more perfectly or abundantly what probably will be his future wants, than those objects would otherwise exist" (Rae 1834: 81–2). Technological change has been brought about and a new instrument created. Imbedded in Rae's very definition of "instrument" are all the inventing–realizing stages, 1–4, which have brought the "instrument" about. In the following quotation, the components, in their different ordering within his definition, are identified by means of a number in square brackets to indicate the particular stage:

> [4] all those changes which man makes, [3] in the form or arrangements of the parts of material objects, [1] for the purpose of supplying his future wants, and [2] which derive their power of doing this from his knowledge of the course of events, and [3] the changes which his labor, [2] guided by his reason, [4] is hence enabled to make in the issue of these events, may be termed instruments.
>
> (Rae 1834: 87)

A first glance then at the micro or individual scale of Rae's theory of the history of technological change might present only the initial realization of an invention as constituting technological change. While each new adoption of a technology by each new individual is in a very real sense for Rae a change for that person, what he does not hesitate to argue, nonetheless, is that the long-term historical impact of that change may be insignificant.[8] His example of the production of the flail comes to mind. Even if all "the persons employed in the operation of threshing" were over time to adopt the flail and production of flails were to be able to meet that demand, the adoption of the flail, by all would have little impact on technological change (Rae 1834: 19–20). His reasoning was that once the needs of the threshers for flails had been met, there would presumably be nothing about the instument itself, its design, or the means of its production which could change. Only with the introduction of an invention, a new instument, would there occur technological change.

### *Rae's macrotheory*

Rae's microtheory of technological change was but one part of the whole. Rae did not consider history to report that the thoughts and actions of inventors have been the only determinators of technological change. Although the inventor's activities might be important mavericks of the larger social context, Rae saw "the general course of action of the individual" also as the result of "circumstances determining that of the society" (Rae 1834: 127). Rae was convinced that the general course of individual adoption or rejection of technological change was largely the causal result of greater social conditions. It interested him therefore what at any particular time the disposition of human culture or part of it was, particularly with respect to aspects of technological change. "The subject would not therefore be fairly exhausted, until all the circumstances of the moral and intellectual state, and other particulars of the condition of every people, had been examinied" (ibid. 163). This led him to note and theorize as well about instances of nonchange and attitudes counter to technological change.

As a starting point for his macrotheory, Rae seemed to have believed that at least one condition had to exist within a specific human culture for technological change to occur at all. He referred to this condition as "the principle leading to the formation of instruments," the desire to accumulate. Since Rae observed "the effective desire of accumulation" to be "of different degrees of strength . . . in different societies, as compared with each other," as well as "in the several individuals composing the same society as compared together" (Rae 1834: 130), he probed the reasons for this difference and arrived at the following conclusion:

> The desire to accumulate would then seem to derive strength, chiefly from three circumstances:
>
> 1. The prevalence throughout the society, of the social and benevolent affections, or, of that principle, which under whatever name it may be known, leads us to derive happiness, from the good we communicate to others.
> 2. The extent of the intellectual powers, and the consequent prevalence of habits of reflection, and prudence, in the minds of the members of the society.
> 3. The stability of the condition of the afffairs of the society, and the reign of law and order throughout it.
>
> It is weakened, and strength given to the desire of immediate enjoyment, by the three opposing circumstances:
>
> 1. The deficiency of strength in the social and benevolent affections, and the prevalence of the opposite principle, a desire of mere selfish gratification.
> 2. A deficiency in the intellectual powers, and the consequent want of habits of reflection and forethought.
> 3. The instability of the affairs of the society, and the imperfect diffusion of law and order throughout it.
>
> (Rae 1834: 124)

To this list of three favorable and three unfavorable circumstances for the accumulative principle to exist, he also added: (4) "motive to exertion" or "a want of motives to exertion," and (5) "the principles and habits of action which would lead to effective exertion" or "a want of the principles and habits of action which would lead to effective exertion" (ibid. 134–5).

Rae could have argued that any part of the human experience which might serve as an empirical source for his theoretical assertions would date from prehistory. On the contrary, however, his interest and confidence in his claims derived from contemporary societies of North America. Given that the circumstances for that initial step toward a chain of technological transformations of one's natural and social environment seem to be as demanding as:

1 a sensitivity to a relationship between happiness and benevolence,
2 intellectual reflection and prudence,
3 social stability and law,
4 motivation to expend effort, and
5 knowledge about and practice in expending effort,

Rae quite rightly, it seems, contemplates how any social group could have become (or remained) technological: "instead of there being any reason for surprise at the hunter of the woods disdaining the labors and rewards of civilization, it is rather our business to inquire how he could ever have been led to adopt them" (Rae 1834: 148).

In part, Rae seems to be saying that the answer lies outside the realm of the historian – or even theoretician – of technology, strictly speaking. If, however, the argument is firmly that once the above five conditions are met, technological change will ensue, it does become the task of the theoretician of such change at the very least to be able to verify that claim. Without any real use of historical data, Rae feels he can do so for each condition. Circumstances 1 and 2 are closely linked. Where intellectual powers, and the consequent prevalence of habits of reflection, and prudence, are manifest in the minds of the members of the society, there is where invention can and will occur. Nonetheless:

> Abstract and scientific truth can only be discovered, by deep and absorbing meditation; imperfectly at first discerned, through the medium of its dull capacities, the intellect slowly, and cautiously, not without much of doubt, and many unsuccessful essays, suceeds in lifting the veil that hides it. The procedure is altogether unlike the prompt determination, and ready confidence, of the man of action, and generally unfit, to a greater or less degree, for performing well the part. He, again, who dwells in the world of possible moral beauty and perfection, moves awkwardly, rashly, and painfully, through this of everyday life, he is ever mistaking his own way and jostling others in theirs.
>
> (Rae 1834: 213–14)

Hence the first condition must also hold: "it were, perhaps, *enough in answer to observe*, that the existence of genius among a people" (emphasis added), requires and implies at least, both a motivation on the part of the inventing genius, posited to be "the good arising from communicating good and the consequent desire to be a benefactor in the most extended possible manner," and the existence within the social setting of "the diffusion of a tincture of generous feelings, somewhere throughout the mass" such that the eccentric genius element is benevolently tolerated within the society (Rae 1834: 212, 210).

Rae's evidence for circumstance 3, social stability and law, as the context for technological change is also not exactly historical, though he does single out the Roman Empire to exemplify a society whose wars led to a diminution of the accumulative principle and hence technological transformations (Rae 1834: 158–61). His assertion is very simply elaborated and by the contrary: "whatever disturbs, or threatens to disturb, the established order of things, by exposing the property of the members of society to danger, and diminishing the certainty of its future possession, diminished also the desire to accumulate" (ibid. 222).

The essentiality of circumstances 4 and 5 is perhaps the most problematic for it lies on the fringes of the dispute between Rae and Adam Smith over the role of the division of labor in technological advance. According to Rae's claim, however, it is merely the effort and know-how of the individual to make "almost all the instruments he himself or his family exhaust", not the subsequent "division of employments," which is essential (Rae 1834: 173). Obviously the "effort and know-how to make instruments" entails a certain level of technology. Rae would undoubtedly have responded by wondering what effort does not. "It is seldom, that even the most common laborer is not assisted in his operations by some implement or another" (ibid. 91).

In this case, Rae would further see the initial implement as reflecting an art "so rude, and accumulation so little advanced" that it could hardly be considered a link in the chain of technologcal change. As a reflection of this position, Rae's histories of sequential technological change never start earlier than the devising of a specific instrument or a specific end for an instrument. For example, he writes of "domesticating the ox, and teaching him labor," that it cannot have had a direct historical path:

> *To suppose that men*, while the whole of that species of animals were yet wild, *conceived the project of domesticating them, in order that they might apply them to the various purposes they now serve, were a conjecture altogether unwarranted by any event in the history of mankind and of art*. We have rather reason to believe that in this, as in other instances, *they must have been led on to the object gradually, by the intervention of circumstances, each carrying them a certain way towards this great end*. [emphasis added]
> (Rae 1834: 251–2)

Circumstances 4 and 5, the motivation and the undertaking of an effort, must thus be prerequisites for division of labor and not the result, as Rae considered Smith to have argued. For Rae, the sequence of events is as follows:

> in the early stages of human society, some persons, more ingenious than the rest, make discoveries and improve the natural products in a variety of modes, whence gradually arise the division of labour, the difference of professions . . . *From making clothes and utensils for his family, the man of an inventive mechanical turn will be led by degrees to a profitable employment of his time and talent in working for others.* [emphasis added]
>
> (Rae, 1825: 195–6)

Rae does admit that "in an advanced state of society, very few wants are supplied but by articles or instruments which have passed through many hands." The farmer, for example, transfers his fleeces on and "after they have passed through the hands of the carder, the spinner, the weaver, the fuller, &c. part of them returns to him again in the shape of cloth for some garment that he is in need of" (ibid. 166).

Rae continues his theoretical sequence of ideas by reflecting on the causes which determine the degree of 'technologization' of any society, at least in terms of "the amount of instruments," once the conditions for the initial technological presence are present. The issue of the quality of the instruments seems also to be addressed inexplicitly thereby:

> The causes determining the amount of instruments, formed by any society, will, I believe, be found to be four:
>
> 1. The quantity and quality of the materials owned by it.
> 2. The strength of the *effective desire of accumulation*.
> 3. The rate of wages.
> 4. The progress of the inventive faculty. [emphasis added]
>
> (Rae 1834: 109)

The first of the four causes of an increased use of technology by any society Rae noted was "the quantity and quality of the materials owned" by it. Rae declared quite early in his work that "Every society possesses a certain amount of materials capable of being converted into instruments" (Rae 1834: 99). Since this is one of three points Rae chose to itemize as "circumstances arising from the institution of society" (Rae 1834: ch. 3), it would seem to emphasize that *every* society has some materials available in sufficient quantity for making instruments and also in a quality which allows them to be made "submissive" to becoming instruments.

It is however, not the mere existence of materials in certain quantity and quality which determines the degree of technology of a society, but more importantly, for Rae, the diversity of them. Rae argues that the degree to which individuals use different materials, their society's technology improve:

> *This diversity of materials seems to have been the great exciting cause to the progress of art and science*, men having been every now and then compelled or induced to adopt new materials, and, as they changed from the one to the other, to have been gradually led from the knowledge of the most simple and obvious qualities, and powers, to a perception of those which are more complex, and difficult to discern.
>
> Tracing any invention upwards to its first beginnings, we shall discover, that these have been exceedingly rude and imperfect, preceding from the simplest, and what would seem to us, the most obvious observations; and that it has advanced towards perfection, *by having been led to change the materials with which it originally operated*, and passing from one to another, has at each step of its progress discovered new qualities and acquired new powers. [emphasis added]
>
> (Rae 1834: 224)

In his theory of the "history of inventions," Rae emphasizes the distinct ways in which use of a diversity of materials comes about to cause technological advance. According to one scenario, when "arts change materials," the difficulty or downright impossibility to obtain "the materials with which they had been accustomed to operate" causes human beings perforce to adopt different materials. According to a second, when "different arts adopt the same materials," new materials are selectively chosen over the ones formerly used. In the case of the first scenario in which individuals have been compelled to use different materials, it is their combining their retained knowledge of "the qualities and powers of the old" materials with those of the new which brings about a positive technological change. The second scenario differs from the first in that change derives from individuals having been induced or "encouraged to operate with new materials" because the new ones appear "evidently better suited to their purposes than the old."

Rae presents his theoretical scenarios both as if deriving from his histories of technology and as if offering examples of them. With his histories, Rae both posits and provides documentation for his assertions that use of a diversity of materials, whether "compelled or induced," causes changes in one of two ways: either in conjunction with the purposeful integration of scientific ideas into the technical "arts," or due to the observations of an instrument's new qualities and powers.[9] Metallurgy reflects the latter type of progress from "rude and imperfect" results to highly advanced ones through the experiential adoption of different materials, gold, silver, copper, and iron.

> There are few arts, either, in which the processes have probably at first been more rude, in which they have ultimately attained greater perfection of skill, or in which the progress has been more gradual, and more dependent for its advance on the variety of materials opened upon.
>
> (Rae 1834: 226)[10]

The example of the plough is of a similar type, in which "the change of materials of which it is formed" seems "to have been the occasions of its successive improvement" (ibid. 229). His histories of the regular mill and steam power exemplify the other kind of stages in which the diversity of materials causes technological change through the introduction of scientific ideas into the technological base.

There is further a theoretical correlate to Rae's assertion that the availability and use of specific materials is one of the causes of technological advance. He underlines that geography and technological change are inherently interrelated, in two respects. It has been observed that in certain areas the readiness with which "the most difficult materials" can be formed into instruments is remarkable, whereas in others, quite the reverse, and that this is a result of the geographical setting of the materials (Rae 1834: 154) The second kind of relationship stems from the geographical instances of materials: where they exist, they have the potential to, and often do effect changes. Water-driven mills could be constructed only where (and when) "there was a current suited to the purpose." Steam power was notably first applied to pumps in mines where water was both overly available to be raised out of the mines and sufficiently available to be used as the pump's power source. Its later application to riverboats occurred specifically where the geography made the demand the greatest:

> [T]he peculiar circumstances of the North American continent, may, with propriety, be said to have been the exciting cause producing steam navigation . . . That country is full of great lakes and rivers, affording the easiest, and often the only means for transport of the larger quantities of agricultural produce, that its interior sections yield. . . . The point, too, in North America, where it did first actually take place, is also, as it were, particularly marked out for it. The transport between New York and Albany, by sailing vessels on the Hudson river, was both very expensive, and pecularily tedious.
>
> (Rae 1834: 248–9)

In the context of his discussion of the applications of steam power, Rae made one of his most generalized theoretical extrapolations. It seems to be tightly linked to his assertion that the geographical presence of specific materials was one of the most important causes of technological change:

> *It is to be observed, however, that, whatever it* [the steam engine] *has performed, has proceeded in the order we have indicated, and which, I believe, almost all inventions have followed.* The diversity of climates, territories, productions, and other circumstances of different regions and nations, has helped it, as them, forward, and been to it as it were steps, by which it had gained the rank it holds in the modes of human industry. [emphasis added]
>
> (Rae 1834: 248)

Rae proceeded to support his theoretical claims for the other three conditions of the technologization of a society. Unfortunately more space than is alloted would be required to discuss each one, but they leave little doubt about the causative nature of his theory of the history of technological change and the elements which make up that causative chain. Also, through the causes he determined to be effecting technological change Rae drew connections to natural history, in the guise of geography and human individual and social behaviour, to capital theory, in the guise of labour wages, and of course, to the history of technology itself.

## Conclusion

Rae's theory of technological change, like all causative theories, entailed results. One of those results was that the process of technological change had been charted. It held for the transformations of the past and would hold for those of the future:

> In conclusion I may observe, that I believe it will be found, that there is no art in existence which we may not find means to trace, with greater or less certainty, to the rudest and most simple principles, and which may not be shown to have attained perfection by continual changes from place to place, and material to material, and by encountering consequently alternate difficulties and facilities, the former developing its powers, the latter extending their field of action, and both, by helping to introduce general principles, weakening the restraining power of the tendency to servile imitation, and advancing the progress of science.
>
> (Rae 1834: 253)

The other main result was that Rae felt he had established that technology was the source of a society's prosperity. This result cannot be attributed to Rae's theory of the history of technological change alone. Several other of his studies played a part in his establishing this result. Nonetheless, he attributed it quite specifically to his study of the history of technologies and would certainly have counted it among the conclusions of that study

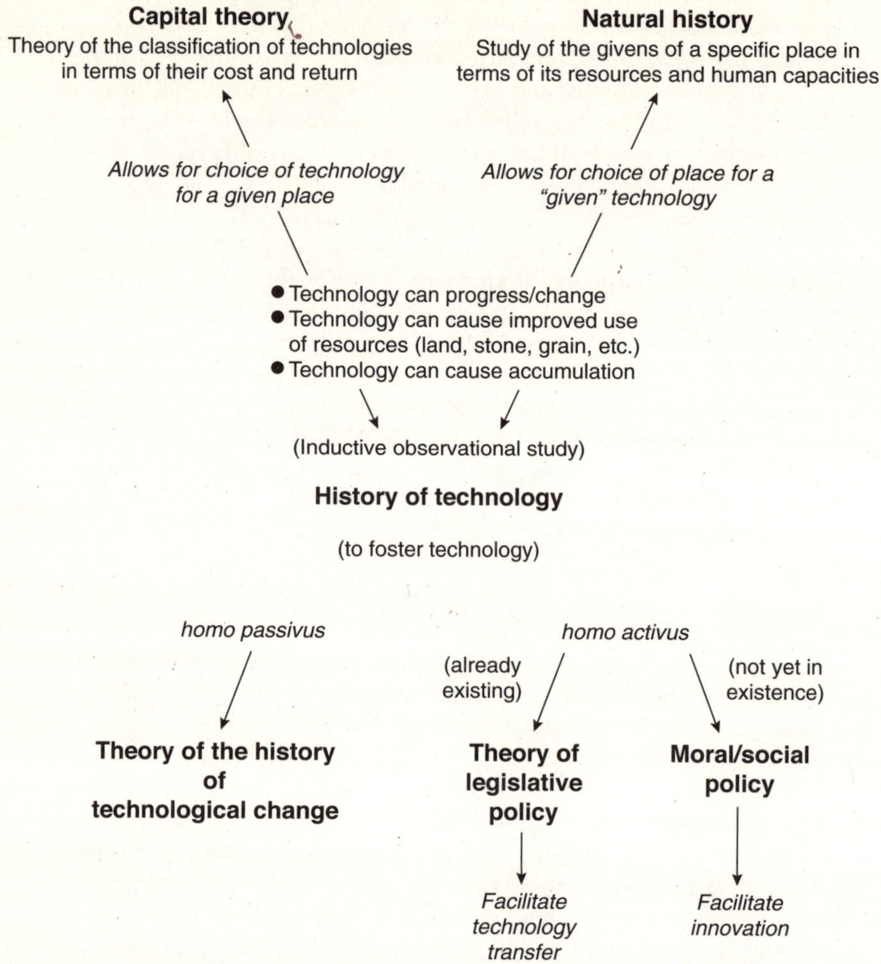


*Figure 4.4* The place of history and theory of technology in Rae's classification of ideas

to serve as a premise for a theory of technological change. "This successive passage of the same arts from country to country, and from one into another, seems to be the great exciting cause of the progress of them all" (Rae 1834: 253).

Rae left no doubt that he saw in technology the root cause of a society's prosperity. His study of history had provided the demonstrative instances that this was the case, and he was able to build a theory which could explain most of the pertinent steps in historical progression. Rae constructed an elaborate chain of causation for many whys: why a technology would be employed at one time and not at another, why one technology would give way to a different one, and so on. At the base of all technological change was, for Rae, the individual, the inventor, the realizer, and the adopter. The social context for the individuals was, however, critical. It had to be one fostering of the accumulative desire and comprised of specific circumstances. When all the conditions coincided, rude technology became an instrument and began its course of change and improvement:

> The wants of mankind are few when population is small; but they gradually encrease with the numbers of the species and with its progress in civilization. New desires, the offspring of new wants, in their turn, give birth to new arts, which mark the advancement of society, introducing the conveniences and elegancies of life by the agency of mechanics and manufacturers who prepare the rude produce of the earth for the use and gratification of their fellow men.
>
> (Rae 1825, in James 1965a, 1: 195–6)

The true believer Rae was, he would probably not have allowed for this less-than-reverent reworking of Genesis, "and Rae saw technology and he saw it was good." Nonetheless, it was the case. "I shall content myself," Rae wrote, "with adducing a sufficient number of instances to show, that this continual change has been a circumstance operating very beneficially and efficiently, in enlarging the bounds of human knowledge and power" (Rae 1834: 225). Not only did he reveal his conviction in that goodness, but also the absolute integralness of technology to all of human existence and expression. An attempt has been made to capture this in Figure 4.4 where the relationship of those studies to which Rae devoted much of his intellectual energy is schematically laid out.

## Notes

1 See Price (1996).
2 See Rae (1834: 229) on the "example" of sacred architecture; (ibid. 237) on the "example" of "the same arts changing materials" and of "those which we have now to attend to . . . of different arts adopting to same, or similar materials"; and (ibid. 240) on the "particular instances" of power generation in mills, etc.
3 For example, "Such was probably . . ." (Rae 1834: 228); "They were probably . . ." (ibid. 231); "the art was probably . . ." (ibid. 234); "Such was probably the earliest plough and those that are used in many parts of the east, to this day, differ not much from it" (ibid. 227); "Without pretending to say what those circumstances were, it is at least probable that one may have been the keeping these animals in enclosures . . . This we know, in more recent times, to have been a custom in some eastern countries" (ibid. 252).

4 Rae has either Watt or a "Dr. Black" in mind as the "distinguished individual" who has been recognized as having pointed out steam power "as capable of producing the greatest effects" (Rae 1834: 246).

5 This was not the only of Rae's forays into inventing: "Another of Rae's projects was a device for feathering the paddle wheels on steamboats. His scheme was to feather the blades vertically so that they would move through the right angle made by a vertical plane parallel to the keel and surface of the water. This was before the days when feathering was used and the idea was ingenious enough, although the device later adopted provided for feathering parallel to the axis of the wheel. Modern aircraft propellers embody the kind of feathering principle Rae apparently had in mind." (James 1965a, 1: 8–9.)

6 "Though not convinced [by Dr Hamilton's objection to his scheme] I was obliged to yield and let it go, as I did not wish to irritate my father . . . He [Dr Hamilton] judged of the ocean from fanciful ideas he had got sitting in his elbow chair. I knew something of it then, and have lived on it many a long day since, and can see nothing absurd in the project" (Rae, draft of a letter to Hugh Bowlby Wilson, *c.*1850–65, in James 1965a, 1: 112).

7 This is also where the distinction between invention and innovation might be placed by some economists.

8 It might also, however, be important depending on the capital required to acquire the already current technology by another would-be user. Rae contrasts flails with threshing machines (Rae 1834: 20–1).

9 See Price (1996) for Rae's two types of histories of technology which seem to divide along similar lines.

10 Rae (1834: 226) goes on at length about the contribution which is metallurgy: "None of the arts which are not necessary to the preservation of human existence itself, has probably had a greater influence on the modes which that existence has assumed, than metallurgy. Without the metals, it would be impossible for the series of instruments to be continued from which the wants of civilized society are supplied, and without them, consequently, mankind could never have emerged from barbarism."

# 5

# JOHN RAE AND CONSPICUOUS CONSUMPTION

*Roger Mason*

## Introduction

John Rae's treatment of luxury consumption in *New Principles* (1834) added to what was then a meagre literature on the subject, for few political economists had considered such behaviour to be a matter of any real significance in the development of economic thought up to that time.

Ostentatious economic display had long been recognized, however. Before 1500, it had been seen as an indulgence of the rich and privileged which, kept within reasonable bounds, was acceptable as a necessary mark of rank and status. Only when such privileges were usurped by the less deserving or newly affluent were sumptuary laws introduced to suppress it. For the great majority, however, the means and opportunity to indulge in any ostentatious display of wealth was denied them; moreover, the Church was quick to condemn any such ambitions in those who might choose to emulate their social and economic betters.

After 1500, the case against luxury consumption was further extended, for not only was it then claimed to be morally wrong to indulge in ostentatious display, but also seen to be against the commercial interest. To the Mercantilists, who dominated economic thinking after 1500, there was a clear correlation between frugality and prosperity; high levels of savings, properly invested in domestic and international trade, were seen to provide the motor for economic growth. While the ostentatious excesses of the ruling elites were, for political purposes, still accepted and excused, any conspicuous waste on the part of the emerging, and increasingly wealthy, merchant classes was condemned by political economists as being against the national interest. The higher moral condemnation of the Church was now reinforced by a more pragmatic belief in the economic values of thrift and investment.

After 1600, this emphasis on thrift as the motor of economic development began to be questioned. There was, in reality, little if any evidence to support the argument that the suppression of luxury expenditure acted as a stimulus to economic growth; to the contrary, too much emphasis on saving seemed to lead to economic stagnation and unemployment.

The first attack of any substance on the supposed virtues of thrift and frugality came with the publication of Bernard de Mandeville's ([1714] 1924) *The Fable of the Bees; or Private Vices, Publick Benefits*. Mandeville, living in London but a Dutchman by birth, claimed that the economic prosperity of the Dutch Republic in the seventeenth century had been strengthened rather than weakened by the high levels of luxury consumption enjoyed by the merchants of Amsterdam and other large towns – patterns of consumption which were, in turn, emulated by others, and which could be found, to varying degrees, at all social and economic levels. Such expenditures, argued Mandeville, might well be seen as private vices which lacked any moral justification; the reality was that they generated employment and prosperity and so worked to the public good.

Mandeville's views were, at the time, roundly condemned as an attack on established moral and economic doctrines. In England, *The Fable of the Bees* was declared "a public nuisance" by a Middlesex grand jury in 1723. Later, Hume ([1752] 1955) attacked the idea that human "vices" could in any sense be beneficial to social and economic development. Adam Smith also argued that Mandeville's ideas were "in almost every respect erroneous," but was more guarded in his views of status-driven consumption. To Smith, those of real social status – the rich and the great – could legitimately conspicuously consume as a statement of their social and economic superiority. This ostentatious consumption then needed to act as a spur to others, not to imitate such behaviour, but to work harder. Over time, this hard work would then generate the wealth by which deserving individuals could join the ranks of the rich and successful, and could then legitimately display their new social status through personal consumption. Only a vain man would seek to emulate his betters in the presence that he was of equal wealth and status, and such idle vanity could never be condoned.

Smith, therefore, saw the ostentatious consumption of the rich as a spur to greater national effort. In condemning the vanity of those who attempted to "buy" social status, however, he conceded that Mandeville was right to claim that such ambitions were widespread within society. He also admitted that, at any given social level, it could be morally and economically legitimate for a man to protect his existing position in society through some necessary conspicuous display. To accommodate this concession, Smith defined "necessaries" as "not only those things which nature, but those things which the established rules of decency have rendered necessary to the lowest rank of people." Such consumption, he argued, could not and should not be considered extravagant because it was necessary to secure the dignity of life among social equals.

Smith's views were at one with the teachings of the Church, which, throughout the period, continued to condemn excessive and unnecessary ostentatious display. This academic and religious rejection of conspicuous consumption was to persist for many years, and was only weakened when conflicting commercial interests and a growing desire to consume for status began to put strains on a doctrine which was beginning to look increasingly irrelevant and outdated.

## *New Principles* and conspicuous consumption

In *New Principles*, John Rae focused on the role and importance of capital accumulation and on the inventive faculty as principal generators of economic development and national wealth. At the same time, he identified several "contrary principles" which, to his mind, worked against national well-being, including the tendency of many individuals to indulge in high levels of luxury consumption. Demand for luxury goods, he argued, channelled money and effort into immediate gratification rather than into the savings and investment which served longer-term economic prosperity, and in so doing, worked against the national interest. Rae's case against luxury consumption, however, was also concerned with wider moral and ethical issues. Rae defined luxury, very selectively, as "the expenditure occasioned by the passion of vanity." Vanity he defined in turn as:

> The mere desire of superiority over others. . . . A purely selfish feeling; its pleasures centre on the individual; and if it does not endeavour to diminish the enjoyment of others, it is never directly its object to increase them . . . Its aim in all cases that concern our subject, is to have what others cannot have.
>
> (Rae 1834: 265–66)

Such vanity was satisfied, argued Rae, only when the luxury consumption which it encouraged was "conspicuous." As evidence, he cited examples of the excesses and extravagances of earlier civilizations – from Babylon and the Roman Empire to the "Asiatic Monarchies." Such excesses had already been well documented and Rae's restatement was in no sense original, but it served his purpose in establishing that luxury consumption, as he had chosen to define it, needed always to be socially visible.

Rae's views on conspicuous consumption were influenced to a great extent by two political economists in particular. Certainly, Adam Smith's views on the subject carried considerable weight. Like Smith, Rae recognized that, however much it was to be condemned, vanity and the wish to appear superior or to maintain social status within the community was easily observed, and affected all members of society. And the fact that such behavior was commonplace, and often perceived as necessary, meant that resort to such expenditure was, at the least, understandable:

> No blame can attach to individuals, for compliances with follies to which the passion of vanity prompts. It were a great mistake to imagine that even its absurdities are easily avoidable. It is in vain for any one man to oppose general opinions and practices, however ridiculous. If he does so, he is sure to encounter greater evils than a compliance with the customs of society would inflict. It is the business of the poor to stand well with the world, else he will scarcely make his way through it. It is his business, too, to avoid a display of poverty.
>
> (Rae 1834: 281)

In those less-than-ideal societies where conspicuous display had been made socially important, therefore, Rae conceded that no blame could attach to individuals who felt a need to consume conspicuously in order to protect their position in society. "A physician, unless dressed in silk and cow's hair," he admitted, "passes for ignorant and is employed by no one" (Rae 1834: 282). Such expenditures had to be seen as necessaries rather than luxuries; only when luxury consumption was excessive and not central to sustaining social position could it be considered to have no merit and to be damaging to the community at large.

While Rae recognized this need to conform, his view was somewhat at odds with that of Smith, for while Smith implied that socially inspired conspicuous consumption had been, and would continue to be, a part of the modern world, Rae saw it as unnecessary and as something to be resisted. In this view, he was undoubtedly influenced by his active involvement with, and commitment to, the Presbyterian Church, which had always taken a strong stand against vanity and conspicuous display at whatever social and economic level. Rae, indeed, had himself attacked the Anglican Church for tolerating Adam Smith's "liberal or loose system" of morality, and had no sympathy with arguments which, to his mind, sought to defend or justify excessive acts of ostentatious display.

A second major influence on Rae's views of luxury and luxury expenditure is perhaps more surprising, for considerable attention is given in *New Principles* to the work of Heinrich von Storch, in particular to his treatment of luxury consumption in his *Cours d'Economie Politique*, published in 1815. Storch, born in Russia of German parents, was a less than distinguished economist, whose work was heavily criticized in its day. Nevertheless, Rae quotes extensively from *Cours* and was clearly impressed with Storch's analysis of *le luxe d'ostentation* as an expression only of vanity. Storch had, in fact, been a tutor in political economy to the sons of Tsar Alexander I, and must have seen excessive levels of conspicuous consumption at first hand. It was this experience, perhaps, which lent greater credibility to his opinions and observations in Rae's eyes.

Rae's view of conspicuous consumption was that it fed off vanity and had no redeeming features. At the same time, he did not see this passion of vanity as something which need be in evidence in all societies. Vanity, he argued, was always opposed by two countervailing forces which kept conspicuous consumption within bounds. First, when the "social and benevolent affections" were strong, man's actions were not destructively self-centred but were directed towards the well-being of others within the community. Second, when "intellectual powers" predominated, money was spent on objects of "permanent excellence," rather than on the wasteful conceits of personal vanity.

In those most civilized of societies where both the social and benevolent affections and the intellectual powers were strong, conspicuous consumption was seen to be at a minimum. Such societies were also typically those where the effective desire for accumulation was high, and where, consequently, rates of material and spiritual progress were at their strongest. However, Rae argued that, in many societies, one of the virtuous powers tended to dominate, and this imbalance itself determined the nature and direction of vanity-driven conspicuous display.

To Rae, Mandeville's earlier descriptions of the ostentatious expenditure of the seventeenth century Dutch Republic demonstrated the nature of conspicuous consumption in a society where the intellectual powers were dominant and where expenditures were made on articles of quality and permanence. He also associated the contemporary conspicuous consumption of North America as being dominated by these same intellectual powers, reflected in expenditures on fine houses and, lower down the social order, on gold watches of enduring value. In contrast, he saw Britain as a country where intellectual values were weaker and where the social and benevolent affections came to the fore. Here, shows of vanity were consequently focused more on luxuries associated with hospitality, with rare wines, and with extravagances associated with the "dainties of the table."

In an idealized society, Rae saw the social and benevolent affections and the intellectual powers as strong, equal partners working to ensure that any vanity-driven conspicuous consumption was kept within manageable levels. At the same time, he saw other factors at work which either raised or lowered levels of luxury consumption. First, there was a demographic dimension to such behaviour. Pernicious luxury, he argued, prospered in the towns and cities of Europe and America, where populations were large, relationships largely impersonal, and where most inhabitants were strangers to one another. Under such conditions, conspicuous consumption was inevitably seen as a means of communication and as a signal of success and status. In contrast, scattered rural communities, where generations of inhabitants were well known to each other and where discretionary incomes were significantly lower, encouraged greater productive activity and far lower levels of ostentatious display. In effect, individual and family status is always known in such small communities and can not be "bought" with goods and services.

Rae believed also that the conditions pertaining in "new" countries tended to lower the overall propensity to conspicuously consume. Again, the population was scattered, the accumulative drive was heightened, and a necessary preoccupation with hard work distracted individuals from thoughts of status-seeking conspicuous display. To Rae, such societies were to be commended:

> There is hence no better school for the dissolute European than the backwoods. After a dozen years' residence in them, or in the clearings to which he has helped to convert them, he comes out a completely altered man.
>
> (Rae 1834: 281)

Turning to the nature of luxury goods themselves, Rae's view was that their whole value derived from scarcity. However, product scarcity (and hence status value) was often reduced over time because of improvements and innovations which made the manufacture or production of a particular article less costly and so lowered market price. As price fell and availability increased, so the good in question lost its prestige value. In this way, the classification of luxury goods changed periodically as relative scarcity itself changed.

To Rae, all pure luxuries represented a loss to society – they supplied no real wants, and did not increase overall well-being (one man's gain being another man's loss). However, when luxury goods contained a substratum of real utility, their increased production over time could then bring benefits to society at large, for as they became more widely available and affordable, so their "real" utility value was correspondingly increased and a greater number of individuals were able to benefit from their consumption. This, claimed Rae, had been the case with such products as soap, silk, cotton fabrics, and glass, all of which had initially been seen as luxury goods, but had subsequently become widely available and now served valuable roles as utilitarian consumer goods.

## Vanity and the process of economic decline

Rae held strongly to the view that excessive conspicuous consumption was morally reprehensible. At the same time, he believed that the consequences of such behaviour extended beyond morality into the economic sphere, arguing that vanity and personal indulgence inevitably led to national economic decline.

In those societies where both the social and benevolent affections and the intellectual powers were strong, so community values dominated to the benefit of society at large. Within the family, mothers were concerned not with ostentatious display, but with the well-being of their home and children. For men, similarly, marriage served to focus attention on the family, and did not encourage them to think and act too far above their proper station. While some limited conspicuous consumption was understandable as a means of securing improvements in a family's social standing and to advance the interests of future generations, such spending was kept within the limits necessary to ensure that the "effective desire for accumulation" remained strong enough to see the economy as a whole prosper. Society remained stratified, but this ensured that the distance between social groups was kept stable over time.

This social and economic stability was threatened, in Rae's view, when those forces which worked against too great a level of conspicuous display were weakened and ineffective. Under such conditions, the capitalist class which, to Rae, had the greater propensity to consume conspicuously, would then begin to indulge more freely and openly in ostentatious consumption. This self-indulgence would eventually and inevitably deteriorate into acts of conspicuous expenditure, fueled not by any desire to secure a proper level of personal or family reputation, but by personal vanity alone. As such acts of vanity increased, so the social and economic distance between capitalists and labourers widened and social cohesion was lost.

This vanity was not only morally and ethically unacceptable, but had significant economic implications, for the labourer, now faced with what he saw as an unbridgeable gap between himself and higher social groups, would then abandon all hopes of gradual upward mobility and improvement over time, turn away from saving and accumulation, and seek to gain status among his peers through wasteful expenditures on "the purchase of fineries, in treating his companions at the ale-house, and in similar extravagances." This "dissipation," in turn, brought with it various evils: the family was neglected and kept short of necessaries; the labourer himself became workshy and ultimately dishonest; little or no attempt was made to save in good times to make provision for future possible hardship, so exaggerating swings between prosperity and poverty; the inventive faculty was diminished – in short, the moral and economic well-being of society was seriously undermined.

It was the vanity of the capitalist class which, in Rae's opinion, led directly to the social and economic degeneration of society, with all its consequences for economic growth and renewal. When the middle and higher classes of society indulged in excessive conspicuous consumption, they unknowingly destroyed the industry and ambitions of the lower class on which they rested; and "when decay infects the foundation, the structure must fall." Vanity and its attendant evils were, therefore, a root cause of national decline and, as such, had to be rejected on both moral and economic grounds.

## Policy, prescription, and cure

Rae conceded that, in reality, vanity and the conspicuous consumption it generated could be found to varying degrees in all nations, and that luxury goods, whether domestically produced or imported from overseas, were commonly used to service an ostentatious consumption which was a reflection of society's inability to keep vanity in check.

Luxury goods derived their value from their relative scarcity – a scarcity secured by high prices and limited availability. Rae therefore proposed that taxes on "pure" luxuries should be increased, for this would serve not only to add to the scarcity and status value of the good in question, but would at the same time raise additional funds for the Exchequer which could then be used for the betterment of society as a whole. At the same time, he was against encouraging any new domestic investment in the production of these pure luxuries, and also supported protectionist policies which would restrict or even eliminate the importation of such products from abroad. These import restrictions, coupled with domestic legislation to prevent attempts at import substitution, could then only work to the wider public good, as they would channel both domestic business and overseas trade into the production and exchange of goods possessing real utility value.

For those luxury goods with a substantial substratum of utility, Rae argued that increasing levels of competition, achieved by the removal of manufacturing restrictions and any other barriers to trade, would encourage higher levels of domestic production, would lower costs and prices, and would increase availability. This would have the effect of driving out any residual appeal to vanity as the goods lost their scarcity value and would ultimately produce commodities of real value to the community at large.

While Rae, therefore, had policies and prescriptions to ameliorate what he saw as the twin threats of luxury production and conspicuous consumption, he was more concerned to tackle the root cause of the problem – that of vanity itself. If vanity could be eradicated, then luxury consumption as he had defined it would itself disappear over time.

Rae believed that man's behaviour, and, in particular, much of his economic behaviour, was conditioned by prevailing social attitudes, but that these attitudes were in no sense fixed or immutable. They could be changed, he argued, by two forces which, taken together, worked to ensure that a society's values were both positive and productive. First, strong religious beliefs led individuals to be more concerned with furthering the well-being and prosperity of the community, rather than with themselves. Without this necessary religious foundation, then "vanity, vice and folly" came to exert a pernicious influence on the individual and on the capital accumulation and inventiveness of any society. With "the Church in the house," however, the proper moral and ethical foundations were laid. Rae wrote to the *Montreal Gazette* as follows: "Religion, say they, and we most cordially assent to the proposition, ought to form a main object of attention in the education of youth" (quoted in James 1965a, 1: 178).

Religious education, and the moral values it secured, were seen then as essential elements in the proper ordering of society. To Rae, however, these religious and moral values were necessary but not sufficient conditions, for societies also needed to achieve the highest standards of general education in order to succeed. "The power of knowledge," Rae wrote to the *Montreal Gazette*, "is irresistible in advancing the best interests of the human race." Taken together, religion and education kept vanity and conspicuous consumption in check, and ensured the proper ordering of society.

## Reaction and response after 1834

In the years immediately following publication of *New Principles* in 1834, Rae's analysis of luxury consumption passed largely unnoticed and without comment. Nassau Senior was to read and be impressed by the book (Bowley [1937] 1967: 161 n.), but his interest focused on Rae's theory of capital accumulation and the process of economic growth, rather than on the nature and management of conspicuous consumption. Senior later recommended the book to John Stuart Mill, who paid tribute to Rae in his *Principles of Political Economy* ([1848] 1965), but again it was Rae's work on capital accumulation which particularly impressed Mill. However, he was also clearly aware of the treatise on luxury consumption, in particular as it related to taxation policy.

Rae had argued that any increase in price caused by the taxation of goods which were being purchased only to display wealth would not adversely affect demand, for the high price of such products was the real measure of value in the eyes of conspicuous consumers. Mill agreed that this was an ideal way of raising public revenues to nobody's disadvantage. And if, by any chance, such taxes were to reduce demand, then they had served an equally useful social purpose in acting as "a kind of sumptuary law" and reducing expenditures on needless trivia.

Rae was certainly flattered by Mill's several references to his work, and corresponded with him through the early 1850s. At the same time, he was clearly disappointed with the overall reception of *New Principles* and the book's general lack of impact. He had thoughts of producing a new, revised edition, and wrote to Mill:

> Were I visiting in England, what chance would there be of my making an impression by publishing there a new edition of my *Principles*, or by breaking the book up, and giving it a more practical form? Suppose I were to put forth my views on capital, on money, currency and banking, on rent, on the wages of labour, and, perhaps, on population, each in short works – stating only obvious facts, and venturing on no excursive reasoning, – what chance of success do you think I would have?
>
> (Draft of letter of J.S. Mill, *c*.1854, quoted in James 1965a, 1: 428)

This proposal for a revised edition is interesting for what Rae proposed should be omitted from the revision, rather than for what he intended to include. It suggests, in fact, that he considered the sections on luxury which appeared in the original edition may have detracted from the book's perceived merits, and he was seemingly prepared to discard them if this would add to a new edition's prospects of success. It is clear that Rae sought the approval of mainstream economists, and was concerned that discussion of anything so "trivial" as conspicuous consumption may have seriously prejudiced the book's reception in the years after 1834.

While Senior and Mill had read and applauded Rae's contribution to political economy in *New Principles*, the book attracted little attention through the middle and later years of the nineteenth century. In so far as luxury expenditure was concerned, it is in any event doubtful that Rae's views would have been more widely debated even if *New Principles* had itself found a wider audience, for any extended discussion would have raised issues inimical to the interests of two influential groups, both powerful yet working to very different agendas.

First, moral and economic condemnation of luxury expenditures was not at all welcome to many business interests which, as early as 1840, were beginning to see great commercial potential in encouraging conspicuous consumption at all social and economic levels. Not surprisingly, they enlisted the widest support and worked to make status-driven consumption acceptable on both moral and economic grounds. In Germany, Friedrich List, like Rae sympathetic to the protectionist cause, but also leader of the General Association of German Manufacturers and Merchants, declared emulation and luxury consumption to be a necessary stimulus to economic growth and to the future development of consumer goods markets. In his *National System of Political Economy* ([1841] 1974), he defended conspicuous consumption and status-seeking expenditure, arguing, like Mandeville many years earlier, that such consumption was a positive asset and a significant contributor to the public good; any moral objections had to be put aside in the wider public interest.

Others, more cautious and less partisan than List, were also persuaded that conspicuous consumption could be a force for good when economic conditions allowed for the widest possible participation. Past debate about the morality of such consumption was often dismissed as sophistry. Roscher ([1854] 1877) argued that "when a political economist declares for or against luxury in general, he resembles a doctor who should declare for or against the nerves in general." To Roscher, conspicuous consumption at all social levels was acceptable in civilized societies where growing affluence had created a more equitable distribution of wealth and income. Indeed, because emulation could itself serve under such conditions as an equalizing tendency, it was defensible not only on economic but on moral grounds. Only when nations declined and the distribution of income once again became markedly unequal did luxury consumption become unacceptable.

Any greater publicity for Rae's belief that conspicuous consumption could not be defended and needed to be eliminated rather than encouraged would have worked against the interests of a business community which was increasingly concerned to cultivate and develop new commercial markets. Moreover, the market for luxury and status goods was particularly attractive as it was prepared to tolerate, and often actively welcomed, high prices as a mark of increased prestige and status value; manufacturers of socially visible goods and services, therefore, had every reason to encourage consumer ambitions in this area.

A second group which also had little interest in looking too closely at the nature of luxury consumption lay within the academic community itself. After 1840, the foundations of neoclassical theory were being laid, leading, via Menger, Jevons and J.M. Clark, to publication of Alfred Marshall's *Principles of Economics* in 1890. A central tenet of neoclassical doctrine relating to consumer demand theory was the assumption of independent consumer preferences – the assumption that an individual's demand for any product or service was in no way influenced by the opinions or consumption of others. Given this assumption, economists could then safely adopt the concept of "additivity," which allowed aggregate demand to be calculated from the summation of individual demand schedules.

Conspicuous consumption, whether motivated by vanity or by wider social considerations, posed a considerable threat to this concept of additivity, because it vividly demonstrated the importance of interpersonal effects on consumer demand when considerations of social prestige and status entered the utility function. The early neoclassical writers sought to avoid this potential embarrassment by playing down the real significance of such behaviour. Cournot (1838) acknowledged that some goods were, in fact, purchased for their social and symbolic value, but argued that "objects of this nature play so unimportant a role in social economy that it is not necessary to bear in mind the restriction of which we speak." Jevons ([1871] 1965) also recognized that consumption could indeed be motivated by social considerations, but, again, made casual reference to such behaviour and never attempted to incorporate such considerations into his economic analysis. Marshall (1890) himself did not deny the existence of conspicuous consumption, but expressed serious reservations about how such tastes and preferences could sensibly be incorporated within economics. Like Cournot and Jevons before him, he argued that such effects were, in any event, trivial and more properly the concern of sociologists and social psychologists. Although he was later challenged by Pigou (1903, 1910, 1913) and others, he continued to make few concessions to those who believed that the concept of additivity was flawed, for to do so would have been to call into question the legitimacy of neoclassical aggregate demand measurement.

John Rae's discussion and analysis of luxury expenditure and conspicuous consumption, therefore, received little attention through the nineteenth century for two reasons: first, because *New Principles* itself had enjoyed a very limited readership after publication in 1834; secondly, because it was, in any event, not in the commercial or neoclassical interest to encourage further discussion of the subject. By the end of the century, however, Gilded Age ostentatious display in the United States had reached such proportions that the nature, morality, and effects of conspicuous consumption could no longer be ignored. The amounts being spent to secure social position became so great that the public reacted. Sensing this reaction, the press began to take a more hostile attitude to such behaviour and conspicuous consumption became a political issue (Mason 1981). This popular and political concern then found expression in the academic world with publication of Thorstein Veblen's *The Theory of the Leisure Class* in 1899 – a book which brought the phrase "conspicuous consumption" into everyday usage and which developed many of the ideas which John Rae had expounded some sixty-five years earlier.

Veblen's analysis of pecuniary emulation and of conspicuous consumption certainly seems to owe much to Rae's earlier work, although Veblen himself never cited Rae as a source. He was certainly aware of Rae, referring to him in 1909 as a "good and authentic. . . . utilitarian theorist." And others certainly came to suspect that *New Principles* had provided Veblen with material on conspicuous consumption which was subsequently reworked in *The Theory of the Leisure Class*. Dorfman (1973) records an incident told to J.M. Clark in 1924 by a student who, with Veblen, had attended a party at a colleague's house. Asked if he knew of Rae's work, Veblen replied that he did and that "some people have accused me of stealing my ideas from him." He was clearly sensitive to such charges and put on the defensive when asked about Rae. In fairness to Veblen, the treatment of conspicuous consumption in *The Theory of the Leisure Class* is more comprehensive and sophisticated than that offered by Rae in 1834. At the same time, there are surprising points of similarity in the writings of the two men (Edgell and Tilman 1991), and it is difficult to believe that Veblen was not, at the very least, aware of Rae's work when formulating his own ideas on the subject.

Rae's reputation, nonetheless, has lagged far behind that of Veblen. His wish to see *New Principles* reprinted was realized when Mixter (1905) published an edited version under the title *The Sociological Theory of Capital*. Unfortunately, this further retarded Rae's reputation for, as Mair (1990) has pointed out, the new title alone "was likely to be the kiss of death for any book in economics wishing to be taken seriously." In truth, Rae always believed that a significant part of economic activity had to be seen from a sociological viewpoint, but this had had the effect of moving his work out of the mainstream of economics and had done nothing to secure greater recognition of his work.

## Summary

John Rae's writings on luxury laid great emphasis on moral and spiritual considerations. He believed strongly that conspicuous consumption, fuelled by vanity, threatened both social stability and the economic progress of nations. It was a conservative thesis, entirely opposed to Mandeville's belief in the compatibility of private vices and public benefits and in the gains to be made from status-seeking consumption.

Although Rae was sympathetic to much of Adam Smith's treatment of conspicuous consumption, he held more strongly to the view that man could never allow himself to indulge vanity, and should always be sensitive to the importance of preserving a proper balance between various social and economic groups – a balance which ensured the long-term stability and prosperity of the community as a whole. His views were, without question, heavily influenced by his Presbyterian faith and by the strictures of the Church against all forms of ostentatious display.

Rae, like Mandeville before him, must be credited with presenting an original thesis on the form and effects of conspicuous consumption, although the two men took radically different views of such behavior. Veblen's subsequent contribution to the debate would also have found little sympathy with Rae, for *The Theory of the Leisure Class*, being first and foremost an attack on the evils of American finance capitalism and informed by a quasi-socialist rather than a religious and moral agenda, offered a very different analysis of conspicuous economic display. Yet it is *The Theory of the Leisure Class* which is today seen as the definitive work on conspicuous consumption, and the term "Veblen effects" which has entered the economic literature to describe such behaviour. It has been John Rae's fate to have made a significant contribution to work on luxury expenditure and status-seeking consumption, yet to have seen his work overshadowed by Thorstein Veblen's later exploration of pecuniary emulation and the formation of tastes. Belatedly, some greater recognition is now being given to Rae and to his contribution to economic thought on matters relating to the conspicuous consumption of goods and services.

# Part III

# CAPITAL AND RELATED ISSUES

# 6

# RAE, BÖHM-BAWERK, AND FISHER ON THE SUPPLY AND DEMAND OF CAPITAL

*Syed Ahmad*

## Introduction

In at least two recent papers, two eminent economists, Dorfman (1993) and Samuelson (1994), compare Böhm-Bawerk's (1889) and Fisher's (1907) contributions to capital theory. Both, somewhat surprisingly, since not many historians of capital theory have done so in recent years, refer to John Rae (1834) as a sort of forerunner of their protagonists even if in a somewhat lukewarm fashion. The protagonists themselves, however, had assigned a much greater role, and status to Rae. The dedication of Fisher's ([1907] 1982) main work on the subject reads, "To the memory of John Rae who laid the foundations upon which I have endeavoured to build," and his view remained unchanged after twenty-three years, when he wrote in the Preface of its revised version. "*Every* essential part of it [his theory] was *at least* foreshadowed by John Rae in 1834" (emphasis added) (Fisher [1930] 1970: p. ix). And Böhm-Bawerk ([1884] 1959: 208) had this to say:

> It was on the subject of the theory of capital . . . that Rae held a number of exceedingly original and remarkable views, and those views exhibit unmistakable similarity to views which were developed about half a century later by Jevons and myself.

Since according to Dorfman, Fisher's ([1907] 1982) *The Rate of Interest* and Böhm-Bawerk's ([1889] 1959) *Positive Theory of Capital* are the *Ursprunge* [origin, extraction] of modern neoclassical theory of capital, the minimum claim that can be made on behalf of Rae on the basis of the above is that he provided the foundation of the origin of this theory.

In this chapter, I shall attempt to go beyond (although not necessarily exclude) the opinions *on* Rae expressed by Böhm-Bawerk, Fisher, or for that matter by anybody else, and to examine directly the contributions made by the three through the study of their texts – Rae (1834), Böhm-Bawerk ([1884] 1959) and ([1889] 1959), and Fisher ([1907] 1982) and ([1930] 1977) – on capital theory, particularly under its two main themes: the determination of the rate of interest or profit, and that of economic growth.[1]

The objective of this examination is to assess the areas in (if any) and the extent to which:

1 Böhm-Bawerk and/or Fisher borrowed from Rae;
2 they developed original ideas, or made significant advance over Rae; and
3 Rae still presented a clearer or more relevant view than either of the other two.

It will be convenient to have some classificatory scheme for this discussion. We will do so by modifying the classification used in a recent evaluation of Rae's contribution. Niehans (1990) says: "Rae's specific contribution to economic theory is the first correct description of the interplay of *capital productivity* and *time preference*" (emphasis added). Even though "time preference" and "capital productivity" do provide the required classification, they are perhaps too closely associated with Fisher for an "impartial" use, so to say. Hence I shall rename them with a pair of older and more neutral terms – the "supply" of and the "demand" for capital respectively. This is, of course, not to claim that these terms, or the term "capital" itself has been used in the same sense even by the three economists we consider here, let alone by the profession as a whole – in fact, quite to the contrary, as we shall briefly see in the Appendix. In the main text, however, we use them in the above sense, which has not only the merit of being more easily understandable to modern nonspecialists, but also of being used by Mixter (1902: 386), who was not only responsible for reigniting interest in Rae at the turn of the last century by claiming that Rae was a forerunner of Böhm-Bawerk, but perhaps also interesting Irving Fisher in Rae. In the text of the chapter I shall use the expressions "supply" and "demand" of capital without further qualification or clarification.

## Supply of capital

### *John Rae*

Rae gives a great deal of attention to the supply of capital, particularly to the reasons that determine its magnitude. He then goes on to consider its role in the economy, and, to a limited extent, the policies needed to promote it.

The factors which, in his view determine the magnitude of the supply of capital, are scattered throughout his book, but at one place he provides a numbered list of six factors. In effect, however, these represent only three items, since the other three are their exact counterparts. The first three are:

> 1. The prevalence throughout the society, of the social and benevolent affections, or, of that principle, which, under whatever name it may be known, leads us to derive happiness, from the good we communicate to others.
> 2. The extent of intellectual powers, and the consequent prevalence of habit of reflection, and prudence, in the minds of the members of the society.
> 3. The stability of the condition of the affairs of the society, and the reign of law and order throughout it.
>
> (Rae 1834: 124)

These items are supposed to encourage the supply of capital (saving). The remaining three numbered items are simply the reverse of these, and thus are postulated to discourage saving (the supply of capital).

However, the above statements are no more than a summary of his immediately preceding arguments. In the rest of the book he refers to other items which promote saving or militate against it, the most significant of which are as follows:

4 income (ibid. 11);
5 uncertainty about the future, including a person's expected length of life (ibid. 119);
6 habit (ibid. 103);
7 fashion (ibid. 123, 278);
8 vanity (ibid. 275, 297, 369).

Except for 4, the rest are supposed more or less to discourage saving.

This skeletal description does not do justice to the richness of Rae's argument and illustrations, which elicited the highest level of praise from Mill ([1848] 1927),[2] who cited him extensively, and concluded:

> On the Subject of Population, this valuable service [of providing detailed analysis] has been rendered by the celebrated Essay of Mr. Malthus, and [on the accumulation of capital] I can refer *with equal confidence* to another, though less well known work, *New Principles of Political Economy*, by Dr. Rae. [emphasis added]

For Rae, saving is an important and independent factor in economic development, but its status is essentially of a supporting nature.[3] We return to this later. Furthermore, in his view (Rae 1834: 148), the intensity of the desire to save also marks the place of a society (or perhaps even individuals) in the scale of civilization! Among the societies of his own time, he placed the European nations at the top of the list, then came the Asiatics, with the Indians of the Americas at the bottom. Over time, however, he awards the booby prize to the Roman society of Rome's declining days, which, in his view only accumulated little or nothing like the American Indians, but in fact decumulated extensively (ibid. 157–8).

### *Böhm-Bawerk*

Of Böhm-Bawerk's ([1889] 1959) three famous "Reasons" for the existence of a positive rate of interest:

1 the pattern of the flow of income over time;
2 the systematic underestimation of the future utility; and
3 the technical superiority of the present over future goods,

the first two can be treated as factors influencing the supply of capital. However, he also mentions elsewhere some other factors or the amplifications of the above factors which make his views closer to Rae's. One of the minor differences is that he excludes risk premium from being a part of the interest rate, thus not allowing Rae's item 5 (see above) to have any effect on this rate (Böhm-Bawerk [1889] 1959: 263). But his very acknowledgement of the existence of the risk premium is an acceptance of Rae's position that uncertainty can affect the *supply and demand* of saving.

On the whole, Rae's view on the factors behind the supply of saving is much richer than Böhm-Bawerk's, with one important exception. There is no counterpart in Rae of Böhm-Bawerk's "First Reason"; the pattern of the flow of income is not mentioned by him as a determinant of saving, although, as we noted, the level of income is (in the simple Keynesian fashion). Böhm-Bawerk's argument is that with the expectation of rising income over time, saving will be smaller, and vice versa. We return to this in the concluding remarks in this section.

### *Irving Fisher*

Fisher's relation to Rae's theory of the supply of capital is much more direct, as one would infer from the dedication in his book. Fisher quotes Rae extensively, and the factors that in his view influence the supply of saving match closely Rae's. In the *Rate of Interest*, Fisher enumerates five of them ([1907] 1982: 103) beside the income stream: foresight, self-control, habit, expectation of life, and concern for other persons. In the revised version of the book (Fisher [1930] 1970) under the title *Theory of Interest*, however, he adds a sixth item, fashion. A comparison of the factors enumerated by Rae and Fisher immediately shows how closely Fisher has followed Rae.

However, there is again one crucial exception. Fisher also analyzes – in fact, very thoroughly – how the time pattern on income affects the rate of interest, exactly as Böhm-Bawerk does, and reaches the same conclusion. Nevertheless, as noted earlier, Rae does not refer to this.

### *Conclusions on the supply of capital*

Thus, except for the one factor of the time pattern of income, Rae's discussion of the supply of capital is richer, if anything, than Böhm-Bawerk's or Fisher's. Fisher, in particular, follows Rae very closely. So much so that "fashion," the item he adds in the *Theory of Interest*, is one of Rae's points that, for some reason, Fisher did not include in the earlier version of his book. In fact, while each of them claims originality for his contribution to the theory of demand for capital, both Böhm-Bawerk ([1884] 1959: 239–40) and Fisher ([1930] 1970: 182) disclaim any in their contributions to the theory of supply of capital. One result is that both of them accept without question Rae's proposition that the "social and benevolent affections" *increase* the supply of saving. Fisher does so, in spite of Mixter's (1905) fairly early objection to the effect that such "affections" can have two opposite effects. The affections, for those living in the period in which the decision to save is made, are likely to *reduce* saving, while for those belonging to the future generation, they will increase it. Hence the net effect of "affections" on the supply of capital would be ambiguous.

Finally, we return to the exception noted above. Both Böhm-Bawerk and Fisher consider the time pattern of a person's income as an important factor in determining his or her saving. This is Böhm-Bawerk's "First Reason," and Fisher uses extensive numerical charts and diagrams to make the same point. As noted above, Rae does not even mention this. The question is whether this omission is simply an oversight, or whether it can be explained with something more substantive.

One plausible explanation may be given through the difference in their respective theories of value – Rae's was a modified classical version, while the other two subscribed to the neoclassical theory. Crudely speaking, in the classical approach, a good is a good is a good – its possible diminishing marginal utility is not a part of the argument, and hence the difference in income stream would not have any significance other than the "defective telescopic faculty" represented by Rae's item 2, and also Böhm-Bawerk's item 2 and Fisher's first (foresight) and second (self-control). On the other hand, in the world of diminishing marginal utility of income[4] and the equalization of the utility at the margin after suitable discounting, the difference in the income stream will obviously have additional significant effect on the saving behavior.[5]

## Demand for capital

### *John Rae*

Rae's contribution to the theory of demand for capital,[6] can be conveniently studied under two headings. One is a clear, even if, to a modern reader, unfamiliar, statement of the diminishing marginal productivity of capital, *with the given state of knowledge*. The other is the manner, the means, and the policy required to increase this knowledge through "invention" – which shifts up this marginal product curve.[7] Rae's contribution under both these headings is very impressive and important. However, while the former can be traced back to Turgot ([1770] 1911), the latter, in spite of Ricardo's chapter on machinery and some earlier references to this, is very much Rae's distinctive contribution.[8]

To discuss the demand for capital, Rae defines the concept of "instruments," which consist of all goods, consumption (with some qualification) and production, as well as land. He then develops the concept of the "order" of these instruments (Rae 1834: 100, 195).

This concept can be most easily understood in, and strictly applies to, a point input-point output framework. An input (instrument) of value 200 units of labor at one point of time, yields an output at another point of time which has a value of 400 units of labor[9] – twice that of the original input. Then, if the time interval is one year, the "order of the instrument is A or 1, if two years it is B or 2, and so on. This in now known to be an alternative way of representing the marginal product of capital (see e.g., James 1951). If $r$ is the marginal yearly rate of return on capital, and $n$ the order of the instrument – that is, the number of years in which the value doubles – then:

$$(1 + r)^n = 2$$

gives the relationship between $n$ and $r$. If $n$ is known, the marginal product of capital, or more precisely, its yearly rate of return:

$$r = 2^{1/n} - 1$$

Obviously $r$ and $n$ are negatively related. Rae, in fact calculates the corresponding $r$'s for some $n$'s: for $n = 1$, $r = 100$ percent, for $n = 2$, $r = 42$ percent and so on (Rae 1834: 195), using, of course, the compound interest concept.

Rae clearly sees that given the technical knowledge, the marginal return to capital ultimately diminished. He bases his argument on the generalization of Ricardo's idea that labor and capital are used on the better quality "land" first, then on the lower quality land, hence leading to "diminishing returns." The generalization consists in applying this argument to every productive opportunity, and not only to land. Capital will first be used in the opportunity with higher returns, then in that with lower returns, and so on:

> [I]f we suppose them to acquire *no additional knowledge* of the powers of those materials, and yet add continually to the amount of instruments they form out of them, [they] must *at length* have recourse to such, as are either operated on with greater difficulty, or bring about the desired events more sparingly or tardily. [emphasis added]
>
> (Rae 1834: 113)

Near the end of the chapter dealing with this issue, he says:

> This progress [increase in the quantity of the instruments], *while art itself remains stationary,*, would, however, undoubtedly, gradually carry instruments to more and more slowly returning orders. [emphasis added]
>
> (ibid. 117)

As can be seen in the above quotations, and several other passages (e.g. ibid. 108) tardiness is treated on par with higher cost.

It is, however, the theory and policy on "invention," that changes in knowledge which are assumed constant in the above analysis, to which Rae makes his most powerful contribution (see Brewer 1991; Ahmad 1993, 1996a). In the context of the theory of demand for capital, he asserts that invention raises the marginal product curve of capital in the relevant range. In the process of this discussion, Rae throws light on various aspects of invention, such as its labor-augmenting (Rae 1834: 92) or capital-augmenting nature, and the related issue of learning by doing, and *perhaps the most significant, the externalities generated by invention*, (ibid. 51–2), to some of which we return later.

### *Böhm-Bawerk*

Böhm-Bawerk's "Third Reason," the technical superiority of the present good over the future good, relates to the demand for capital. It is well known that he was the first to attempt a systematic formal presentation of the time-structured production process, even if only for the flow input-point output cases. This was an advance over Rae's formal presentation, since Rae's "order" of instrument was formally presented only in the point input-point output framework, a special case of Böhm-Bawerk's. The other time-structured frameworks, the point input-flow output or the flow input-flow output ones were suggested by both of them, but not systematically presented by either.

In his flow input-point output framework, Böhm-Bawerk defines formally a measure of "capital intensity" in units of "time," in contrast to the more usual measures, which are given either as capital–output ratios or capital–labor ratios (see e.g., Ahmad 1991 for details). This is Böhm-Bawerk's well-known "average period of production," defined as the weighted average of the period for which inputs at various times (he explicitly envisages only labor inputs leading to the suggestion that he had a wage-fund theory ([1889] 1959: 365, 377)) remain in a flow input-point output production process, the weights being the quantities of these inputs. Formally:

$$A = \frac{\sum_{i=0}^{t} a_i t_i}{\sum_{i=0}^{t} a_i}$$

where $A$ represents the average period of production, $a_i$ represents labor input in period $i$, and $t_i$ the time interval between the input of $a_i$ and the production of the output.

It is obvious, that *in this form* the "average period of production" cannot be obtained for the point input-flow output cases. This, however, is only a deficiency not an error in the concept. The error lies in its implying a zero rate of interest. In a concept the main purpose of which is to prove the existence of a positive rate of interest, this implication, to say the least, is ironical. It is true that his argument can go through even with a simple (non-zero) rate of interest, but he does not explicitly postulate or even use this assumption.[10] However, even the simple interest approach is not acceptable on purely logical grounds (see e.g., Ahmad 1991). One may note that Rae in his numerical discussion, albeit of the simpler point input-point output case, does use the correct compound interest approach.

Böhm-Bawerk's attempt to define capital intensity in units of time was to support his contention that the roundabout method (longer average period of production) is more productive (the message of this Third Reason). However, this is clearly undermined by his admission "Exceptional cases may occur, in which a roundabout method is not only *better*, but also *quicker*" (emphasis in the original) ([1889] 1959: 82). If one is generous, one could say that in most cases his general position would be right, but even then, his attempt at pseudo-precision by defining a numerical measure was, to say the least, ill-judged.[11]

Finally, we may briefly turn to Böhm-Bawerk's discussion of invention as an element in the demand for capital. Most of his discussion of the change in technique is simply that of a movement along a production function, with given knowledge, which is of course not Rae's "invention." Even when he mentions something resembling invention – a change in knowledge – he sometimes only repeats Rae's argument (Böhm-Bawerk [1884] 1959: 365), but mostly his objective is to illustrate that even in these cases a larger output is obtained by prolonging the period of production – the argument is parallel to but not the same as implying that the invention is capital-using – and is not for the purpose of introducing a new element affecting the demand for capital.

### *Irving Fisher*

Fisher, not unlike Böhm-Bawerk, claims originality for his contribution to the demand aspect of capital theory, rather than to the supply. In his basic exposition, he uses what one may call the production possibility curve between the present and the future goods, the tangent price line (based on the rate of interest) to it, and confronts this line with the indifference curve obtained from the supply-side analysis. From this he obtains the conditions for the individual and overall equilibrium,[12] more or less along the lines of the basic textbooks on the theory of international trade. However, his idea that has drawn much more attention in recent years, is that of the "rate of return over cost," or for him an interchangeable term, the "internal rate of return." He defines this in the following words:

> This hypothetical rate of interest which if used in calculating the present worth of the two options [of income stream] compared would equalize them or their differences (cost and return) may be called the *rate of return over cost*. [emphasis in the original]
>
> (Fisher [1930] 1970: 155)

Using symbols, we can write this rate of return over cost as $r$ in the equation

$$Q_0' + \frac{Q_1'}{1 = r} + \frac{Q_2'}{(1+r)^2} + \dots + \frac{Q_n'}{(1+r)^n} = Q_0 + \frac{Q_1}{1+r} + \frac{Q_2}{(1+r)^2} + \dots + \frac{Q_m}{(1+r)^m} \tag{6.1}$$

where $Q_i$ and $Q_i'$ are the elements of the income streams negative or positive, for period $i$. Written in this way, the $r$ may be interpreted as a switch point between two techniques if, following Fisher, the two sides of the equation are interpreted as net income streams representing two given techniques. If two values of $r$ satisfy the equation, we have reswitching, something Fisher does *not* consider in this context, although he brings this up in another. We return to this below.

On the other hand, if the values for all periods other than 0 on the left-hand side of the above equation are eliminated and $Q_0'$ is interpreted as the point input (but considered positive), the equation (6.1) becomes:

$$Q_0' = \frac{Q_1}{1+r} + \frac{Q_2}{(1+r)^2} + \dots + \frac{Q_m}{(1+r)^m} \tag{6.2}$$

and *r* can then be formally interpreted as Keynes "marginal efficiency of capital" (leaving aside the finer points of the concept).[13]

Fisher, as noted above, is not aware of the reswitching in his general "rate of return over cost" case (equation (6.1)). This is somewhat ironical, since in another context, in his criticism of Böhm-Bawerk, he gives example of reswitching ([1907] 1982: 352). Equal-valued input of $a is used in both techniques in year 0, but Technique I produces goods worth $5 in year 10 *and* worth $100 in year 100, while Technique II produces goods worth $15 in year 25 only (see Table 6.1). This is reswitching; since he finds that at 5 percent Technique II will be chosen, whereas if at 1 percent or 25 percent, Technique I will be chosen. What Fisher does not see is that this is simply another special case of equation (6.1), and hence his own concept of the "rate of return over cost" is susceptible to the same criticism as he directs against Böhm-Bawerk on the basis of the illustration in Table 6.1.[14] Thus both Fisher and Böhm-Bawerk can be successfully attacked through the Cambridge criticism. Rae, on the other hand, cannot be formally faulted on this account, since his formal (numerical) analysis is only of the point input-point output case, in which no reswitching can occur (Ahmad 1991).

Finally, turning to invention, Fisher, discusses this in detail, as one would expect from such an ardent admirer of Rae. Even then he says: "The subject of the economic effect of invention, and particularly of its effect upon the rate of interest, has been fully treated by John Rae, and to him the reader of this book is referred for extended study" ([1907] 1982: 203). In fact, it was he who first noted (1897) that the study of invention was a distinctive feature of Rae's work, and contrasted it with Böhm-Bawerk's in this respect. In his discussion of invention, he is a clear follower of Rae, repeating his argument with different examples, almost reaching lyrical heights in praise of invention and inventors, and even suggesting, following Rae, that the inventor should be subsidized ([1930] 1970: 353)! To Rae's (1834: 15) "Invention is the only power on earth, that can be said to create," Fisher says: "invention is a chief basis for progress in civilization and for the increase in the income of mankind" ([1930] 1970: 354).

Fisher considered his own age to be the age of invention, and ascribed to this the steep rise in the New York Stock Exchange in 1929 (a diagnosis that almost led to his financial ruin)! He does not, however, seem

*Table 6.1* Fisher's example of techniques and rate of return

| | *Years* | | | |
|---|---|---|---|---|
| | *0* | *10* | *25* | *100* |
| Technique I | $a | $5 | $ 0 | $100 |
| Technique II | $a | $0 | $15 | $ 0 |

quite sure whether "invention" belongs to the demand analysis of capital, or is something to be superimposed upon it. It appears that, somewhat unexpectedly, with time he became inclined to the latter view. In his *Rate of Interest* (1907), he treats "invention" as a part of his formal analysis of what we have called the demand of capital, but in his *Theory of Interest* (1930), he places it among the chapters on auxiliary topics.

## Theory of capital

As noted in the first section, there have been two predominant themes in the theory of capital: one, the determination of the *rate of interest*, the other of *economic growth*, and in the neoclassical tradition both have been considered in terms of the supply and demand analysis.[15] Rae was interested in the role of capital both in the theory of interest or profit and in the theory of growth. He writes: "It [political economy] has usually been discussed under the head of [profit of] stock, wages of labor, and rent, and it is to the first of these that our investigations are altogether confined" (Rae 1834: 79), indicating his interest in the theory of profit. But he also says:

> The general tendency of all the circumstances, the nature and causes [note the similarity with the title of Smith's book] of which has been our aim hitherto to investigate, is to advance the wealth of society, the capital and stock of communities.
>
> (ibid. 265)

indicating his interest in the theory of growth.

That for him the supply and demand for "capital" *determine* the rate of interest can be deduced from the following:

> Loans, indeed, pass under the name of money, but money is only the means of affecting the loan, it is in reality instruments that are lent, and they must in return yield not much less than what is paid for their use, otherwise they would not be borrowed, and not much more, otherwise they would not be lent.
>
> (Rae 1834: 197)

and how the *changes* in the supply and demand conditions affect the rate of interest, from the following:

1. *Accumulation* of stock or capital, is the addition made to these, through the operation of the accumulation principle. [supply]
2. *Augmentation* of stock or capital, is the addition made to them, through the operation of the principle of invention. [shifting the marginal product curve upwards]

> 3. Increase of stock or capital, is the addition made to them, by the conjoined operation of both principles.
>
> Accumulation of stock diminishes profits [rate of]; augmentation of stock increases profits [rate of]; increase of stock neither increases nor diminishes profits [rate of].
>
> (ibid. 264)

It is to this analysis of Rae's that Fisher refers in his statement cited earlier (Fisher [1907] 1982: 203).

Although Rae's contribution to the theory of interest provides, by all counts, the fundamental *basis* of the neoclassical theory of interest, it would perhaps generally be agreed that *for him*, this is essentially a prelude to his theory of growth of income and wealth. It is undoubtedly the theory, and the required policy for this growth, and the essential and dominant role of "invention" in it, that provides for Rae the *raison d'etre* of writing his book. His study of profit, of the various aspects of invention, including its "learning by doing" character, and the externalities generated by it, are all essentially only ingredients of this grand theme. This has been discussed in greater detail elsewhere;[17] here, I shall conclude with only one of the immediately relevant points. To follow up on the last sentence of the preceding quotation, in his view the "increase" in capital neither raises nor lowers the rate of profits. In other words, the marginal product of capital remains constant! Of course, it may be reading into it much more than he intended, but still, this may be the first statement of the so-called AK model of endogenous growth (Rebelo 1991).[18]

### *Böhm-Bawerk*

Böhm-Bawerk's overwhelming preoccupation was with the existence and determination of the rate of interest, with little direct concern for economic growth. Of course, in his long discourse on capital, matters relating to growth could not be entirely avoided. For instance, he distinguished between "social capital" and the "private capital," and relates the former to production, the latter to interest rate. One may claim that the former is indirectly related to growth. Gain, he does mention in passing the externalities of invention (Böhm-Bawerk [1889] 1959: 96) and also, more directly, growth through net investment resulting from saving (ibid. 111, 113), which he goes on to suggest is a precondition of capital formation. These are, of course, straightforward conventional positions. What is somewhat unexpected is that he anticipates and considers – and, of course, rejects – the position later taken by Schumpeter (1911) and Keynes (1936), but enunciated much earlier, for example by Lauderdale (1804), that saving, that is nonconsumption, is a nonaction, and hence cannot produce anything (ibid. 117). None of his discussion on growth is very focused, however. In brief, for a capital theorist, his interest in growth was not very extensive.

We have already covered the various ingredients of his theory of interest. These provide the basis of individual equilibrium when the individual maximizes the present (discounted) value of his utility, with the given interest rate, while the interest rate is determined through the usual market clearing conditions. It is interesting that he uses the *compound discount rate* for obtaining the present value of utility, and of goods (ibid. 289, 306) – hence his missing the lecture on compound interest would perhaps account for his decision not to use this in his formulation of the "average period of production."[19]

Since the interest rate is derived from the exchange rate between the present good and future good, for Böhm-Bawerk the theory of interest is a special case of the theory of value (ibid. 347, 381), an idea which was much more fully developed by Fisher, to whom we now turn.

### *Irving Fisher*

Fisher's theory of interest is a most elaborate, as well as elegant, piece of analysis in the neoclassical tradition. He uses what we have called the supply and demand apparatus in his verbal and geometric presentations, starting with the individual, in the manner similar to, but more elaborate than we have noted in Böhm-Bawerk, and ends up on the same manner in determining the market interest rate. He then moves on to a fully-fledged general equilibrium model determining the interest rate and other related present and future variables – not surprising for a mathematical economist of his calibre, who had read Walras.[20] Somewhat surprisingly, not many references have been made to him for this part of his contribution by the modern defenders of the neoclassical position against the Cambridge attack, who have defended this position through resort to the Fisherian general equilibrium approach,[21] while in their ill-fated defence based on the rate of return over cost approach, his name has been invoked in innumerable occasions.

On the other hand, Fisher also does not have much to say about the relation between capital and growth. He does, following Rae very closely, discuss some of the aspect of invention, but, as we have seen, he himself does not have much new to add. His *major* contributions to capital theory, *Rate of Interest* (1907) and its revised version *Theory of Interest* (1930), both pointedly contain "interest" alone as the substantive word in their titles.[22]

## Concluding assessment

First, the basic neoclassical ideas on the supply and demand for capital were provided by Rae, on which Fisher explicitly built both his theory of supply and of demand. Böhm-Bawerk, according to his own acknowledgement, was aware of Rae's contribution on the supply of capital through Mill

([1848] 1871), while his basic ideas on the demand were closely related to, if not based on, Rae. In this respect the statements by Niehans, Fisher, and Böhm-Bawerk cited at the beginning of the paper are amply substantiated.

Second, all three authors provide some technical and formal analysis. Rae does this through his analysis of the "order" or instruments (to be clearly distinguished from the Austrian "order" of goods), leading to the marginal product of capital in (effectively) a point input-point output framework. Böhm-Bawerk does this through his "average period of production," in a more general, flow input-point output framework, and Fisher through his rate of return over cost, in the most general flow input-flow output framework.

As noted above, Rae's framework is the simplest of all, and Fisher's the most general. It so happens, however, that because of its special and simpler nature, Rae's approach is not directly subject to the modern criticism of the neoclassical capital theory on the basis of the possibility of "reswitching" and related concepts, while both Böhm-Bawerk's (even leaving aside the criticism based on his zero interest rate assumption) and Fisher's are. This last statement is not to claim any superiority for Rae's approach, but mainly to record a fact from the history of economic analysis. This is simply an example of the overambitious being punished, but perhaps still opening up new doors.

With the general equilibrium approach, Böhm-Bawerk implicitly, and Fisher explicitly and in detail, did no doubt make significant analytical advance over Rae, an approach which, in addition, has been immune to the Cambridge attack. However, Rae with his Baconian methodological preference would have perhaps attacked this strongly for its singular unsuitability for his cherished, even if not always practised, "inductive" approach.[23]

Finally, neither Böhm-Bawerk nor Fisher, in spite of Fisher's attempt to follow Rae closely on the subject of invention, made any significant contribution to the relationship of capital to growth. They treated "invention" by and large as a once-for-all phenomenon, or, at best, a sporadic one. In this area Rae's contribution remains outstanding, and in relation to the other two, almost exclusive. Many of his ideas on this theme, it seems, have become relevant to the currently burgeoning literature on "endogenous growth."[24]

## Appendix

Capital, its supply, its demand, and other related expressions, have been used in so many different senses in the literature, and so much has been written on them (including the whole of Böhm-Bawerk's ([1884] 1959) volume 1 of *Capital and Interest*, that any attempt to cover them in a brief appendix would be pointless. What I intend to do here instead is to indicate very briefly the way that the three protagonists have defined them and used them in their works. We have not been able to do so in the text, since its purpose was to *compare* their contributions, which would have been extremely difficult, if not impossible, if we presented each of their theories in their own different "language," so to speak.

The term "capital" is often used by Rae in a loose sense, particularly before he defines "instrument," and relates the term to capital. "Instruments," which he also calls "stock," as we noted in the text, consist of all goods, consumers' and producers', as well as "land." "Capital," for him, is not exactly the same thing; it is defined as the instruments minus the consumers goods reserved for immediate consumption (Rae 1834: 171). Following Smith, he divides it into circulating capital and fixed capital, without making much use of this distinction.

Since he looks at capital essentially as a productive agent, the "supply" of capital is the supply of these agents by their producers, or owners, and its demand is by the accumulators of capital (the savers). This is, of course, the reverse of the modern practice, according to which the savers are said to "supply" capital (fund), while those undertaking production "demand" capital (fund). For the sake of the uniformity of treatment, we have, in this chapter, used these terms in the modern sense in which they were also used by Mixter in discussing Rae, as well as by the other two protagonists.

Böhm-Bawerk also defines capital as productive agents, but only what we would call "the produced means of production." Hence he excludes land from the category of capital. He also excludes consumption good that has already reached the consumer, from the category of capital. Hence his "capital" is Rae's capital minus land and the consumers' good that has reached the final consumers, but is not reserved for immediate consumption. It is also interesting to note that in spite of his overwhelming preoccupation with "capital," Böhm-Bawerk excludes it from the category of "factors of production," thus rejecting the classical position. For him, land and labor remain the "only factors of production."

Böhm-Bawerk does use the expression "supply" of and the "demand" for capital, but very rarely, and more or less disparagingly. He thinks, not without good reason, that these expressions are often used in vague and confusing ways. However, whenever he does use them, he does so essentially in the same sense as we have done in this chapter.

Fisher distinguished between "capital goods" and "capital" ([1930] 1970: 14–15). "Capital goods" help produce goods and income, as "capital" does for Rae and Böhm-Bawerk. But Fisher's "capital," is different: it is the discounted value of all the output (income) that can be attributed to a productive agent. In other works, "capital goods" produce output and income, but it is income that produces "capital." Since all "factors" can be expressed in this way, to him, effectively, there is only *one* factor of production, "capital." Land and labor are not separate factors of production; they are all simply "capital." Thus he completely reverses Böhm-Bawerk's position on the definition of factors of production. What Fisher fails to emphasize is that capital measured in this way is not a *measure of capital as a productive agent*, whatever else may be its use for other purposes. It cannot, for instance, be an argument in a production function. As Samuelson (1961), following Joan Robinson (1953–4), puts it: "Such computed totals, it need hardly be said, cannot be fed into production function, kicked at, or leaned against." The unfortunate consequence of Fisher not clarifying this point can be seen to this day, in spite of Samuelson's admonition. Most applied works in this area, including even in the otherwise theoretically uncompromising field of new classical economics, use such "computed values" in their production functions.

Finally, Fisher, like Böhm-Bawerk was not keen on using the expressions "demand" and "supply" of capital, and for similar reasons. But when he does use them, again like Böhm-Bawerk, the usage is similar to that in this chapter.

## Notes

1 It may be claimed that only the former is a part of "neoclassical" enquiry, but not the latter (e.g. Burgstaller (1994)). However, the existence of the neoclassical growth theory, if not a contradiction in terms, would make such a claim untenable, even it is conceded that the problem of growth has been much more of a classical preoccupation than a neoclassical one. In any case, here the term neoclassical will be used in an inclusive sense.

2 It is interesting, and perhaps illustrates the depth of Rae's contributions to economics, that two principal commentators on Rae, question Mill's judgment in singling out this feature of Rae's work as his chief contribution. Ferrara (1956) and Böhm-Bawerk ([1884] 1959), provide their own different candidates for this distinction.

3 Ahmad (1996a). For an earlier and somewhat stronger view see Brewer (1991).

4 Not a necessary consequence of the diminishing marginal utility of goods – an issue into which we cannot go here, but something which is relevant to Böhm-Bawerk's work in a different context.

5 Böhm-Bawerk criticizes Rae, among other things, for his not having "the" correct theory of value ([1884] 1959), but not in the present context. In fact he does this to criticize a view which he mistakenly attributes to Rae. This does not mean that Rae made no contribution to the theory of value. In fact Ferarra (1856) considered this to be Rae's main contribution, and criticized Mill, as we have noted above, for praising Rae for the wrong reason. Ferrara (1856) interpreted Rae's theory of value as a "reproduction cost theory" (see also a more recent work, Guccione (1993)), which ultimately, even in indirectly, implies the idea of the equivalence of goods through their utility at the margin.

6 A reminder that we are using the term "demand and supply of capital" in the neoclassical sense, also used by Mixter in discussing Rae, and *not* in the sense used by the authors themselves. See the Appendix for further clarification.

7 This is not meant to give a complete picture of the effects of invention, but should do for the present. See, for example, Ahmad (1991) for a fuller discussion.

8 In his assessment of Rae's contribution to capital theory, Mixter (1902: 287) places his theory of invention at the top of the list, and the theory of the supply of saving at the bottom. On this see also Brewer (1991) and Ahmad (1996a). Fisher (1897) also claimed that Rae's contribution to the theory of invention made his theory of capital superior to Böhm-Bawerk's. Böhm-Bawerk ([1884] 1959: 239–40), on the other hand, claimed for himself the credit for developing the technical side of the theory (not specifically invention), while conceding that its psychological side (related to the supply of capital) was developed by Rae. For that matter, even Fisher, in spite of his above-mentioned claim for the superiority of Rae of Böhm-Bawerk, asserts the originality for his own contribution to the technical aspect of capital theory. We return to this in the concluding part of this section.

9 The problem of translating physical units into value (which he happens to measure with labor as the numeraire), is something that he does not address, not unlike most neoclassical economists of today. He also gives examples from other frameworks, but assumes that these can be converted into the point input-point output form. His *formal* (numerical) example is always given in this form, however.

10 It has become almost customary to suggest that Böhm-Bawerk uses a simple (non-zero) rate of interest. See e.g., Samuelson (1994), in which he speculates that Böhm-Bawerk had perhaps missed his Law class during the lecture on compound interest! It seems (from a letter from Weizsacker dated February 1, 1994) that the suggestion of his argument going through with simple interest as well was first made by Lutz (1951) and, since, then, it has become customary to attribute this to Böhm-Bawerk.

11 In his related discussion, he postulates diminishing *absolute* returns to time for obtaining an equilibrium solution. This is not essential – the diminishing *proportional* return would do. See Wicksell's ([1893] 1954) "Jevon's Rule."

12 We return to his extending this to a general equilibrium framework with more than two variables.

13 No doubt, both similarities are only formal, and not necessarily of substance. For a discussion of the possible substantive difference between Fisher's internal rate of return and Keynes' marginal efficiency of capital, see, for instance, Dimand (1988).

14 Thus the claim (e.g., by Yeager (1976)) that the problem of reswitching can be treated as an example of the multiplicity of the internal rate of return is valid only for the internal rate of return defined in the original Fisherian sense – one equating the present value of two processes. The internal rate of return corresponding to the Keynesian marginal efficiency of capital is not conceived in this form, hence my conclusion in 1991 that the problem of the uniqueness of the internal rate of return (obtained from equation (6.2) is not that of reswitching.

Fisher's criticism of Böhm-Bawerk based on the above example is somewhat off the target in any case; it is conceived in terms of the point input-flow output framework, while Böhm-Bawerk's formal analysis was conducted in a flow input-point output framework. Fisher, of course, could easily have chosen the latter for illustrating reswitching, as Samuelson has done in the more recent controversies (1966).

15 The titles of Fisher's books are sufficient evidence of the former and so is the general title of Böhm-Bawerk's two volumes; the first modern formal published presentation of the neoclassical theory of growth, by Pilvin (1953), is evidence of the latter.

16 This may give the impression that for Rae money is just a veil, which it is, but this does not prevent him from making a fairly sophisticated contribution to the theory of money (Rae 1834: 176 ff.).

17 See Brewer (1991), Ahmad (1993, 1996a, 1996b) and, as examples of some earlier views, Spengler (1959) and Dean and Dean (1972).

18 This relation of Rae's work to endogenous growth is, of course, made just in passing. This has been somewhat more fully articulated in Ahmad (1996b).

19 See n. 10 above.

20 In fact, Walras ([1874] 1954) himself had applied the general equilibrium technique to the determination of the rate of interest, albeit in a somewhat different context. However, in the application of the general equilibrium *technique* for specific narrower purposes, Walras is a borrower. Cournot (1838) who should be called the father of the formal "Walrasian" general equilibrium *technique* (including not only the counting of equations and unknowns, but also the derivation and elimination of the dependent equation!), applied this to, of all things, the question of bimetallism.

21 One of the first defenders along these lines, Bliss (1975), for example, does not mention Irving Fisher even once in his entire book.

22 His *Capital and Income*, published in 1906, is essentially only a definitional exercise, clearing the way for the other two books. Its main theme, the conceptual relation between capital and income, is considered in the following Appendix.

23 I have discussed this in somewhat more detail in Ahmad (1996b). See also Hamouda (p. 41) in this volume.

24 My views on the relationship between Rae's writings on growth and those of Adam Smith, as well as the views of some more recent economists, may be found elsewhere (see Ahmad 1993, esp. 1996a, 1996b).

# 7

# INVENTION

*Anthony Brewer*[1]

## The role of invention in the *New Principles*

John Rae's *Statement of Some New Principles on the Subject of Political Economy* (1834) was intended to refute Adam Smith's analysis of the causes of the wealth of nations and the laissez-faire conclusions generally drawn from it. "Invention" plays a central role in Rae's argument. He accused Smith of attributing economic growth exclusively to the accumulation of capital and of attributing accumulation in turn to individual savings decisions.[2] Rae argued that although an individual certainly becomes rich by saving,[3] things are different for a society as a whole. An individual who saves can acquire assets from others, but a society can only use saving productively by creating new capital assets. If all, or the "greater number" of individuals try to save, they may succeed for a time, but as "every branch of business within the society" becomes filled up, the desire to save will be diminished (Rae 1834: 22).

Individuals can invest in doing more of the same, but societies can only continue to accumulate for any length of time by adopting new methods of production, which themselves have to be invented. Rae supported this rather weak argument by appealing to the facts. The national capital of Great Britain, he claimed, had expanded tenfold in a few centuries, as a result of "the wonders and achievements of art, . . . fire and water transformed into our obedient drudges, . . . carrying us over the land with the speed of the wind, bearing us through the ocean against tide and storm" (Rae 1834: 14), and so forth. He concluded: "Invention is the only power on earth that can be said to create . . . [I]ndustry and parsimony increase the capitals of individuals; national wealth . . . cannot be increased but by the aid also of the inventive faculty" (ibid. 15). This makes Rae the first economist to see technical change as the main source of continuing economic growth and, since he saw no limit to the scope for invention, the first to foresee an unlimited potential for future growth.[4]

He was careful not to overstate the extent of his disagreement with Smith. He agreed that "the causes of the wealth of nations . . . are to be found in the improvement of the productive powers of human labor" (Rae 1834: 12), and that capital accumulation is an indispensable component of that improvement. Having defined an "instrument" as any (useful) produced good, lumping consumer goods, intermediate goods, and capital goods together, he devoted much of the *New Principles* to discussing the "amount" of instruments formed, thus effectively identifying growth of output with growth of the capital stock. Syed Ahmad (1996a) suggests that the difference between Rae and Smith might be discussed by looking for the necessary and sufficient causes of growth in their work, but it is clear that accumulation is both a necessary and (in a sense) a sufficient condition for growth for both of them, provided at least that extraneous variables such as the geographical and social environment are held constant.

What is at stake here is not the importance of capital accumulation, but its causes. Both thought that savings were automatically invested, but Smith attributed saving to the "uniform, constant, and uninterrupted effort of every man to better his condition," which is thus "the principle from which public and national, as well as private opulence is originally derived" (Smith [1776] 1976: 343). According to Rae, Smith's case for laissez-faire follows. Since total saving is the sum of individual saving, and since individuals can be trusted to save (in general, if not in every case – there are some "prodigals") any state intervention will reduce saving and hence economic growth (e.g., Rae 1834: 16–17, 63–5).[5] This argument, however, only holds if the determinants of private saving can be treated as exogenous. Rae's case is that they are not, and that Smith treated "what is merely a necessary concomitant for a cause" (ibid. 28). In Rae's story, saving, like population, is endogenous, with invention as the exogenously determined cause of growth. "It is invention, which showing how profitable returns can be got from the one [capital], and subsistence procured from the other [population] that may most fitly be esteemed the cause of both" (ibid. 31).

Rae's case, then, is that:

1 invention is needed to maintain the incentive to save; and
2 invention has causes independent of individual savings decisions, causes which are open to influence by the "Legislator" where individual savings decisions are not.

Rae's treatment of the second point is the main topic of this chapter. The first point requires a little further discussion, though it will not be pursued at length here. Rae's case for the role of invention in permitting continued saving and investment has three components:

1 Savings/investment is responsive to changes in the anticipated rate of return on instruments.
2 Invention increases the rate of return, thus inducing savings and investment.

3 Without invention, the rate of return would be forced down, and accumulation would soon stop.

Of these, item 1 is the subject of Rae's capital theory and his account of intertemporal choice. Individuals balance the return on different instruments against a number of factors such as the uncertainty of surviving long enough to enjoy the benefits, altruistic feelings towards their descendants (who will benefit if the saver does not survive), and so on. Item 2 can be taken as axiomatic – only inventions which raise returns are of interest. Finally, item 3 is partly a consequence of Rae's theory of intertemporal choice – accumulation stops at a (positive and perhaps substantial) rate of return, reflecting the "effective desire of accumulation" of the community – but is also an empirical question: How close is the community to the minimum acceptable rate of return thus determined, and how rapidly would returns be driven down if invention did not restore them? Rae implicitly assumed that established communities are close to equilibrium, so growth would soon stop if invention were to stop. There would be no further movement to slower yielding instruments, because those already in use fully reflect the effective desire of accumulation of the community.

Something should be said here, if very briefly, about the role of the division of labour. Rae did not deny its importance, but (again) questioned Smith's view of the underlying causality. Smith attributed the division of labour primarily to the accumulation of capital (e.g., Smith [1776] 1976: 277). The "extent of the market," often cited as Smith's main explanation for the extent of the division of labor, can itself be traced back to the general level of economic activity in the locality, a result of the accumulation of capital, along with other factors such as favorable location which can be taken as constant over time. Smith did mention inventions as a factor affecting the productivity of labor, but claimed that "the invention of all those machines by which labour is so much facilitated and abridged, seems to have been originally owing to the division of labour" (ibid. 20). The primacy of capital accumulation, and hence of individual savings decisions as the central cause of growth, is maintained.

Rae reversed the causality – the division of labor is the result of invention, not the other way round. Simple technology gives few opportunities for division of labor. The invention of more specialized and complex instruments creates potential gains from specialization. Where Smith argued that specialization made labor more productive, through increased "dexterity" and the like, Rae stressed the more efficient use of instruments, which a specialist uses full time. An unspecialized producer would either not use specialized equipment at all, or would have to leave it idle much of the time (Rae 1834: bk II, ch. 8; see also Ahmad 1996a). Two comments are appropriate here. First, what is at stake, again, is causality – Smith treated the invention of machines as a result, not a cause, of the division of labor, while Rae reversed the causality. Second, the difference between them may reflect real changes in the world they saw around them. In Smith's time, manual skills really were of primary importance, but by the time Rae wrote, more than half a century later, technology was already beginning to be embodied in the design of the machine rather than in the skills of the person who used it.[6]

In sum, Rae's analysis is centered on the role of invention as the primary, independent, causal factor behind economic growth. At any date, the wealth of the nation depends on:

1. the state of knowledge, which is the result of past invention;
2. the effective desire of accumulation, which determines how far that knowledge is employed; and
3. the available materials, that is, the natural environment (Rae 1834: 109).[7] If 2 and 3 are treated as constant over time, the wealth of the nation can only grow as a result of new invention.

## Invention and its causes

Despite its central role in his system, Rae did not define "invention" clearly and explicitly. His examples and passing comments in the early part of the book suggest a fairly broad but reasonably familiar definition. Invention is described as "improving agriculture and the other old arts, or . . . discovering new ones" (Rae 1834: 14, 20, 23). Examples include steam power, the threshing machine, and so on. A summary listing of some of the things which a "Legislator" might do to "direct part of the energies of the community towards the furtherance of this power of invention" gives further clues: the Legislator should support the progress of science, art (that is, technology), the discovery of new arts and of improvements in the arts already practiced, and "the discovery of methods of adapting arts already practiced in other countries" to local circumstances. All of these are said to require "the aid of the inventive faculty" (ibid. 15–16).

The opening paragraph of the chapter on the causes of invention suggests a wider definition, one which goes far beyond mundane economic issues and provides some backing for the apparently wild claim in Book I, Chapter 1 of the *New Principles* that "invention is the only power on earth . . . that can be said to create" (Rae 1834: 15):

> Invention . . . is the great immediate maker of all that is the subject of our thoughts, or ministers to our enjoyments, or necessities, nor is there any portion of our existence, which is not indebted to its antecedent formative power. . . . It is always a maker, and, in a double sense, a maker. From the depths of the infinity lying within and without us, it brings visibly before us forms previously hidden.

> These are its first works. But neither does it intend to stop, nor does it, in fact, stop here. The forms which its eye thus catches, and its skill "bodies forth" into material shape, pass not away; they remain. Things of power, true workers, drawing to themselves, and fashioning to their semblance, the changeable and fleeting crowd . . . they are, in truth, the only permanent dwellers in the world, and rulers of it. In this, the double power of his works, the mathematician is as much a maker as the poet, and the poet as the mathematician, and genius in all its manifestations, may . . . be considered as the same power, and as excited to action by similar causes.
>
> (Rae 1834: 208)

The idea that invention is a maker "in a double sense," of the "double power" of the works of invention may seem puzzling at first sight. It makes sense if it is taken with the distinction that Rae drew, much earlier in the book, between the poem of "Childe Harold" and the paper on which it was printed (Rae 1834: 14). He can be read as saying that the inventor or creator produces something physical and time bound – a manuscript, a prototype, or something else that can serve as an example – but that this physical embodiment of something new can be distinguished from its lasting content, which is perpetuated by subsequent copying or by serving as the basis for further development.

He admitted that his subject, political economy, "leads us to attend to invention merely as it concerns itself with the physical world," but this is only one form of the work of "real discoverers, in any of the regions over which the power of this principle extends" (Rae 1843: 208–9). "Invention," it seems, is anything that adds to the stock of knowledge, defined broadly enough to encompass a poem or a work of art.

Rae went to extreme lengths in the opening pages of the chapter on the causes of invention both to emphasize the gap between the mass of mankind and the "man of genius,"[8] the inventor or creator, and to dramatize the tribulations he faces. The context is his claim that "man is essentially imitative" (Rae 1834: 209). The inventor is one who does not imitate. "Among the men with whom he lives, he lives as not of them" (ibid. 219). Novelty is misunderstood and resented. "The personal history of most men, who, in modern times, have brought into being those arts by which human power has been so largely advanced, is little else but a narration of misfortunes, and ingratitude" (ibid. 217). (Rae must surely have had his own rather unhappy life in mind.)

He clearly set himself a problem with this extreme formulation. How is invention to be explained? If novelty and creativity are not rewarded, what motivates invention? His first shot at an answer is heartfelt but unconvincing:

> We in vain search for any sufficient motive exciting to this course of action [invention], unless the good arising from communicating good, and the consequent desire to be a benefactor in the most extended possible manner . . . When strongly felt, it irresistibly impels those who are conscious of capacities equal to the attempt, spite of every obstacle to be overcome, or pain to be endured, to task themselves to the performance of works of permanent and diffusive utility.
>
> (Rae 1834: 210–11)

Invention is a moral choice, and its rewards are not of this world. Since Rae included poetry and mathematics among the works of invention and emphasized the gulf between the man of genius and the common herd, one might expect him to argue that the poet, at least, is driven by an inner need to write poetry for its own sake, regardless of others. Not so – Rae consistently presented invention as the result of a calculated choice. The inventor balances benefits against costs but his calculation of the benefits is shaped by altruistic feelings towards humanity at large.

He had earlier argued that saving and thus capital accumulation depend on a willingness to wait for rewards. If people were rational and immortal, there would be no problem, but they are neither. A saver cannot be sure of living to benefit from the full fruits of investment. The "effective desire of accumulation" thus depends on altruism, on a concern for the welfare of one's descendants. Willingness to devote oneself to invention demands an even wider form of altruism, a concern for the welfare of the whole community over an indefinite future. Intelligence too is required for the future benefits of both investment and invention to be appreciated and valued. A high effective desire of accumulation and a willingness to invest thus tend to go together. If the community as a whole feels a duty towards the future, then inventors may be rewarded, or at least admired. The resentment of novelty, which he had earlier stressed may be reversed, and a desire for fame, if not fortune, can drive invention. Economic success is, it seems, an index of (and a reward for) the moral and intellectual standards of the community.

In Rae's discussion of more directly economic cases, a rather different picture emerges. Take, for example, the discussion of advances in the use of steam power in Britain (Rae 1834: 245–7):

> As the progress of order, civilization, and art, covered the island of Great Britain with a numerous population, the stores of fuel . . . were by degrees exhausted . . . Necessity thus taught its inhabitants the use of coal.
>
> (ibid. 245)

As coal mines were driven deeper, drainage became a problem, but the use of steam power to drain mines came to the rescue. Rae set out the factors which brought about the first use of steam power, "an agent . . . far greater than any which has hitherto been placed within the hands of man" (ibid. 246). The need was urgent, the materials were available, previous improvements in machinery had paved the way, and the funds were available. The previous progress of science, in particular the concept of latent heat, may have played a role. Rae admitted that practical inventors could have progressed without the theory of latent heat, but if (pure) science had only helped to bring forward the progress of steam power by a few years, that was valuable enough (ibid. 247–48). The inventor in the broader sense of the opening pages of the chapter thus plays some role, albeit a small one.

The progress of steam as power source 'may be said to have been inevitable' (ibid. 247). Steam navigation emerged on the inland waterways of America, because the circumstances there were particularly favorable (ibid. 248). The creation of steam-powered railways, again, is explained in terms of the context – horse-drawn railways were already in use and steam power had come into use in mines. What was needed to bring the two together was a lighter and more compact steam engine to pull a train.

> The undertaking was commenced with full assurance that it would accomplish the desired improvement, though the manner how was not known . . . Had not Great Britain existed, metal railways and steam carriage might have been still in only the category of possibilities.
>
> (ibid. 249)

The tortured genius of earlier parts of the chapter has vanished, to be replaced by a story in which invention proceeds logically and smoothly, with "full assurance" of success. This version of Rae's story could even be forced into a Smithian mould – capital accumulation, it could be said, by pressing on resource constraints, creates both needs and opportunities. The division of labor ensures the existence of specialists to respond to them, and technical advance follows. Rae would, of course, have rejected this reading, since he always insisted that invention was primary and capital accumulation and the division of labor were secondary, but it does seem at the least that one could describe growth in terms of a sequence of inventions following each other in a predictable fashion, without drama and without any need for state intervention.

## Import substitution

What seems to be the main line of Rae's story, already sketched in earlier parts of the book, emerges towards the end of the chapter on the sources of invention. In this, the emphasis is on the transfer of technology from one industry to another (the account of the development of steam power could be in this context), but above all on the transfer of technology from one place to another, with consequent adaptation and change.

> I believe it will be found that there is no art in existence which we may not find means to trace . . . to the rudest and most simple principles, and which may not be shown to have attained perfection by continual changes from place to place, and material to material, and by encountering consequently alternating difficulties and facilities, the former developing its powers, the latter extending their field of action, and both, by helping to introduce general principles, weakening the restraining power of the tendency to servile imitation, and advancing the progress of science. *This successive passage of the same arts from country to country . . . seems to be the great exciting cause of the progress of them all.* [emphasis added]
>
> (Rae 1834: 253)

Circumstances are different in different places, so importing techniques from elsewhere is never a matter of simply copying. In any case, the procedures which are to be copied are those of somewhere far off. In a new location the normal desire to stick to what is familiar is ruled out, opening the way for improvement and adaptation. Setting up an industry in a new location both requires and stimulates invention.

Rae emphasized the potential gains from setting up an industry in a new location, but he also stressed the difficulties involved. The individual who takes the lead must have special qualities, even if they are not quite those of the "man of genius" who "lives apart," as in the earlier part of the chapter. "Very few individuals have a thorough knowledge of every different part of any complicated manufacture." The "director" has to "preserve the economy of the whole, and to search out the individuals best fitted for carrying on every part" (Rae 1834: 47). In a new country, this means finding and bringing in people with the necessary skills, and either importing machinery or having the equipment constructed locally, where it is, of course, new and unfamiliar. The costs and risks are correspondingly high.

Rae stressed that it is not simply a matter of copying what is done elsewhere – adaptation is needed to set up production in a new location where circumstances are different. The new industry can and (according to Rae) often does surpass established centers, given time. The "director" himself presumably cannot do the adapting, since we are told that no individual knows all parts of a complicated manufacture, but he plays the key initiating and organizing role. The relation between specialists and director is reminiscent of Schumpeter's distinction between inventor and innovator, discussed below.

Import substitution provides the main context for Rae's case for action by the "Legislator," that is, for state intervention. Throughout the *New*

*Principles* he pointed to what we would now call the public-good character of invention, thus laying the basis for a wholly coherent case for state intervention. It is, however, rather difficult to see quite what the state can do to promote genuine novelties which must, by their nature, be difficult or impossible to foresee. Rae's pessimistic attitude to the reception of genuine novelties makes the problem worse. If the community, as a whole is mistrustful or actively hostile to real invention, as Rae claimed, how can the "Legislator," the representative of the community, be expected to promote invention? Rae recognized the problem but dealt with it rather limply, saying that only a community which values intelligence and scores high on altruism towards future generations is likely to be willing to support invention (Rae 1834: 378). It is clear that he did not see such communities as the norm. In the case of import substitution, however, the opportunities and incentives for the Legislator to act are much clearer. The aim is to establish a domestic industry to produce a familiar (imported) product with an established market, while those who have most to lose, the existing suppliers, are foreigners.

Rae argued the case for state intervention to support infant industries strongly, but qualified it carefully – he was not against markets or trade in any general way. He urged the Legislator to be cautious, to assess the potential benefits carefully, and to support only industries that were likely to succeed. Support for new industries could take several forms: premiums for those individuals who first establish a new domestic manufacture, bounties (subsidies) for home products, or duties on imports. Rae suggested premiums first, to test the water, then bounties or duties to build up a full-scale industry (Rae 1834: 367–8).

Import substitution, then, plays an essential role in Rae's story. His first version of the sources of invention seems too pessimistic – if novelty is always rejected and despised, how can development ever happen? The second version, implicit in the story of the development of steam power, on the other hand, makes the process of development appear more automatic than Rae wanted, and seems to leave no rôle for state intervention. His focus on import substitution as the main motor of development neatly avoids both Scylla and Charybdis.

## Rae, Schumpeter, and the incentive to innovate

There are obvious parallels between Rae's ideas and those put forward much later by Joseph Schumpeter. Both emphasized the importance of habit and routine in everyday life, but argued that real economic development was the result of the efforts of those few who could break out of customary patterns of thought and introduce real novelties. Thus Schumpeter ([1911] 1961: 8, 85, 66) argued that "everyone will cling as tightly as possible to habitual economic methods," and that "carrying out a new plan and acting according to a customary one are things as different as making a road and walking along it," while development "is defined by the carrying out of new combinations." No other significant figures in the history of economic thought shared this very specific view of economic development. Schumpeter must have been influenced by Rae, but the difference in context and in the state of development of the subject is such that the influence is at the level of what Schumpeter called "vision" rather than analysis. Whatever Schumpeter took from Rae he remade completely in his own analytical framework. I shall not pursue the question of influence – I bring Schumpeter in here simply because the comparison between the two throws a useful light on some of the distinctive features of Rae's viewpoint.

Schumpeter drew a sharp distinction between invention and innovation:

> As long as they are not carried into practice, inventions are economically irrelevant. And to carry any improvements into effect is a task entirely different from the inventing of it . . . besides, the innovations which it is the function of entrepreneurs to carry out need not necessarily be any inventions at all. It is therefore not advisable, and it may be downright misleading, to stress the element of invention as much as some writers do.
>
> (Schumpeter [1911] 1961: 88–9)

Innovation, in Schumpeter's terms, means the introduction of something that is economically, rather than conceptually or technically, new. The entrepreneur, the central character in Schumpeter's story, is an innovator, but not necessarily an inventor.

Rae's concept of invention, stretching as it does from music and poetry to import substitution, is much broader than Schumpeter's concept of innovation. It is not even clear that Schumpeter's "innovation," in its pure form, would count as "invention" in Rae's terms at all. Suppose one individual thinks up a new technique but, for some reason, never puts it to use, while a second individual, a Schumpeterian innovator, takes it up and introduces it on a practical scale. Is the second an "inventor"? It is not clear from Rae's text, though the "director" of a project to start local production of something produced abroad (see above) seems very close to a Schumpeterian entrepreneur. Rae evaded the issue by arguing that some "invention" was always needed to adapt production to local circumstances. If Rae had made some distinctions on the lines of Schumpeter's it might have clarified his very confusing account of the causes of invention.

In Schumpeter's story, innovation is followed by copying, but the innovator has a temporary lead over imitators and can gain a corresponding temporary profit before competition is restored and the gains from innovation spread among the generality of consumers. This provides the incentive for innovation. Whether this incentive is sufficient to ensure an optimal level of innovation – a matter of great concern to Rae – is a question that Schumpeter did not address directly. The returns to innovation do not constitute a "supply price" of entrepreneurship, he argued, since such a thing does not exist (Schumpeter [1911] 1961: 154). They may be much greater than is required to call forth the amount of entrepreneurship actually observed (which, of course, says nothing about whether the observed level of innovation is optimal), even though the possibility of success acts as a "stronger incentive than is rationally justified by its magnitude multiplied by the coefficient of probability" (ibid. 155). Entrepreneurial profit is the main source of upward social mobility in a capitalist society; the "rich" are the successful entrepreneurs and their heirs (ibid. 155–6). One might add that the ability to innovate successfully was, in Schumpeter's view, rare, but even in a business cycle downturn it takes only "one or a few" of these rare individuals to turn the tide and pave the way for more (ibid. 228). Given this perspective, a lack of incentives to innovate does not seem a matter of concern.

Rae's view was quite the opposite. He stressed the extra costs incurred by the first to do something new, especially (as noted above) the costs involved in starting local production of previously imported goods. These costs he saw as virtually prohibitive for the individual, even where the potential long-run gain to the community as a whole would amply justify the costs. This makes perfect sense in his framework. The gains from invention last for ever (though they are, presumably, eventually incorporated into later developments) and accrue to the whole community. More specifically, those who copy can appropriate the benefits without incurring the special costs faced by the innovator. One can readily translate this argument into the language of modern economics – innovation has the character of a public good and the free-rider problem inhibits individual provision or, to make the same point from a different point of view, there are positive externalities attached to innovation, so social benefits exceed private benefits. In some cases, he argued, the potential benefits may eventually rise so high that the return to the individual "projector" is enough to justify investment, but in this case the potential social benefits must have been positive much earlier, so even where private initiative does do the job, it does it too late (Rae 1834: 54).

What can be said about these conflicting views? It is clear that the total social benefit accruing from an innovation is only partly captured by the innovator. That much seems to be common ground – one might see the difference between Rae and Schumpeter as the difference between saying a glass is half full or half empty. Schumpeter's approach would be appropriate for the case in which an innovation depends on an almost costless, albeit rare, act of creative insight.[9] Provided the return is enough to induce the potential entrepreneur to act, and enough to enable him to raise the money to prove the idea in practice, that is enough. There is no need for the whole of the social gains (which might be very large) to accrue to the lucky individual who had the original idea. Rae's argument, on the other hand, would fit cases in which the outcome is reasonably predictable, but in which there are substantial initial costs. Modern, organized, research and development programs often fit this pattern, but were almost unknown in Rae's time. That is presumably why he concentrated on the case of import substitution, where observation of the foreign industry and of the local market for imports gives a fairly clear idea of the potential private and public gains. His argument also requires a particular structure to the costs of transmission of information – it must be costly to gain detailed knowledge of the processes used elsewhere and/or costly to adapt that knowledge to local conditions (making life hard for the trail-blazer), but cheap to transfer the knowledge from firm to firm within a particular area or country (making copying easy for those who follow). When Rae was writing, his implicit assumptions about the costs of information transfer made sense, since long-distance transport was slow and expensive while the relevant technical knowledge was often embodied in the craft skills of workers, who were reluctant to move far afield but easily tempted to change employers within a single locality.

Rae faced a problem. In order to support his main argument – against Adam Smith and in favour of government support for infant industries – he wanted to emphasize the difficulty of establishing something new, but he made the point so strongly that it seemed almost impossible for anything new to get started at all. He then had to explain how progress had in fact happened. The altruistic genius of the opening pages of the chapter on the causes of invention provided an answer of sorts, but offered no real basis for the desired policy conclusions. His solution was to point to special circumstances in which normal channels of trade were disrupted, for example by war, or in which political upheavals forced skilled workers and other specialists to emigrate, taking their skills with them. Disturbances of this sort are bad for accumulation, since insecurity discourages investment, but good for invention, since the normal bias towards imitation loses its force when the normal sequence of events is broken (Rae 1834: 222). When normal sources of supply fail, people have to make for themselves what they can no longer get from others and they have to find new materials to replace those that have become unavailable. Economic growth proceeds irregularly, with periods when accumulation is interrupted but invention stimulated, followed by peaceful interludes in which accumulation exploits the fruits of (previous) invention.

Government policy, on the other hand, can stimulate invention without the costs which disruption imposes. Rae hoped that the world might become a more peaceful place, so intervention would become the only means of stimulating invention. This is an ingenious solution to the problem, but it is still rather hard to square with some of Rae's examples, such as his account of the essentially smooth development of steam power (discussed above). One might, perhaps, argue that disruption of normal patterns of trade (or government assistance) is needed in the specific but (Rae thought) particularly important case of import substitution, because, in this case, the nascent local industry faces competition from established foreign competitors, while steam power was a real novelty, not just a transfer from elsewhere, and did not need special support.

It is worth noting that Rae's account of the immediate consequences of innovation differs from Schumpeter's. In Schumpeter's story the focus is on a single industry or market. The first with a cost-reducing innovation can sell at the old price to begin with, making a large profit, while an innovator who creates a new market can sell at a monopoly price. Once others copy, the price is bid down. This story goes back to Ricardo and was echoed by Marx, though Marx, in a Rae-like touch, commented on the extra costs facing the innovator, so that "the trail-blazers generally go bankrupt," leaving those who follow on, "the most worthless and miserable sort of money-capitalists," to reap the gains (Marx [1890] 1962: 103).

Rae, by contrast, was very vague about the course of prices and the nature of the gains accruing to the first-comers. He argued that an invention in one industry raises returns generally, though the basis for this claim is very unclear. It must presumably imply a price reduction in the industry concerned, else how would other industries benefit? Take his example of an innovation which cheapens the making of bread (Rae 1834: 259). He claimed that the bakers would have "a small additional profit," the whole society would have cheaper bread, and returns on investment would be raised throughout society. Here the innovator's profits have clearly been eliminated, as the benefits are "very shortly" diffused throughout society. He did not present any detailed discussion of pricing or profits in the intermediate stage in which the innovation has not been generally adopted, though it is hard to see how one can draw useful conclusions about the incentive to innovate without tackling these issues. More generally, Rae had rather little to say about the workings of markets, and was rather clumsy in what he did say. His main discussions of capital and returns are cast in terms of the physical returns, evaluated subjectively by the individual, with the market introduced only later in the argument. His analysis is the weaker for it.

## Conclusion

The structure of Rae's argument in the *New Principles* depends crucially on his claim:

1 that invention has causes distinct from (and prior to) the current level of saving;

2 that laissez-faire will generate a suboptimal level of invention; and
3 that state intervention can and should redress the balance.

His attempt to demonstrate these points is somewhat confused, because he did not make clear distinctions between different types of inventive activity, and because he described the motivation of the inventor and the rewards of invention in a variety of different ways. It is, of course, reasonable to think that there may be real differences between the relevant factors in different cases, but the fact that Rae did not distinguish clearly between the different cases he considered makes him appear simply inconsistent. Taking a very broad view of invention and focusing on scientific and artistic creativity led him to an overpessimistic view in which it is hard to see how invention can progress at all. Consideration of British development led to the opposite conclusion – invention seemed to proceed smoothly without outside help. Import substitution turns out to be the one case which fits (or can be made to fit) his argument perfectly. It requires and stimulates "invention," but whoever initiates production in a new locality faces exceptional costs, and cannot normally be expected to do so without some form of state support. The potential benefits are visible and readily comprehensible, so the Legislator can reasonably be expected to understand them and to act accordingly – given, of course, an acceptance of Rae's account of the determinants of economic growth in place of Smith's.

## Notes

1 Economics Department, University of Bristol, 5 Woodland Road, Bristol, UK BS8 1TN (A.Brewer@bris.ac.uk). I would like to thank Robert Straw, who made very helpful comments on an earlier draft and participants in the bicentennial conference in honour of John Rae at Aberdeen in March 1996. The errors, of course, are mine.
2 Whether Rae's interpretation of Smith is correct is a secondary issue in this context, since Rae, not Smith is under discussion. For a fuller discussion of Rae's critique of Smith, see Brewer (1991).
3 This can clearly be made true by definition: define wealth as value of assets, define saving as income minus expenditure, and define income so as to include all capital gains and windfalls.
4 Adam Ferguson ([1767] 1967) or even David Hume ([1752] 1955) might be cited as possible precursors of the view that growth is driven by technical change, but neither developed any substantial economic analysis to back up this insight (see Brewer (forthcoming)). Turgot ([1788] 1973) and others perhaps saw unlimited scope for human advance, but in terms of the advance of knowledge rather than in a specifically economic context.
5 Neither Smith nor Rae seems to have considered the possibility that the state could directly affect the aggregate rate of saving, say, by saving itself out of tax revenues, or by somehow compelling individuals to save.

6 Though I will argue later that Rae's discussion of import substitution implicitly assumes that setting up a new industry required far more than just importing the necessary machines.

7 Population and labour supply are treated as endogenous, as in Smith. The socially determined subsistence wage affects the return on investment and hence the equilibrium stock of instruments, but Rae said little about the determinants of wages.

8 The masculine ("man" of genius) is Rae's. I shall generally use the masculine to avoid artificiality.

9 Take the example (cited by neither author) of the wheelbarrow. This very useful device depended only on the prior invention of the wheel but was unknown in classical antiquity, despite the existence of large building projects where it would have been very valuable. Once the idea came to some anonymous person in the Middle Ages, the use of the wheelbarrow spread rapidly throughout Europe.

# 8

# RAE'S THEORY OF CAPITAL AND GROWTH

*Thomas K. Rymes*[1]

## Introduction

John Rae stressed technical progress as the primary source of capital accumulation and growth. Was technical progress to Rae a given, or was it to some extent endogenous, a product of the human activities of accumulation and thrift? In a capital theoretic context, that is the central question of this chapter.

Rae begins his critique of Smithian economics by arguing that, since capital or wealth results from fundamental human activities, one should not study them as Rae suggests Smith did, but rather those individual and collective activities which give rise to capital and wealth. He argues that Smith:

> in great measure misses that which is the real object at which his inquiry aims, the investigation of the true nature and causes of national wealth, . . . [and] falls into the error of taking, what in truth are the results of general laws governing the course of this class of events for the laws themselves, and of so elevating effects into causes.
>
> (Rae 1834: 4)

On what would be called now a more normative note, Rae also says that his main object is:

> to show that that notion of the exact identity of the causes giving rise to individual and national wealth, on which the reasonings and arguments of Adam Smith all along depend, is erroneous, that consequently the doctrines he has engrafted on it, cannot thus be maintained, and are inconsistent with the facts admitted by himself.
>
> (ibid. 8)

One basic point common to optimum neoclassical and neo-Keynesian growth models is that capital is *endogenous* to the growth process. In a simple neoclassical optimum one-commodity growth model, where labour force growth is ignored, one has, as first-order conditions, the two equations of motion:

$$-\mu \frac{\dot{c}}{c} = q_k(k) - \delta - (n' + \rho)$$

which may be called the Ramsey–Keynes condition (Blanchard and Fischer 1989) or perhaps the Champernowne formula (Hicks 1965: 258), and:

$$\dot{k} = q\ (k) - (\delta + n')k - c$$

where the standard notation has $\mu$ as the elasticity of the marginal utility of consumption with respect to consumption, where $c$ and $k$ are consumption and capital, all expressed in Harrod, rather than Solow, units, where $q_k(k)$ and $q(k)$ are the standard technology statements, where $\delta$ is the carrying costs of capital, $\rho$ is the rate of time preference and $n'$ is the Harrodian rate of technical progress (sometimes erroneously referred to as only labour augmenting).

In steady state, when $\dot{c}/c = 0$, the real rate of return, $R$, defined as $q_k(k) - \delta$, equals the rate of growth of technology plus the rate of time preference.[2]

Once the behaviour of the capital intensity, $k$, in particular the idea of generalized diminishing returns to capital is questioned, one can shift over to endogenous neoclassical or neo-Keynesian growth theory. In the exogenous growth theory, $n'$ is given and $\rho$ determines $R$. In the endogenous growth theory, $R$ is given and $\rho$ determines $n'$. The central neoclassical case in the endogenous growth literature is the so-called $AK$ or von Neumann models.

One writes:

$$Q = AK,\ Y = AK - \delta K = (A - \delta)K$$

so that:

$$R = Y/K = A - \delta$$

Considering then

$$-\mu \frac{\dot{c}}{c} = R - \rho = A - \delta - \rho,$$

it follows that, given $R$, the greater is the rate of saving, that is, the lower is $\rho$ (the rate of time preference), the higher is $\dot{c}/c$. Since the growth rate of the labour force is zero, then $\dot{c}/c = A - \delta - \rho = n'$, with $\mu = -1$, that is, the greater the rate of saving, the greater the rate of technical progress. Some of this new classical literature has imperfectly competitive firms generating higher $R$'s, so that firms with market power experience higher $R$'s and such rents encourage and permit higher rates of technical progress (Barro and Sala-I-Martin 1995: chs 6 and 7; Aghion and Howitt 1994).

In simple neo-Keynesian growth models

$$s\,rk = s(q_k(k) - \delta)k = n'k$$

where $s$ is the propensity to save out of returns to capital (all wages are consumed).

Then:

$$Sr = s(q_k(K) - \delta) = n'$$

$$r = (q_k(k) - \delta) = n'/s'$$

such that $\rho = 0$ entails that $s = 1$ and $R = n'$.

A more general neo-Keynesian growth model would have:

$$n' = n'(R^*)$$

where the rate of technical advance through accumulation would be positively related to the expected rate of return, and:

$$R^* = R^*(R)$$

with expected rates of return being positively but diminishingly related to actual levels of rates of return. Thus:

$$R = n'/s$$

and:

$$n' = n'(R^*(R))$$

such that the higher the rate of saving (the lower the rate of time preference), the *lower* would be the rate of return and the rate of growth (Robinson 1962; Rymes 1989).

These simple models illustrate that growth rather than being the mere expansion of the wealth of nations depends fundamentally on technical progress and that rates of return to capital depend more on rates of technical progress and saving than on any static conditions of overall capital intensity.

Rae holds *some* insights. Since, for him, capital intensities did not determine growth rates or rates of return to capital, he became involved in an argument that an overall measure of the time structure of capitalistic production is a determinant of the real rate of return, rather than the other way around. More importantly, however, by focusing upon what one would now call endogenous rates of technical progress and rates of saving – what Rae calls the inventive faculty and effective accumulation – he was carrying on the classical program of developing a theory of the rate of capital accumulation and the rate of return to capital, and the mutual interaction between these two fundamental determinants of economic growth.

We know, from the Cambridge Capital Controversy, that static comparison of techniques of production will not permit us to infer anything about the relationship between overall capital intensities and rates of return. Rather, we should be examining the two-way relationship between rates of technical change, rates of accumulation, and rates of return to capital.

I argue that, aside from an Austrian sideslip, Rae essentially was concerned with the individual and collective activities which codetermined rates of technical advance and rates of return to capital (and rates of growth and capital accumulation) in the neoclassical way. He certainly had nothing to say about the Keynesian problem.[3]

## Rae's statics

Part of Rae's analysis was based upon applications of Austrian point input–point output analyses. It is argued that we can array aggregate capital inputs in terms of their average periods of production. In Rae's language, a given application of labor today in the construction of a capital good would result in a certain product, in labor equivalents, a number of periods hence. All other capital goods, requiring the same labor input, associated with lower products in labor equivalent units in the same periods are hence not viable. Rae argued that the further into the future the labour equivalent products would be, the lower relatively speaking would such equivalent products be. Given some rate of time preference, Rae argues, with marginal capital inputs – or instruments, to use Rae's phrase – just meeting the test of time preference, the given rate will be either greatly more than covered by capital goods with immediate product (accumulation in them eliminating profits), or simply more than covered by capital goods with less immediate products (again accumulation in them eliminating their profits).

If Rae's analysis were general, then the lower the rate of time preference, the greater would be the average time period of production for all capital inputs. Techniques of production would be more round about or more capital intensive. In terms of the neoclassical exogenous growth model, from $q_k(k) - \delta = R = n' + \rho$, the lower is $\rho$, the lower is $R$, the greater is $k$ and the lower is $q_k(k)$. In this sense, Rae is strongly neoclassical. The capital intensity of production would grow until the diminishing marginal physical product of capital would be equal to the rate of time preference. Thus, in Rae, given $n'$, $R$ is determined by the rate of time preference and the overall capital intensity of the economy adjusts until $R$ is equal to $n' + \rho$. If the aggregate *stock* of capital were conceived of, not as an index of the *flow of the services of the stock of capital goods*, but rather as *the flow of the services of waiting*, then the lower the rate of time preference, the greater the aggregate capital intensity of production, or the greater the aggregate flow of the services of waiting.

Small wonder then that Böhm-Bawerk ([1884] 1959), Fisher ([1930], 1970), and Schumpeter (1954: especially 468–9) praised Rae.

Once the time structure of production has greater complexity, the Cambridge Capital Controversy showed that, in general, no such relationships between aggregate stocks of capital or waiting, rates of time preference, and real rates of return to capital need exist.

That capitalistic production involves time and that such production involves waiting, points which Rae makes, remain incontestable. Though Rae certainly set out the conditions for which he can be interpreted as suggesting they would permit such well-behaved aggregate capital constructs, his analysis exists without such aggregates being maintained. Niehans (1990: 85) is perhaps overly generous when he states that Rae "seems to have realized . . . that the concept of an aggregate capital stock is redundant."

## Rae's dynamics

Rae emphasized technical progress as being the primary source of growth. Anthony Brewer (1990: 291) says that Rae was the *first* "to place technical change, not capital accumulation, at the centre of a theory of growth and development, and to work out its implications rigorously," and that "Rae's conception of growth as wholly driven by 'invention' was genuinely original" (Brewer 1991: 11).

Wealth, or the stock of capital or instruments, in any society was owing, thought Rae, to:

1. The quantity and quality of the materials owned by it.
2. The strength of the *effective desire of accumulation*.
3. The rate of wages.
4. The progress of the inventive faculty.

(Rae 1834: 109)

By quantity and quality of materials, Rae meant the given powers of the soil. Rae maintains a constant real wage rate in his analysis (ibid. 97–8). He does say, however, that, though he had assumed "the wages of labour constitute an invariable quantity," yet in a society subject to augmentation of stock through invention and accumulation of stock through the effective desire of accumulation, real wages "should rather be continually increasing, the labourer as well as the capitalist, gaining something by the improvements which the progress of invention produces" (ibid. 327).

I assume Rae would have been prepared to argue that materials and labor, that is, nonproduced means of production, could be taken as given, not fixed, but given independently of the variables with which he was concerned. His whole focus is on the growth of produced means of production, since the world he saw around him (even in Canada!) was one in which the key fact requiring explanation was ongoing and nondiminishing capital accumulation.

Without the progress of the inventive faculty, Rae expressed no doubt that capital accumulation would be carried out to the point where, in modern language, the net rate of return would equal the rate of time preference, with the strength of the effective desire of accumulation determining the rate of time preference. It is true that for Rae the stronger the effective desire of accumulation the more roundabout, the more capital intensive, capitalistic production would be. Without progress of the inventive faculty, however, the rate of capital accumulation would assuredly diminish. With progress – technical progress, we would say – for Rae the process of capital accumulation could go on forever. Knowledge, it would seem, to Rae, exhibits nondecreasing returns. It is not just in terms of technological advance: advances in knowledge exhibit no diminishing returns, so that the diminishing returns to capital, which might be exhibited in a world without advances in knowledge, would not be experienced. The more we learn, the more learning is possible. Inventive faculty begets more inventive faculty. Learning by doing would seem, in Rae's argument, to suggest that capital accumulation could take place for sometime without any diminishing returns being experienced. Extensions of art beget extensions of art, and assuming that art does not remain stationary, generalized diminishing returns to capital may be permanently set to rest. Rates of return to capital would be a function of the rate of advance of inventive faculty.

On inventive faculty, Rae writes:

> [I]t is not so easy to conceive how, or for what purpose, a general increase of these means or instruments [a general increase in capital] should take place without some accompanying discovery of an improvement in their construction by which they may put additional stores within the reach of the nation.
>
> (Rae 1834: 19)

Rae is setting out here in his most general introductory statement the idea of "learning by investment." It is that one really cannot separate capital accumulation and technical progress. One cannot conceive of capital accumulation going on either across a set of techniques given and orderable in terms of their capital intensities (the static argument), or across a set of techniques steadily improving (the dynamic state), independently of the capital accumulation going on. That is, in the standard neoclassical growth model, where $n'$ is zero, one can think of the economy moving through a sequence of temporary equilibrium with ever-increasing capital intensities until the rate of return equals the rate of time preference and the economy stops growing. In that same growth model where $n'$ is given, greater than zero, but *independent of the rate of capital accumulation*, the same analysis applies. The sequence of temporary equilibria involves ever-increasing capital intensity until the rate of return equals the rate of time preference and the given rate of technical progress. Certainly, as Brewer so cogently argues, for Rae technical progress is the source of steady growth.[4] Yet I believe Rae is also arguing that the greater the rate of accumulation the greater the rate of technical progress. In an accompanying argument, Rae (1834: 19 ff.) discusses flails as instruments in agriculture in which accumulation takes place. At one point, the threshing machine was "invented" (ibid. 20). Now one can say that the concept "invention" is consistent with the view that, in Rae, technical progress– that is, invention – was exogenous. Rae argues throughout his work, however, that the pace of invention is not a given, but is a function of the resources devoted to such activity, that is, the rate of technical progress is not independent of the rate of capital accumulation.

Rae writes:

> It is invention, which showing how profitable returns may be got from the one [capital], and how subsistence procured from the other [population], that may most fitly be esteemed the cause of the existence of both; and hence this power has most title to be ranked as the true generator of states and people. It is certainly, therefore, very far from being a self-evident truth, that the legislator, *by employing the resources of the country in rousing this principle to activity*, necessarily retards, instead of advancing, the increase of wealth and the prosperity of the state. [emphasis added]
>
> (Rae 1834: 31)

Thus, the rate of technical progress is not a given, but is a function of the rate of accumulation devoted to the development of new and different instruments, or capital.

At a technical measurement level, flails are replaced by threshing machines, as the economy advances. Not only do new techniques appear which are more flail intensive, but which are also characterized by threshing machines. In a technically progressive economy it seems difficult if not impossible to distinguish movements along production functions from shifts in them (Hicks, 1973: 120 n. 3).

Later on in his work Rae argues:

> *The capacity which any people can communicate to the materials they possess, by forming them into instruments, cannot be indefinitely increased, while their knowledge of their powers and qualities remains stationary, without moving the instruments formed continually onwards in the series ABC & c* [Rae's description of the static Austrian ordering of the capital goods]*: but, there is no assignable limit to the extent of the capacity, which a people having attained considerable knowledge of the qualities and powers of the materials they possess, can communicate to them, without carrying them out of the series ABC & c., even if that knowledge remains stationary.*
>
> (Rae 1834: 109)

One can derive, I think, from Rae, $R = R(n')$ such that the higher the $n'$ the higher the $R$ and the greater will be the rate of capital accumulation. One can also write that $n' = n'(R)$ such that the higher the rate of return, the higher will be the rate of accumulation and the higher the rate of technical progress.

Now technical progress entails novelty, the adaptation of old and new techniques of production to new knowledge and learning, and a deeper understanding of existing knowledge. One cannot have a theory of true novelty. Some part of the rate of technical progress has to be taken as just given. Nevertheless, some part is endogenous, in the sense that it is positively related to capital accumulation (e.g., embodied technical progress), which is a function of rates of return to capital. One could say therefore that $n' = n'a + n'b$, where $n'a$ is pure novelty for which one has no theory. Yet, if $n'b = n'b(R)$, one can, in general, write $n' = n'(R)$.

What of the complement to invention, the effective desire of accumulation? In a given state of knowledge, the greater the effective desire of accumulation, the lower would be the rate of time preference and the greater the rate of saving. As I have indicated, Rae worked out the static consequences of this in a given state of technology. Capital intensity would be greater, and generalized diminishing returns would entail $R$ determined by $\rho$. To this can now be added that the effective desire of accumulation would drive $R$ down to $\rho + n'$.

Rae defines the effective desire of accumulation as, "the determination to sacrifice a certain amount of present good, to obtain another greater amount at some future period" (1834: 119), or precisely $\rho$, the rate of time preference. Thus the greater the effective desire of accumulation, the lower would be $\rho$ and the more people would save from the net output of the economy.

From the neoclassical endogenous growth theory, we know that in a world in which diminishing returns to capital have been set aside, a higher rate of saving, a lower rate of time preference, would be associated with a higher rate of growth. If Rae is interpreted as working within a model in which his dynamics suggest generalized diminishing returns to capital can be set aside, the AK models of endogenous growth say

$$-\mu(\frac{\dot{c}}{c} + n') = R - \rho$$

such that a greater effective desire of accumulation, a lower $\rho$, given $R$, will be associated with a greater rate of technical progress, $n'$, and accumulation of capital, providing $\mu$ is unaffected by changes in $\rho$. In short, the lower the "takeout," the higher the rate of growth.

Thus there is in Rae the argument that $n' = n'(R)$. From the static argument, one would think that a lower rate of time preference would lead, via increased capital intensity to lower rates of return and therefore lower rates of growth. Rae was, I think, arguing that an increased desire to accumulate would not necessarily be associated with a lower $R$ from greater capital intensity. This result would hold in a given state of knowledge, but because greater thriftiness would lead to greater accumulation of capital, it would be associated with greater inventive faculty, with a greater rate of technical progress.

In the neo-Keynesian models, a higher rate of saving associated with a lower rate of time preference, leads, given $n'$, to a lower $R$ and hence, through $n' = n'(R)$, to a lower $n'$. Such a result exhibits the problem of Keynes thrown into the long run. Since Rae did *not* deal with the problem of Keynes, there is no way Rae can be interpreted as an early Keynesian growth theorist.

For Rae, then, we have from inventive activity:

$$R = R(n')$$

and from effective accumulation:

$$n' = n'(R;\rho)$$

and, in steady state:

$$R = n' + \rho$$

This is shown in diagrammatic terms in Figure 8.1.

Consider the benchmark case where $R = n'$, where the rate of growth equals the rate of return to capital. That case is that for which $\rho = 0$, where the effective desire of accumulation is at its maximum (excluding

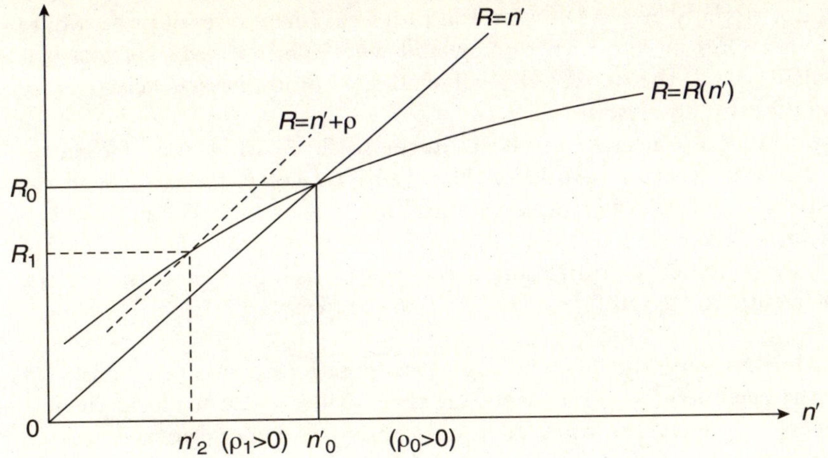


*Figure 8.1* Rae's growth model

the possibility of a negative price of waiting). Consider a second case where $\rho > 0$. Then $n'$ is less than before, and rather than $R$ being unchanged or affected somehow by changing capital intensities, $R$ is lower because it is a function of $n'$, and the lower is $n'$, the lower is $R$.

Thus, there can be wrinkled out of Rae the two arguments:

$$R = R(n')$$

and

$$n' = n'(R;\rho)$$

together with the steady state condition $R = n' + \rho$. If correct, then one can solve Rae's system of thought for $n'$ and $R$. In Rae, there is the beginnings of a general theory of the determination of the rate of technical progress and the rate of return to capital.

## Conclusion

Rae sought to work out a theory of a capital accumulating economy in which the rate of technical progress and the rate of return to capital would be mutually determined.

I am no doubt being too generous. I have dealt only with simple cases and not those where there would be many rates of technical progress and many rates of return to capital. Indeed, outside the steady state, we would be talking about economies where the many growth rates of accumulation would not trivially be rates of technical progress, where rates of profit would replace net rates of return to capital, and where the carrying costs associated with capital, the $\delta s$, would involve all the ambiguities associated with depreciation by obsolescence.

Certainly, Rae conceived of capital in the static Austrian way. He recognized, however, that in a world of the inventive faculty, the concept of the generalized diminishing returns to capital need not apply. When linked to his effective desire of accumulation, the rate of time preference, we obtain the theory of the codetermination of the rate of technical progress and the rate of return to capital I have set out. Rae states:

> It thus appears, that it is through the operation of two principles, – the accumulative, and inventive, that additions are made to the stocks of the communities. It would contribute something to accuracy of phraseology, and therefore to distinctness of conception, to distinguish their modes of action by the following terms:
>
> 1. *Accumulation* of stock or capital, is the addition made to these, through the operation of the accumulative principle.
> 2. *Augmentation* of stock or capital, is the addition made to them, through the operation of the principle of invention.
> 3. Increase of stock or capital, is the addition made to them, by the conjoined operation of both principles.
>
> Accumulation of stock diminishes profits; augmentation of stock increases profits; increase of stock neither increases nor diminishes profits.
>
> (Rae 1834: 264)

I add two final comments on Smith. Rae explicitly denies that the division of labor, though certainly a function of the extent of the market, is a source of growth. He allows as to how it is the effect of the two forces of invention and waiting, but not a cause. He cannot thus be considered a supporter of the view that endogenous growth is associated with increasing returns to scale stemming from the division of labor (see Rae's (1834: 352–7) appendix to Book II: "Of the Principle of the Division of Labour").

What does Rae say of the role of the state? There are arguments in Rae about infant industries and the like. The most powerful role for the state emerges when he discusses the fundamentals lying behind the effective desire of accumulation. Rae states:

> The desire to accumulate would then seem to derive strength, chiefly from three circumstances.

1. The prevalence throughout the society, of the social and benevolent affections, or, of that principle, which, under whatever name it may be known, leads us to derive happiness, from the good we communicate to others.
2. The extent of the intellectual powers, and the consequent prevalence of habits of reflection, and prudence, in the minds of the members of the society.
3. The stability of the condition of the affairs of the society, and the reign of law and order throughout it.

It is weakened, and strength given to the desire of immediate enjoyment, by three opposing circumstances.

1. The deficiency of strength in the social and benevolent affections, and the prevalence of the opposite principle, a desire for mere selfish gratification.
2. A deficiency in the intellectual powers, and the consequent want of habits of reflection and forethought.
3. The instability of the affairs of the society, and the imperfect diffusion of law and order throughout it.

(Rae 1834: 124)

The effective desire of accumulation, the rate of time preference, is both an individual and social phenomenon.[5] [6] Collectively much can be done, then, in Rae's view to cause the rate of technical progress and rate of return to capital and the rate of capital accumulation to be higher than they would be in a solely individualistically determined equilibrium. Rates of time preference and rates of technical advance are partly social phenomena.

## Notes

1 Department of Economics, Carleton University, 1125 Colonel By Drive, OTTAWA, Ontario K1S 5B6, 1–613–520–2600–3771, Fax 1–613–520–3906. Visiting Professor, Department of Economics, University of Adelaide, ADELAIDE, SA 5001, Australia.

2 From the two equations of motion:

$$-\mu \frac{\dot{c}}{c} = q_k(k) - \delta - (n' + \rho)$$
$$\dot{k} = q(k) - (\delta + n')k - c$$

for steady states, one has:

$$q_k(k) - \delta = R = n' + \rho$$
$$q(k) - (\delta + n')k = c$$

and for maximum consumption steady states:

$$q_k(\delta + n') = 0 \textit{ entails } R = n', \text{ or } \rho = 0$$

Sometimes where utility is a function of consumption in natural rather than Harrod units, these equations of motion appear (Barro and Sala-I-Martin 1995: 70–1) as:

$$-\mu \frac{\dot{c}}{c} = q_k(k) - \delta - (\rho - \mu n')$$

$$\dot{k} = q(k) - (\delta + n')k - c$$

and for steady states:

$$q_k(k) - \delta = r = \rho - \mu n'$$

and

$$q(k) - (\delta + n')k = c$$

For maximum consumption steady states:

$$q_k(k) - (\delta + n') = 0 \textit{ entails } R = n'$$

but in this case:

$$\rho = 0$$

will entail a steady state where:

$$R = n'$$

if

$$\mu = -1$$

3 One needs to integrate into the analysis Rae's work on monetary theory, in particular his work on banking. Rae's banking theory is, I believe, an integral part of his contribution to the idea of endogenous growth theory. Mair (1990: 285) argues that for Rae "the proper use of banking was essential to the growth of real income and capital stock and the augmentation of a country's wealth." See also Neill, "The Economics of John Rae, 1822–34" (1991: ch. 4).

4 In the neoclassical growth literature, a confusion exists. In steady state models, growth in output per unit of labor input, it is said, can be decomposed into capital accumulation per unit of labor and Hicksian or Solovian technical progress. This is wrong. All the steady growth is due to Harrodian technical progress, which is why growth magnitudes must be expressed in Harrodian terms (Steedman 1985; Cas and Rymes 1991).

5 See Rae (1834: 203) for an argument that whatever is saved must be invested.

6 The argument informed Mill (Hollander 1987: 231).

# 9

# PRODUCTIVE SAVINGS, INVENTION, AND INVESTMENT SUPPLY IN RAE'S GROWTH THEORY

*Michael J. Gootzeit*[1]

## Introduction

John Rae's *New Principles* (1834) contained much analysis of the savings motive in its relation to capital accumulation. In fact, Rae looked at savings on two levels: the personal and the social[2] or national. The first part of this book criticized *The Wealth of Nations* and its rationalization of free trade for putting too much emphasis on the importance of the individual in both the choice of work and consumption/savings decisions. Rae wanted to emphasize instead that the "social entity" or nation's goals were sometimes quite different from the individual's. Furthermore, the former has what really mattered for capital accumulation and growth. If a correct social prescription for national growth were followed, individuals would also be much better off in the future, rather than if personal initiative was given the highest priority. These ideas led Rae off the beaten early-nineteenth-century track so much that his ideas were neglected until the early 1900s, when they were revived by Mixter (1897, 1902) and Böhm-Bawerk ([1884] 1921: ch. 11). Yet, especially the latter neglected Rae's main focus on what economic policies a nation should follow to become and remain strong, and focused instead on the discussion of Rae's theory of capital and how it differed from his own. In this chapter I will attempt to rationalize Rae's emphasis on the "social" sector, the "community" or "nation," and show how it related to his ideas on business and personal savings.

Rae's ideas on savings gave an important role to the business sector. For only the business sector, rather than the personal sector, could supply what might be called "productive" savings – savings that would increase the nation's capital stock, and ultimately, national wealth. Rae was certainly not part of the Smith–Mill–Marshall–Keynes tradition which focused on personal savings as productive, and held that mainly through it increasing could the nation's capital stock increase – the primary requirement of economic growth. Instead, Rae's ideas on savings were much more in the Senior–Cairns tradition, largely neglected in modern economics since the late 1800s, which concentrated much more on business savings as the chief force behind national expansion (see Gootzeit 1995).[3] This tradition treated "abstinence" as the motive which caused savings, but it did not always make it clear that the source of these funds would be the business sector. Rae made it much clearer than the other two writers, but without formally using the concept of abstinence,[4] that businesses had a hidden (or invisible) social responsibility, in that they, rather than individual savers/consumers, were looking out for the truly national interest. Paradoxically, this argument seemed to have some commonality with Smith's idea of the "invisible hand," except for the fact that Rae gave businesses the role that Smith gave to individuals for promoting the social or collective goal of national growth.

## Rae's concept of productive savings

Rae never used the term "productive savings," but his ideas implied that business was more productive than personal savings. This idea was related to Rae's approach to the relationship between "individual and national interests," the general topic of Book One of his *New Principles*.[5] Mixter referred to this topic as the difference between "public and private capital" (Mixter 1897: 170), although Rae did not formally use these terms in the first chapter of Book I (1834: 12–15), to which they were referenced by Mixter. Rae was trying to make the anti-Smithian point that because personal and national interests were generally not the same, the formation of private and public capital by savings would be subject to different incentives. Since Rae believed growth depended on the size of the nation's or the community's capital stock, he attempted throughout his book to give examples of the proper type of savings which should occur in order to increase it. This is what may be called "productive savings."

Rae downplayed the role of personal savings. He referred to how an individual attempted to "gain wealth" by "acquiring a portion of the wealth already in existence" (Rae 1834: 15). So personal savings, even if it did lead to an increase in a person's wealth stock, would mean that the accumulator used his savings to outbid another personal saver, who would not be satisfied. The way for a nation to increase its wealth stock was for "creation" to take place and this could only be done on the "national" level (Mixter 1897: 171). In order to explain how an increase in the "community's wealth could take place" (Rae 1834: 15), Rae described the important role of the business sector in supplying national savings. He regarded this type of savings as the only form which could lead to a nationally expanding capital stock; it was the only true form of productive savings.

Rae's prescription for growth emphasized the social organism: the "nation" or the "community." The growth of productive capacity described invention as a necessary condition for an increase in the nation's capital stock: "the increase of *national* capital [n]ever does, in fact, proceed, unless in conjunction with some successful effort of the inventive faculty, some improvements of some of the employments formerly practiced in the community" (1834: 22, emphasis added). But, invention would only work through the business, not the personal sector, by causing businesses to construct new "instruments":

> The capital of a state is a mere instrument in the hands of its industry [business sector], to enable it to draw forth the riches, with which the conjoined powers of nature and art have endowed it. A multiplication of instruments is of no avail, unless something additional be given on which they may operate. When invention succeeds in discovering these additional riches, the mere view is sufficient, in every well regulated community, to induce its [business] members to form the new instruments, necessary to draw these riches forth.
>
> (Rae 1834: 29)

The term "industry" referred to the business sector of the community. Rae was telling us that new capital instruments could only be formed from the increased profit of business or direct business savings which would flow from invention or improvements in the mode of production.

For Rae, personal savings led to the formation of personal instruments, which appeared to have the character of durable consumption goods, while business savings led directly to the formation of business instruments, which Rae called "capital":

> Even the poorest beggar has some clothes to cover him; the opulent have houses, furniture, . . . etc. This part of the whole instruments possessed by individuals or communities is termed a *stock reserved for immediate consumption*. The remainder of the general stock of instruments of individuals and societies, with the exception of land . . . is termed *capital*.
>
> (Rae 1834: 171)

Instruments were also formed instantaneously from savings, without a significant time lag.[6] The interesting phenomenon, however, was that unproductive (personal savings) was kept segregated from productive (business savings) in Rae's treatment of the formation of instruments. Only business saving could form capital which was the source of growth. Unlike later mainstream writers in the nineteenth and twentieth centuries, Rae minimized the role of personal savings in capital formation.

## The role of invention in interest rate formation and investment

Rae did not refer exclusively to the "business" sector in his analysis of the source of investible funds and its relation to capital formation. In fact, Rae sometimes discussed capital as if it were only meant for the use of "individuals and societies" and he also stated that capital goods were "instruments" which would "supply the future wants of *individuals* owning them" (1834: 171, emphasis added). Yet, the most consistent source of investible funds for Rae, both in the short and longer periods, was higher business profits generated from "the progress of invention" in society.[7] It was also Rae's focus on invention that led to his perception of the lending and borrowing of "instruments"[8] as the crucial element of capital accumulation.

Invention played a very important role in Rae's analysis of economic growth, especially since "Rae was an amateur inventor of considerable talent" (James 1951: 151).[9] Rae's ideas on the importance of invention are scattered throughout his *New Principles* and they are commented on in various ways by his chief interpreters.[10] But, although hinted at, Rae's use of his ideas on invention to give business savings an important role in capital formation, has not been much emphasized by the literature. In fact, Rae clearly separated invention from what he called "parsimony," which is personal savings.[11] Rae made it clear that invention was responsible for the "augmentation," as opposed to the "accumulation" of stock (Rae 1834: 263–4). But, Rae never made it clear that the only way in which improved quality capital goods may find their way into the economy was through the mechanism of business savings from current profits.

If Rae's concept of "augmentation of capital" is carefully examined, one may see that business, not personal savings, was responsible for capital formation:

> [Rae] saw clearly that individuals might increase their wealth by saving but that *the formation of capital by societies* was influenced decisively by technical progress. He disputed vigorously Adam Smith's view that a country's wealth was determined by the willingness of its inhabitants to save. On these grounds, Rae saw a legitimate role for governments in stimulating invention encouraging capital formation. [emphasis added]
>
> (James 1951: 148)

This quotation shows clearly the low esteem in which Rae held personal savings when it came to determining the rate of growth for the economy.

The Keynesian tradition, beginning with J.S. Mill and Marshall, held that personal savings was the most important cause of increases to the nation's capital stock, which modern economists call "current investment":

> Our definition of income also leads at once to the definition of *current investment* . . . the current addition to the value of the capital equipment which has resulted from the productive activity of the period. This is, clearly, equal to what we have just defined as [personal] saving.
>
> (Keynes 1936: 62; see also Gootzeit 1995)

Keynes, chiefly concerned with his definition of aggregate demand, defined aggregate personal savings as income minus aggregate personal consumption (1936: 63). There was little discussion of the role of business savings and its importance in capital accumulation to be found in most late-nineteenth and early-twentieth-century writings on macroeconomics.[12]

Rae's emphasis on "improvement" in the nation's capital stock as the principal driving force behind capital accumulation centered on the business sector. This was because Rae regarded the general profit rate of society as the main cause of economic growth: "The high rate of profit, which follows the introduction of improvement, is indicative of an immediate proportional augmentation of the absolute capital of the society" (Rae 1834: 263). This new stock would come about because "every improvement animates industry, and . . . [it] shows that the members of the society really estimate them higher than [if] they . . . work up . . . similar materials more laboriously" (1834: 262).

Rae's aggregate production function may be stated as follows:

$$Q = Q\ (L,\ C,\ R)$$

where $L$ = labor, $C$ = the total quantity of capital, and $R$ = raw materials and land.[13] The production function for the "augmentation" of the fixed capital stock is as follows:

$$\Delta\ CF = C\ (P_{RE})$$

where $P_{RE}$ = the expected general (or average) profit rate in the production of society's capital instruments, and

$$P_{RE} = P\ (T)$$

where $T$ is a measure of society's technical progress or new invention.

$P_{RE}$ may also be expressed in terms of the market interest rate ($i$) or business borrowing/lending rate, as:

$$P_{RE} = i + Wc$$

where $Wc$ = the wage of the capitalist = "the return that has to be made for the mental exertion and anxiety, and bodily fatigue, of the owner of the stock" (Rae 1834: 195).[14]

Since $Wc$ *has to be made*, it may be regarded as a necessary cost, assumed to be constant in the short, although it may vary in the long period.[15] If $P_{RE} - Wc = i$, the borrowing/lending process with $T$ increasing (constant technical progress), will be shown to expand smoothly leading to an increase in the capital stock. But, Rae also implied a process whereby even constant technical progress may not insure an increase in the capital stock.

Rae did not describe in detail the lending process, but he did clearly see that there was a difference to be noted between business savings (new *instruments retained*) and businesses direct lending to other businesses (new *instruments given on credit*), for although all "loans [and direct business investment] pass under the name of money, but money is only the means of effecting the loan, it is in reality instruments that are lent" (Rae 1834: 197). Apparently, the lending and borrowing process of business when profit expectations were rising would lead directly to new capital formation, without the intervention of the banking system or any other intermediary. There would be no lag between business savings and investment and, furthermore, all savings leading to economic growth was generated by the business sector.

It appeared from the definition of $P_{RE}$ that any increase in the interest rate would be exactly reflected in $P_{RE}$ and vice versa. Rae even stated that: "We may then assume the rate of interest as a fair measure of the real average rate of profits, in any country" (1834: 196). He recognized, however, that if the prevailing or prospective "yield" on instruments was too low, they might *not be borrowed*: "[instruments] must in return yield not much less than what is paid for their use, otherwise they might not be borrowed, and not much more, otherwise they would not be lent" (1834: 197). This statement meant that even though increases in $i$ would mainly reflect increases in $P_{RE}$, $i$ may increase an even greater absolute amount than increases in $P_{RE}$. If this happened, the "net" yield on the proposed investment ($P_{RE} - Wc$) may become $< i$, where $i$ is what would be "paid" for the use of the borrowed funds, so the net yield (the yield after the wage of the capitalist is paid) may eventually become too low in relation to the borrowing cost and this would choke off borrowing for the construction of new investment goods.

In order to describe this process, let $i = k\,(P_{RE} - Wc)$, with $k \geqslant 1$, and let $Is = I\,(i)$, be a positively sloped function where $Is$ = actual (not desired) investment supplied, flowing from firms which finance investment in instruments by borrowing investible funds from other firms within the business sector.[16] When $Wc$ is constant, if $(P_{RE} - i)$ decreases, the slope of $Is$ would gradually fall toward zero. This type of relation illustrates that Rae considered the profit and interest rates as separate, but related, entities when analyzing whether invention might lead to economic expansion. Although the profit rate helped to determine the market interest rate, $i$ could very well increase a greater absolute amount than the increase in $P_{RE}$.

Figure 9.1 illustrates a linear version of Rae's investment supply model. Its components were derived from *New Principles*, chapter 3, on capital accumulation[17] and chapter 10, on invention.[17] We have three equations and three unknowns ($P_{RE}$, $i$, $Is$):

$$P_{RE} = G\ (T) \tag{9.1}$$

where $G$ is a constant and $(0 < G < 1)$. $G$ = the average profitability of technical improvement.

$$i = k\ (P_{RE}) - Wc \tag{9.2}$$

where $k$ is a positive parameter and $Wc$ is a short-run constant.

$$Is = v\ (i) \tag{9.3}$$

where $v$ is a positive constant. Substituting (9.1) into (9.2), we get:

$$i = (GT)k - Wc \tag{9.4}$$

Subtracting (9.4) from (9.1), we get:

$$(P_{RE} - i) = GT(1 - k) + Wc \tag{9.5}$$

Equation (9.2) represents quadrant II of Figure 1. If $k = 1$, the 45 line represents equation (9.2); if $k > 1$, the line becomes flatter as $k$ increases. If $k = 1$, equation (9.5) simplifies to:

$$(P_{RE} - i) = Wc \tag{9.5a}$$

where $Wc$ is a constant, so the differential between $P_{RE}$ and i remains constant when $T$ increases.

The expected profit rate is a perfect predictor for the interest rate and the borrowing/lending process proceeds smoothly. Call $I_{1s}$ the "steady state" investment supply function; it has a constant first and a zero second derivative (a straight line). This is the straightforward theory of short-run investment supply advocated by Rae.

If $k > 1$, $(1 - k) < 0$, and when $T$ increases in equation (9.5), $(P_{RE} - i)$ falls toward zero as $i$ increases faster than $P_{RE}$. The interest rate is determined to some degree by forces other than $P_{RE}$; the greater is $k$, the smaller is the direct relation between $P_{RE}$ and $i$. As $k$ increases, the borrowing/lending

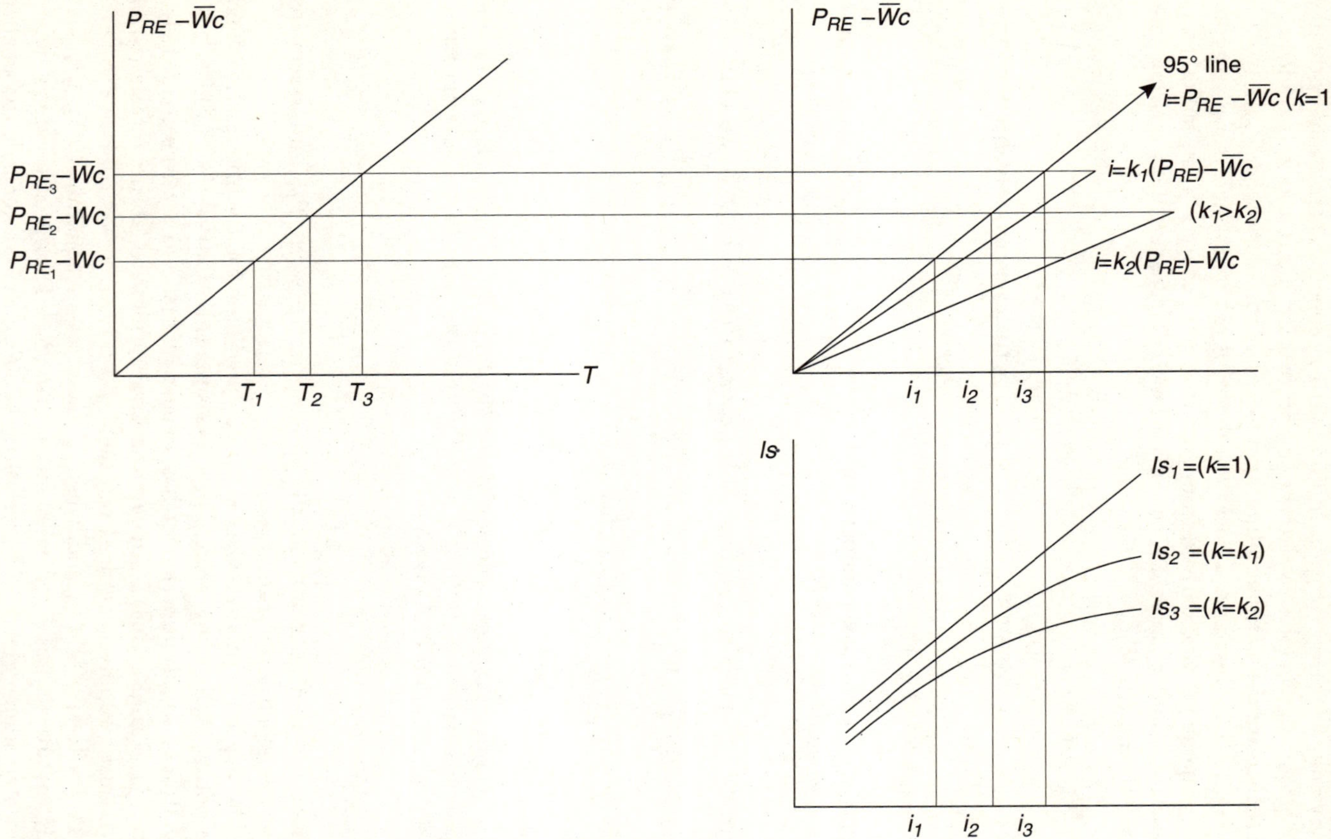


*Figure 9.1* Rae's model of investment supply with sustained technical progress

process may proceed less smoothly; eventually it may grind to a halt, because borrowing cost increases in relation to the expected profit rate from the purchase of new capital goods. Although the first derivative of the investment function remains positive, its second derivative may become negative and $Is$ would approach a maximum. It would approach a maximum more quickly as $k$ increases. Although this description of investment supply is not as straightforward in Rae, it is strongly implied by his description in chapter 8 of *New Principles* of how the functioning of the borrowing/lending process might be disturbed.

## Rae's focus on the business sector's role in growth

That the business sector responded to invention by using part of higher potential profits for simultaneous savings and investment in improved equipment was not always clear. Instead, much of Rae's analysis was couched in terms of analyzing how "the members of society" will respond to a new higher profit rate. But the argument only makes sense if Rae was referring to new business spending from profits, which would not decrease total expenditure in the current income period:

> At length . . . an improvement began to be perceived. What do we find to be the most prominent accompaniment of this change? Is it a diminished expenditure – an increased parsimony – a frugality before unknown? I believe not. Any great diminution of the expenditure of the whole community, it will be difficult to trace, but we shall always discover that invention has somehow or other been busy, either in improving agriculture and the other old arts, or in discovering new ones.
>
> (Rae 1834: 23)

Rae was saying that the funds for any new investment which followed from invention would not be provided from the personal sector (personal frugality would not increase). Instead, invention drew funds from within the business sector "somehow or other" by improving its profit potential. Unfortunately, neither did Rae distinguish the business sector clearly as the motive force behind investment nor did he tell us how the funds for new investment, would be generated.

This so-called augmentation of the capital stock by the business sector of the aggregate economy was a totally different process from the "accumulation" of durables by individuals, because individuals buy the same old things over and over:

> We perceive not so readily the numerous small improvements, which have been gradually . . . spreading themselves through every

> department of the *national* industry . . . [They] . . . sufficiently account for the manner in which the national capital has been augmenting . . . without the necessity of supposing that it ever has augmented precisely as that of *individuals* . . . by a simple multiplication, under the same form, if any or all the items, of which its amount was before made up. [emphasis added]
>
> (Rae 1834: 23)

We can take the term "national industry" to mean the business sector. The new investment which took place in the business sector of the aggregate economy over time as a result of invention was much more important for the nation than the sum of what each individual undertook as his personal "accumulation" of capital. Even though Rae regarded "individual" purchases of durable consumption goods as capital, he regarded such old goods of "the form" to have a lower priority in increasing the size of the "national capital" stock than "augmentation" accomplished by the business sector. Rae was trying to show that "individual and national interests were not identical," title both of Book One of *New Principles* and of both of its chapters. He was arguing against the principle of "providential harmony." Although each individual wished to accumulate instruments (durable consumption goods) that may be used for future consumption, this action will not benefit society (the economy) so much as businesses working together to install new instruments (improved capital goods):

> The capital of a state is a mere instrument in the hands of its industry [businesses] to enable it to draw forth the riches, with which the conjoined powers of nature and art have endowed it . . . When invention succeeds in discovering these additional riches, the mere view is sufficient to induce its [society's business] members to form the new instruments, necessary to draw these riches forth.
>
> (Rae 1834: 29)

Rae has compartmentalized the process by which instruments are formed. Both individuals and businesses purchase instruments; but only the latter purchase technically improved capital goods, the most productive instruments. Both individuals and businesses save, and savings is a necessary condition for the formation of instruments: "It is also true that [the real wealth of a country] cannot advance but as its capital advances and that its capital can only advance by more being saved than is spent" (Rae 1834: 28). But, only business or "national industry" savings can lead to the purchase of those capital goods most likely to cause the economic advance of a nation.

Mixter (1897: 172) implicitly recognized Rae's compartmentalization of instrument formation, when he quoted this dramatic conclusion: "Invention is the only power on earth, that can be said to create. It enters as an essential element into the process of the increase of national wealth, because that process is a creation, not an acquisition" (Rae 1834: 15). Mixter left out the rest of this statement: "It does not necessarily enter into the process of the increase of individual wealth, because that may be simply an acquisition, not a creation" (ibid.). Hence, by default, invention helped to increase the stock of productive instruments in the business sector; however, it had little to do with causing individuals to increase their consumption of existing durables, which, in any case, did little to create new national wealth. Mixter also interpreted Rae to mean that invention would be undertaken by businesses, or at least by entrepreneurs:

> I will state one fact pointed out by Rae which often escapes observation. In our world, he says with truth, the rapid march of invention depends in great measure upon the presence in our society of a body of men of property, who are as a class "bold in enterprise, and accustomed to stake their funds freely."
>
> (Mixter 1897: 172–3)[19]

Mixter failed to add in this analysis, that only if potential profits were large enough, could these risk-takers afford to make the appropriate investments.

Rae's ideas on capital formation in the short period emphasized the risk-taking behavior of businessmen who saw invention as a bold new way to increase profits, which meant that after invention took place, businesses would immediately desire to raise their rate of savings and invest in the new and improved capital goods. Business saving in the presence of technical progress was identically equal to new investment in the current period. The nearly immediate conversion of business savings into investment was not unrealistic, because financial intermediation was not necessary when firms used their own net returns for expansion or even when interbusiness lending occurred. Rae's short-run analysis of how invention affected capital formation did not recognize, however, that such a lag was built into the relation between personal savings, what Rae called "parsimony," and eventual consumer spending on all goods, including durable instruments. Rae's analysis neglected what would happen over a longer period, so he did not describe the possibility that financial intermediation of personal savings could cause a significant delay in current consumption spending.

Rae did not even explore the possibility that personal savings could eventually be channeled by financial intermediaries into the business sector, thus downgrading the importance of what he sometimes called "simple" savings. In a made-up debate between an investment adviser and the proprietor of a large estate, Rae emphasized the importance of business and minimized the importance of personal savings by attempting to show that "there are other means of augmenting capital than simple saving" (Rae 1834: 66).

Throughout the analysis (1834: 65–6), the adviser took the position that "expenditure of [the estate's] revenue" is not saving because it "prevents your augmenting capital" (1834: 66). Rae, however, believed that such an expenditure could be regarded as identical with saving from revenue since the estate owner could be regarded as a business, and with greater "personal superintendence" (1834: 65) or management supervision, the existing expenditures from revenue would produce more revenue almost immediately: "I hope so to improve [the productiveness of my estate] by a more judicious regulation of it, that the same power will produce a far greater effect" through the augmentation of capital (1834: 66). Personal saving would do little, but new business saving would rapidly improve the quality of the capital stock if it were accompanied by better management that could include the use of more technically advanced capital goods.

Rae's short-run emphasis on how investment would expand caused him to focus on the fact that the key to economic growth was a risk-taking business sector which responded almost immediately to the potential of new invention. How would the interest rate fluctuate in the short period after invention occurred, though? If business saving was identically equal to new investment, the real interest rate should stay constant. According to Böhm-Bawerk ([1884] 1921) and Mixter (1902), however, Rae believed invention would cause the real interest rate to rise in the short period.

## The effect of invention on interest variations

Rae regarded the personal sector to be inferior to the business sector as a cause of the increase in the stock of national capital in response to invention. In fact, personal savings (parsimony) was rejected as an important cause of a nation's growth. The incentive for businesses to retain profits for investing, and to enter the credit market for investment loans, was derived mainly from the expected increased profitability of installing technically improved equipment. Mixter described Rae's analysis of the relationship of this improved profit potential to the interest rate as "the particular gains of the individual owners of capital" which may be classified as: "the problem of the emergence of pure capital earnings or interest" and "the problem of the variation of the rate of profits or interest, for short periods as well as long periods" (Mixter 1902: 386). Yet, according to Mixter, Rae was not concerned much with the first "and to an even less degree with" the second problem (1902: 387)[20] Mixter believed, however, that when Rae discussed invention he attributed to it a direct effect in the short period and an indirect effect on interest in the long period:

> For short periods, interest rises from bursts of discovery and invention, from rapid advance in general industrial and commercial efficiency. Interest is hardly likely to rise or continue stationary at

> a high point for considerable periods of time from this latter cause, owing to the fact that the new wealth created by the inventions and discoveries so vastly increases the savable fund. In a developed and healthy society much of what is savable is actually saved, and a lower standard rate of interest than obtained before the era of invention will come about as the final result.
>
> (Mixter 1902: 390)

Böhm-Bawerk criticized Rae's capital theory, beginning in his second edition (1900) of *History and Critique of Interest Theories* (Böhm-Bawerk 1921: ix and ch. 11). His criticism was prompted by Mixter's "rescue [of Rae] from limbo" (Böhm-Bawerk 1921: 209), in which Mixter stated that Rae "anticipated Böhm-Bawerk's theory of interest, in the substance of its leading features and in many of its details, and even to a great extent in the exact form of its expression." (Mixter 1897: 190). Part of this criticism was directed to disprove "what Rae has to say about the relationship between new inventions and an increase in the rate of interest" (Böhm-Bawerk [1884] 1921: 233; see also 234–5). Böhm-Bawerk thus agreed with Mixter that Rae's view was of a direct relation between invention and interest. Nevertheless, Böhm-Bawerk tried to show that such a relationship would only hold in the long period, contrary to the short-run prediction of Mixter's interpretation of Rae's views. Böhm-Bawerk's view was that the interest rate would vary directly with long-run "surplus value" in the production mechanism:

> in the *long run*, a price rate is of necessity established . . . It must reimburse the entrepreneur for his expenditures and yield a *surplus value* which is satisfactory in terms of the relative value of present and future goods . . . That surplus value becomes *originary interest*. [emphasis added]
>
> (Böhm-Bawerk 1921: 225)

If invention added to surplus value in the long run, only then would the interest rate rise; it would not rise immediately after invention occurred, as Mixter interpreted Rae to believe.

It is also important to examine Rae's theory of interest in the light of Fisher (1930), who dedicated his famous book (see his title page) to Rae and Böhm-Bawerk. Fisher seems to have used Rae's ideas in various chapters of his book, but what is relevant to the current discussion is described in chapter 16, "Relation of Discovery and Invention to Interest Rates" (ss. 1–4, pp. 341–7). Section 1 is entitled "The First Effect of Each Important Discovery and Invention Is to Increase the Rate of Interest." Fisher referred to the nominal interest rate as "the rate of return over cost" (1930: 341), which is similar to what Böhm-Bawerk called "surplus value," but he concluded that, in the short period, invention will cause a temporary rise in the interest rate:

> It is important to emphasize the *temporary* nature of the effects of invention and discovery in raising the rate of interest. The effect in raising interest lasts only so long as the rate of return over cost continues to be high and so tempts society to distort greatly its income stream in time shape.
>
> (Fisher 1930: 345)

Thus, without quoting Rae directly, Fisher confirmed the conclusion cited by Mixter and Böhm-Bawerk, that Rae believed invention will cause the interest rate to rise in the short period.[21]

The problem with this literature is that Rae never explicitly stated in his Book II, chapter 10, "Of the Causes of the Progress of Invention, and of the Effects Arising From It," that invention would cause the interest rate to rise. He did state: "The high rate of profit, which follows the . . . introduction of improvement, is indicative of an *immediate* proportional augmentation of the absolute capital of the society" (Rae 1834: 263). This only meant, however, that businesses would tend to invest new profits "immediately" (in the very short run) in improved capital equipment, an identity between business savings and current investment; it did not mean that the higher profit rate would also cause the interest rate to rise. Rae had indicated in Book II, chapter 3, (1834: 196) that the interest rate was determined by the profit rate, but in Book II, chapter 10, Rae did not refer to this relation and only emphasized the connection between the profit rate and capital accumulation by business.[22]

Böhm-Bawerk argued against what he thought to be Rae's position, predicting that the interest rate would stay constant, not rise, in the short period because surplus value would also stay constant:

> Furthermore, I cannot see that it follows, nor why it follows, that where value and costs are thus equally reduced [by new inventions], the difference between them, which is the source of interest, should have become any greater than before.
>
> (Böhm-Bawerk 1921: 234; see also 235)

Mixter's conclusion that Rae believed invention would cause the interest rate to rise in the short period was made even though he believed "[Rae's] theory of interest does not stand forth from his pages as clearly as it otherwise might" (Mixter 1902: 391, see 389–92). After introducing his own theory of short-term interest variation using a loanable funds approach that depended on "the ups and downs of the savings market by changes either on the side of savings or on the side of field of investment" (1902: 390),

Mixter attributed to Rae the conclusion (above) that in the short run, invention and interest would vary in the same direction. He then stated:

> This is in outline a theory of the rate of interest which may be fairly called Rae's theory; although the terminology is somewhat different, and the problem is approached from a different side. Rae himself, for the most part, omits consideration of the market; and, as far as he does deal with it, he contemplates the market for formed capital ("instruments") rather than the market for would-be capital or savings.
>
> (Mixter 1902: 391)

So, according to Mixter, Rae omitted a true loanable-funds or market-determined explanation of interest from his model, and therefore could not have predicted that directly after invention took place, excess investment demand would increase, causing the predicted increase in the interest rate.

The only theoretical mechanism left to Rae for making such a prediction was that invention caused the expected profit rate to rise and that this somehow contributed to the interest increase. Yet, this conclusion was not mentioned by Rae in Book II, chapter 10, and Mixter did not reference its earlier appearance. Mixter's conclusion that Rae believed in a short-run direct relation between invention and the rate of interest appeared to be offered without sufficient justification; yet subsequent authors have taken it up without carefully examining the evidence in Rae's *New Principles*.

Perhaps this is because the implication of a short-run direct relation between invention and the rate of interest comes directly from the investment supply model developed above from *New Principles*. Substituting equation 9.1 into equation 9.2, we get:

$$i = kGT - Wc \tag{9.6}$$

and

$$di/dT = kG - dWc/dT \tag{9.7}$$

If $Wc$ is constant ($dWc/dT = 0$) in the short period after which invention occurs, $di/dT$ would be positive and if $k = 1$ (for continuously positive investment supply), $di/dT = G > 0$; the interest rate rises at a rate determined by the constant average profitability of technical improvement ($G$). If $k > 1$, $i$ increases even faster than average profitability, which tends to dampen the rate of growth of ex-post investment. If we allow $Wc$ to be variable upward in the longer period after investment takes place (something that Rae never considered, but is hinted at by his treating $Wc$ is a necessary cost which presumably adapts slowly to real economic changes):

$$Wc = W(T) \text{ and } dWc/dT > 0 \qquad (9.8)$$

So, from equation (9.7), if $k = 1$, $di/dT = 0$, if $dWc/dT = G$; the interest rate would stay constant in response to technical improvement if the implicit wage of the capitalist increased at the rate determined by the constant rate of average technical profitability, $G$. If $Wc$ increased even faster and $dWc/dT > G$, $i$ would actually fall ($di/dT < 0$). If $G$ may also be regarded as an index of physical productivity, the interest rate would stay constant as long as the average productivity increase following from a given percent improvement in technology yielded the same percent increase in real $Wc$. It should also be pointed out, however, that even though Rae never formally stated these conclusions regarding what would cause $i$ to increase or stay constant after technical improvement occurred, since the short-period model regarding investment supply predominated in his writings (see Figure 9.1), there was a strong presumption built into it that new invention would cause the market interest rate to rise. Böhm-Bawerk's argument, which implied that $i$ would stay constant in the short period and only rise in the long period, could not be correct in the light of Rae's model of investment supply. Furthermore, in the longer period, with the "steady-state" relation ($k = 1$) in equations (9.2), (9.4) and (9.5), only if $dWc/dT < G$ (the wage of the capitalist increased at a slower rate than the rate of average technical profitability) could $i$ increase in the presence of new invention.

## Summary

John Rae's[23] book, *New Principles of Political Economy*, has been neglected both during the nineteenth century, when it was written, and also during the twentieth century, except in the first thirty years. Yet, since certain famous personalities such as E. Böhm-Bawerk and I. Fisher have cited this book as an important work in economics, it seemed worth looking at it more closely to examine elements which needed further clarification. Specifically, it was decided to focus on the most important and widely commented-on subject in Rae's book, the theory of capital accumulation, mainly contained in Book II entitled "Of the Nature of Stock."[24]

Since Rae was so opposed to A. Smith's views on free trade and providential harmony, he focused mainly on the "nation," rather than the "individual," as the driving force for economic growth. Mixter's 1905 rearrangement of *New Principles* took cognizance of this fact by using Rae's term "society" in place of the nation and calling the revised book, *The Sociological Theory of Capital*.[25] This paper looks at Rae's theory of capital formation in the light of his national or aggregate focus. Specifically, it examines Rae's ideas on the source of new funds to purchase capital goods. Since Rae did not discuss much how financial intermediaries became involved in the flow of loanable funds, this discussion mainly concerns itself with how an effective supply of investible funds could become rapidly (or even slowly) converted into capital goods. The previous literature on Rae skirted these views by describing his theory of development (Spengler 1959) or his theory of interest (Böhm-Bawerk 1921; Mixter 1902; Fisher 1930); they never accurately described Rae's theory of capital accumulation. Only Brewer (1990) went into much detail on the relation between technical progress and capital accumulation in Rae.

The first part of this chapter looks at Rae's nationalistic view of capital accumulation and illustrates that only "business" and not "personal" savings conforms to his ideas on how savings could lead to an increase in the capital stock. In fact, personal savings was not productive, in that it did not lead to the creation of new capital; instead, it reallocated part of the existing capital stock between people. Thus Rae argued against A. Smith's positive view that personal savings or "parsimony" would lead a nation's capital stock to grow. This view of the relative importance of personal savings, rather than business savings, as the driving force behind economic expansion, was one of the main ideas of nineteenth- and early twentieth-century theories of growth.

All the previous research on Rae confirmed the importance of invention to Rae's description of economic growth. A typical comment was as follows:

> A consideration of the combined effect of all the circumstances which influence the nature and the production of goods brings Rae to a concise contrast of the methods of operation of the two chief forces, the "inventive principle" and the "accumulative principle."
> (Böhm-Bawerk 1921: 224)

Böhm-Bawerk gave Rae's treatment of the "inventive principle" a very high priority in his overall explanation of how nations grow. Yet these interpretations of Rae neglected the direct connection that Rae made between invention and a nearly simultaneous increase of business – not personal – savings leading to a rapid increase in the supply of investment goods.[26] It has been pointed out that this approach by Rae illustrated a simple, one might say "oversimple," description of how the capital stock increased over time. Capital was "augmented," not merely "accumulated," when new invention occurred. This would raise the expected profit and interest rates simultaneously, leading directly to an increase in the production of investment goods (see Figure 9.1).

The only factor that could prevent this process from functioning smoothly was if the differential between the profit and interest rates increased, a possibility left open by Rae. He believed that the interest was mainly determined by the profit rate. They would both move in the same direction in the relatively short period, but not necessarily on a one-to-one basis. This conclusion ran counter to Böhm-Bawerk's view of Rae's interest theory, which held that the market interest would stay constant in the short period and only rise in the longer period after new invention had raised "surplus value." But the "average profitability of technical improvement" was always an important determinant for Rae of how fast the interest rate would increase. In fact, both Mixter and Fisher, as well as Böhm-Bawerk, made commentaries showing that Rae believed invention and the market interest rate would vary directly in the short period. Mixter also pointed out, however, that Rae was not motivated to explain such interest variation, since he "omits consideration of the [loanable funds] market" and focused instead on the augmentation of national wealth. If the implicit "wage of the capitalist" (an opportunity cost) was also allowed to rise with technical progress in the longer period, conditions were also illustrated for how the market interest might be forced to stay constant, even though new invention was taking place. This was a very special case, though, and one that Rae never actually thought would occur, although his consideration of the capitalist's wage as a unique variable made it worth examining.

## Notes

1 Economics Department, The University of Memphis, Memphis, TN 38152 USA (GOOTZEITMJ@CC.MEMPHIS.EDU).

2 See Rae (1905), a rearrangement of Rae (1834), entitled *The Sociological Theory of Capital*.

3 Both Senior and Cairns argued against the mainstream idea described in chapter 14 of the *General Theory* (Keynes 1936: 175), that a uniform or homogenous supply of savings function was handed down to us from "classical" economics, which described aggregate personal savings as a positively sloped function of the market interest rate.

4 Rae's book was published two years before Senior's (1836) and it did not contain any significant discussion of the relation of abstinence to savings as did Senior's. Invention seems to have played nearly the same role for Rae as abstinence did for Senior; more about this below.

5 The general title of Book I was "Individual and National Interests are Not Identical". The two chapters contained in Book I then considered this topic "as a simple" and "as a theoretical principle."

6 Personal savings thus meant durable consumer spending would take place without a significant lag. Business savings seemed also to mean simultaneous new investment, the purchase of new capital goods, so Rae believed in a version of Say's Identity.

7 Rae's (1834) Book II, chapter 10 was entitled, "Of the Causes of the Progress of Invention, and of the Effects Arising from it." Invention, in effect, became a factor of production for Rae. This was similar to Senior's treatment of "abstinence" as a production factor. See Gootzeit (1992: 245 and n. 5).

8 All capital is instruments, but not all instruments are capital; some of them represent "a stock reserved for immediate consumption" (Rae 1834: 171); these are consumer durables.

9 "While he was still in Scotland, he drew up plans for the feathering of paddle wheels and for a device to measure ocean currents. In 1838, he reported on an ingenious experiment on the effect of the heat of the sun in raising a balloon" (James 1951: 151). The author refers to Mixter (1905: xxviii–xxix).

10 E.g., see Böhm-Bawerk (1921: 222–4, 233–5), Spengler (1959: 400–1), James (1951: 147), and Mixter (1897: 172–3) and (1902: 390, 400).

11 Spengler (1959: 399 n. 2) stated that in Rae, invention, not Smith's parsimony, was responsible for capital accumulation. Rae clearly gave a lower priority to parsimony than he did to invention for providing the necessary incentive to future capital accumulation. This was similar to Senior's downplaying of what he called "frugality," also personal saving, which he made equivalent to hoarding. See Gootzeit (1992: 249). Both Rae and Senior believed that business savings, not personal savings, was the key to growth.

12 The tradition of business savings and its role in capital accumulation in nineteenth-century economics has been lost. Instead, personal savings plays the most important role in modern macrowritings on what causes capital accumulation (see Gootzeit 1995).

13 "But labor is the fund which all men have, out of which to supply their wants . . . every man has this" (Rae 1834: 166; see also 167–71). The remainder of the general stock of instruments of individuals and of societies, with the exception of land, considered not as actually cultivated, but as having a capacity for being cultivated, is termed *capital*. The instruments to which this term applies supply the future wants of the individuals owning them, either from being themselves commodities that may be exchanged for articles directly suited to their needs, or by their capacity of producing commodities which may be so exchanged" (Rae 1834: 171).

14 The beginning of the quotation follows: "It is on these principles, that all reckonings are made, not only of instruments given on credit, but of those retained. In the latter case, the annual return is termed profits of stock, in the former interest. There is, however, this difference between the two, that, in the profits of stock, is generally included . . ." (Rae 1834: 195).

15 *Wc* is an opportunity cost; *W* must be equal to or greater than *Wc*, or the capitalist will not invest in the project with retained earnings or borrow to purchase the capital goods.

16 This analysis neglects the supplying of potentially investible or lendable funds from retained earnings. Presumably, as $P_{RE}$ increased, such funds would continue to be made available, but the total volume of actual investment could still decrease if the volume of borrowing fell, causing a decrease in the volume of lending.

17 The actual title of Book II, chapter 3 is: "Of Certain Circumstances Arising from the Institution of Society," and the title of chapter 10 is: "Of the Causes of the Progress of Invention, and of the Effects Arising from it."

18 The actual title of chapter 8 is "Of the Division of Employments, etc."

19 The last ten words are in quotes, but they seem to be a paraphrase, rather than a direct quote from Rae, because Mixter footnotes the whole of chapter 10 of *New Principles*, (Rae 1834: 208–64).

20 Böhm-Bawerk (1921: 224) also agreed with this viewpoint, even though he went on to criticize Rae's theory of interest (see below): "we must . . . keep in

mind that Rae's interests and purposes were concerned with something other than an explanation of interest. His concern is the augmentation of national wealth."

21 Fisher did cite Rae's book (Book II, ch. 10) somewhat vaguely as follows: "The economic effects of invention, and particularly its effects upon the rate of interest, were well treated by John Rae" (Fisher 1930: 345 n. 31).

22 See also Tavlas and Aschheim (1985: 302) who discussed the interest theory of Alexander Del Mar in a similar fashion.

23 See in Mixter (1905: xix) the beginning of a biographical sketch of John Rae (1796–1872), which distinguished among three different nineteenth-century John Raes. See also Schumpeter (1954: 1223).

24 Book 1 (Rae 1834), in arguing against Smith, also discussed Rae's theory of capital accumulation.

25 James (1951: 148) described "Rae's discussion of these *sociological* influences on the accumulation of capital" (emphasis added). Just prior to this description (1951: 147), James quoted from Rae (1834: 124) on "three elements which govern the effective desire of accumulation." These have to do, according to Rae, with "the prevalence throughout the *society* of the social and benevolent affections," "the prevalence of habits of reflection, and prudence, in the minds of members of *society*, and the stability of *society*" (emphasis added).

25 An exception to this general rule was Spengler, who made this comment: "Moreover, invention augmented capital accumulation by pushing up the rate of return on capital and causing individuals with a given 'effective desire of accumulation' to save more; by increasing output; and by making available new productive objects of desire whose purchase generally entailed prior and additional saving on the part of would be purchasers" (Spengler 1959: 400). Spengler, even though he mentioned "individuals" who would "save more," since they "increase output," could just as easily have referred to "businesses."

# 10

# RAE AND INTERNATIONAL TRADE

*Robert W. Dimand*

## Introduction: Rae and trade

John Rae's *New Principles of Political Economy* (1834) is, as its subtitle proclaimed, a work "Exposing the Fallacies of the System of FREE TRADE, and of Some Other Doctrines Maintained in the *Wealth of Nations*." Rae's remarkable treatise was much more than an assault on the classical case for free trade. His pioneering account of "the effective desire of accumulation" (1834: bk.II, chs. 6 and 7) brilliantly prefigured the analysis of time preference and capital accumulation by Eugen von Böhm-Bawerk ([1884] 1959) and Irving Fisher (1907, 1930). Fisher dedicated *The Rate of Interest* ([1907] 1982) "to the memory of John Rae who laid the foundations upon which I have endeavored to build" and held ([1930] 1970: p. ix) that "Every essential part of [my own theory] was at least foreshadowed by John Rae in 1834." Rae's treatment of the role of invention in social development points forward to Joseph Schumpeter's *Theory of Economic Development* ([1911] 1934). Rae's discussion of "commodities of which the consumption is conspicuous, and which cost much labor, though not better qualified . . . to supply real wants" (1834: bk. II, ch. 11) anticipated Thorstein Veblen's analysis of conspicuous consumption in *The Theory of Leisure Class* (1899).

As Douglas Mair (1990: 279) notes, Rae's book was initially "misconstrued . . . as a polemic against free trade and its advocates, principally Smith. This misconception persists to the present day." Reaction to this initial, overly narrow view of Rae's contribution, and recognition of the richness of his theorizing about capital, technological change, and consumption, risks going too far in the other direction. Rae's *New Principles of Political Economy* is far more than a critique of the classical case for free trade, but it is that as well. It was in the context of international trade that Rae distinguished private and social advantage, rejecting Adam Smith's claim that what is prudence in a private household can scarce be folly for a great nation. Recent emphasis of other important aspects of the *New Principles* has contributed to the limited attention given to Rae in literature on the history of trade theory, and to the overlooking of the extent to which Rae's analysis of trade drew on parts of the *Wealth of Nations*, for all the differences in policy conclusions.

With the important exception of Andrea Maneschi (1995), historians of international trade theory have often neglected Rae. He is not mentioned in John Chipman's three-part historical "Survey of the Theory of International Trade" (1965–66), or in surveys of trade theory by Bhagwati, Caves and Corden, or in Jacob Viner's *Studies in the Theory of International Trade* ([1937] 1965). Although Mark Blaug (1978: 225) mentions the infant industry argument for protective tariffs, the only John Rae mentioned in Blaug's book is the one who wrote a biography of Adam Smith. In *The New Palgrave*, Rae's statement of the infant industry argument is noted in K.H. Hennings's article on Rae, but Rae is unmentioned by Gerald Meier on infant industry, Chipman on international trade, or by Ian Steedman on foreign trade.

The only mention of Rae in Haberler or Kemp is embedded in their quotation of John Stuart Mill's statement of the infant industry argument (Haberler 1936: 280–1; Kemp 1960: 65; Mill [1848] 1965, 3: 918–19):

> The only case in which, on mere principles of political economy, protecting duties can be defensible, is when they are imposed temporarily (especially in a young and rising nation) in hopes of naturalizing a foreign industry, in itself perfectly suitable to the circumstances of the country. The superiority of one country over another in a branch of production, often arises only from having begun it sooner. There may be no inherent advantage on one part, or disadvantage on the other, but only a present superiority of acquired skill and experience. A country which has this skill and experience yet to acquire, may in other respects be better adapted to the production than those which were earlier in the field: and besides, it is a just remark of Mr. Rae, that nothing has a greater tendency to promote improvements in any branch of production, than its trial under a new set of conditions. But it cannot be expected that individuals should, at their own risk, or rather to their certain loss, introduce a new manufacture, and bear the burden of carrying it on until the producers have been educated up to the level of those with whom the processes are traditional. A protecting duty, continued for a reasonable time, might sometimes be the least inconvenient mode in which the nation can tax itself for the support of such an experiment. But it is essential that the protection should be confined to cases in which there is good ground of assurance that the industry which it fosters will after a time be able to dispense with it; nor should the domestic producers ever

be allowed to expect that it will be continued to them beyond the time necessary for a fair trial of what they are capable of accomplishing.

Although this paragraph appeared in every edition of Mill's *Principles*, the words "of Mr. Rae" first appeared as an attribution of the cited remark in 1862 in the fifth edition. Haberler (1936: 280), missing the significance of Mill's mention of Rae, claimed that Mill's paragraph "illustrates the correctness of Viner's remark that all economically tenable arguments for tariffs come from Free Traders." In fact, Mill's entire paragraph stating and qualifying the infant industry argument for protection was drawn from the protectionist Rae, not the single directly attributed remark. Viner ([1937] 1965: 72–73) quoted several brief remarks suggesting the infant industry argument from seventeenth- and early eighteenth-century English sources, and referred to similar mentions by Sir James Steuart, Josiah Tucker, Alexander Hamilton, and Friedrich List, but it was Rae who provided a full and clear statement of the argument, which Mill condensed into his much-quoted paragraph. Mill's paragraph with its reference to Rae was quoted in full by Sir John A. Macdonald, then between terms as Canada's prime minister, in his 1876 speech announcing the Conservative Party's adoption of the National Policy of economic development based on tariff protection for manufactures (Neill 1991: 85–91; cf. Goodwin 1961: 57).

## Rae's 1825 sketch of the infant industry argument

Rae first presented his views on the transfer of manufacturing techniques between countries in March 1825 in an unsigned article identified as Rae's by R. Warren James. The anonymous article closely prefigured aspects of Rae's *New Principles*, and was published in a review to which his sister and brother-in-law are known to have contributed. Rae's "Sketches of the Origin and Progress of Manufactures and of the Policy Which Has Regulated Their Legislative Encouragement in Great Britain and in Other Countries" attracted little notice at the time, and the *Canadian Review and Literary and Historical Journal* ceased publication with its fifth issue in 1826, so that Rae's promised sequel, "An enquiry into the expediency of establishing some new branches of industry in the Canadas, more particularly with a view to the employment of women and children in the cities of Quebec and Montreal," never appeared in print. Rae's 1825 article examined the experience of Britain and the Netherlands to emphasize the benefits of government encouragement of new industries using imported technology. The title of his intended sequel indicates that this historical and theoretical investigation was meant to lead to a practical proposal for introducing new manufactures to make use of the underutilized cheap labor of Lower Canadian women and children. Similarly, Rae's *New Principles of Political*

*Economy* was originally conceived as a theoretical adjunct to a large-scale statistical work on the condition and resources of Canada, a successor to the massive, chaotic *Statistical Account of Upper Canada* by the exiled political dissident Robert Gourlay (Gourlay [1822] 1966: Dimand 1992). The completed portions of Rae's works do not fully reveal how firmly what he intended to do was rooted in the context of contemporary Canadian conditions and proposals.

Rae (1825: 198) used the establishment of the woollen manufacture in England to illustrate his claim that, "When the chief materials of a manufacture are native or colonial, and when workmen, machinery and capital can be obtained at rates which promise successful competition with foreigners, such manufacture, if not otherwise sufficiently attractive to individuals, should be encouraged by government." In this passage Rae advanced what came to be known as the Mill test for protecting an infant industry: the promise of future successful competition, given factor prices, even though the industry would not be privately profitable at first. This view of a worthwhile new industry having a prospect of future successful competition even though it would not be currently profitable for private individuals captures the essence of Rae's dissent from the Torrens–Ricardo comparative cost theory of the gains from trade: comparative costs can change as a newly established manufacture acquires experience (learning by doing) and achieves economies of scale (cf. Mill [1848] 1965, 2: 589 n., on Torrens's priority over Ricardo on comparative advantage).

While Rae initially advanced this test only for industries using domestic raw materials, he extended it to the use of imported inputs in the case where the classical assumption of full employment of resources failed to hold. "When agriculture and its kindred avocations; manufactures requisite to support the national independence, and those which are fabricated from native or colonial produce leave part of the population unemployed and the wages of labour below their rates in neighbouring countries, then a manufacture from foreign materials may be safely encouraged," as when Britain and Holland encouraged Huguenot refugees in the silk manufacture after Louis XIV revoked the tolerant Edict of Nantes in 1685 (Rae 1825: 198). Keynes (1936: Ch. 23) similarly invoked the existence of unemployed resources as providing a rational basis for mercantilist efforts to artificially stimulate manufactures. However, Rae (1834: 310–11) later drew back from this rejection of the assumption of full employment, holding that for commodities satisfying real wants (as distinct from luxuries) "the reasoning of Mr. Say is, I conceive, conclusive. A general overproduction is an absurdity . . . The increased provision for wants thus presented, must either be consumed, or applied to the formation of instruments to supply the demands of a more distant futurity."

In contrast to the mercantile system denounced by Adam Smith, government intervention was to be temporary: Rae (1825: 200, 202) held that:

> [when] the elements of useful knowledge are generally diffused, enlightening the great body of the people and directing their genius, talents and industry to the improvements of the useful arts, the patronage of the government may be no longer necessary, but the progress of manufacturing industry may be left to the sagacious superintendence of private industry. . . . When England was gradually raising up that astonishing fabric of manufactures which now exists, various expedients of a temporary and subsidiary nature were adopted, serving the purpose of ladders, frames and scaffolding, which she can now with safety and advantage throw down and forget. But the memory of such regulations remains for the instruction of other nations in the commencement of their manufacturing career.

Rae (1825) endorsed government support for the invention of implements and machines to facilitate and abridge labour by the granting of patents or by payment of compensation for making an invention freely available to the public. Taking a Ricardian view of the costs of the Corn Laws while defending the market for Canadian grain, he urged manufacturing nations to adopt "a liberal admission of the grain of their own colonies or of friendly nations" because "a monopoly which stimulates agriculturalists to waste capital upon poor soils is in the process of time as hurtful to themselves as to the commercial and manufacturing population" (1825: 203).

Rae had thus formulated the core of his position on international trade and the proper role of government by 1825, along with a sketchier anticipation of his later analysis of the importance of invention in augmenting the capital stock.

## The gains from trade

Rae treated "Exchanges between different Communities" in chapter 12 of Book II of his *New Principles*. He analyzed the gains from trade on the basis of arbitrage between countries with differing autarchic price ratios that reflect differing relative pretrade scarcities in two countries: "Let us suppose that three cords of the wood commonly burnt, are equivalent, in the heat given out by them, to one chaldron of coals; if, then, in the society B there be any commodity there equivalent to less than three cords wood, and which, transported to A, will in A be equivalent, considered as an utility, to one chaldron coals, the exchange will be possible, for this difference may pay, or may do more than pay, for the expense of transport" (Rae 1834: 302). Rae's treatment of the gains from trade made no reference to Ricardo or Torrens, although other passages (ibid. 263 n., 346, 389) show Rae's acquaintance with Ricardo's *Principles*. Although Rae's discussion is not inconsistent with comparative advantage, it is not clear that his argument runs in terms of comparative advantage (each good produced where its opportunity cost in terms of foregone output of the other good is lowest), rather than the narrower case of reciprocal absolute advantage (each country exports a good in which it has an absolute advantage, a lower real cost of production).

The crucial innovation in Rae's analysis of gains from trade is succinctly stated in his table of contents: "Increased facility in the exchange of utilities operates in the same manner as the progress of invention and improvement, and carries instruments to the more quickly returning orders; increased facility in the exchange of luxuries has an immediate tendency, on the contrary, to carry instruments to the more slowly returning orders" (Rae 1834: xv). Rae considered the opportunity to make beneficial international exchanges (of non-luxuries) equivalent to invention in allowing increased consumption from the same resources.

Rae (1834: 100) ranked instruments (capital goods) as "part of a series, of which the orders are determined by the period of time at which instruments placed in them, issue, or would issue, if not before exhausted, in events equivalent to double the labor expended in forming them." In the notation of Hennings (1987) this period would be $n$ in the expression $(1 + r)^n = 2$, where $r$ is the internal rate of return or marginal efficiency of capital, with a decrease in $n$ being equivalent to an increase in $r$. Instruments with a shorter period of producing double their cost (equivalently, with a higher internal rate of return) belonged to the more quickly returning orders.

Similarly, "Measured by the length of the period, to which the inclination of its [society's] members to yield up a present good, for the purpose of producing the double of it at the expiration of that period, will extend . . . [T]he determination to sacrifice a certain amount of present good, to obtain another greater amount, at some future period, may be termed the *effective desire of accumulation*" (Rae 1834: 119). Thus, in the notation of Hennings (1987), the effective desire of accumulation is $m$ in the expression $(1 + s)^m = 2$, where $s$ is the rate of time preference, so that a higher effective desire of accumulation is equivalent to a lower rate of time preference. The stock of instruments (capital goods) will be increased as long as the effective desire of accumulation, $m$, exceeds $n$, the order of the available instruments (that is, as long as the internal rate of return on investment exceeds the rate of time preference). Rae criticized Adam Smith and his followers for emphasizing accumulation, the increase of the capital stock due to parsimony (saving), to the neglect of augmentation, the effect of invention in increasing the capital stock by raising the internal rate of return (reducing $n$, creating more quickly returning instruments). Rae stressed improvements in investment opportunities as the driving force in expansion of the capital stock, rather than changes in savings propensities.

Rae equated international exchange of nonluxury goods to invention in its effect of raising the internal rate of return, carrying instruments to more quickly returning orders, and thus creating an incentive to increase the capital stock and productive capacity. Like his infant industry argument, that learning by doing changes comparative costs, this insight of Rae's carries the analysis of gains from trade beyond the static comparative advantage analysis of Torrens and of Ricardo's famous numerical example (Ricardo [1821] 1973, ch. 7). Just as recent work on market structure and international trade has led to renewed interest in Smith's account of international trade extending the division of labour and lowering costs by extending the market, Rae's analysis of dynamic gains from trade belongs in a broadened and enriched heritage of international trade theory. Ricardo himself went beyond his numerical example with his consideration of the effect of the Corn Laws on the profit rate and capital accumulation, and recognized the significance of technical progress in agriculture, but this analysis was limited to agricultural produce and did not stress the analogy between trade and invention as clearly as Rae did (see Dimand 1995).

Rae joined this insight, however, to a claim that trade in luxuries (gratifying vanity rather than satisfying real wants) has the opposite effect of moving instruments to less quickly returning orders, a poorly supported claim made yet more troubling by his admission that: "As it is impossible in almost any case to determine accurately how far any article is or is not a luxury, there is proportional difficulty in ascertaining what are the precise effects resulting from the exchanges actually carried on between any two commodities" (Rae 1834: 310). While at first glance Rae's distinction between the effect of trade in utilities and that in luxuries seems strange and unfamiliar, Ricardo's critique of the Corn Laws makes an analogous point in more familiar terms. A reduction in the price of wage-goods, brought about by free importation of corn, will raise the profit rate (move instruments into more quickly returning orders) and encourage capital accumulation, while a reduction in the price of luxury goods, achieved by allowing free importation, would have no such effect on the profit rate, as it would not alter the wage rate. Unlike Ricardo, however, Rae distinguished luxuries from necessities according to whether the good satisfied a basic need or merely desire, rather than on the basis of what type of income was spent on it.

## Rae and Smith

Although Rae's *New Principles of Political Economy* was presented as a polemic against Adam Smith, and though he held contrary to Smith that division of labour was more a result than a cause of progress (Rae 1834: appendix to Book II), Rae's analysis of international trade is closely linked in spirit to the first chapters of Book 1 of *The Wealth of Nations*, in which Smith discussed the effects of the division of labour (specialization) and then made a case for the benefits of free trade because the division of labour is limited by the extent of the market. The benefits that Smith saw in the division of labour (apart from saving time going between jobs) were the increasing skill, dexterity, and judgement of specialized workers, and the stimulus to the invention of machines to abridge and facilitate labour provided by concentrating on a particular task. The increased skill, dexterity, and judgement acquired through increased experience in an industry and the related stimulus to invention are the heart of Rae's argument for tariff protection of infant industries. Rae may be read as drawing the logical policy conclusions of the first portion of *The Wealth of Nations*.

## The role of the legislator

Rae's rejection of what he read as Smith's identification of saving rather than invention as the mainspring of economic development led him to reject Smith's claim that, if the state were to fail to promote the establishment of a new industry using imported technology, the nation's capital would be just as profitably employed. Rae argued that Smith mistakenly took the amount of capital as given, and held that the creation of new investment opportunities would increase the stock of capital. He also rejected Smith's identification of individual and national interest (to which Smith allowed some exceptions) and Smith's presumption that legislative interference with the workings of the invisible hand would retard economic growth. The concluding Book III of Rae's *New Principles* expounded the un-Smithian policy implications of his analysis, stressing that "The legislator may stimulate invention by the introduction of new arts" (Table of Contents and Summary of Principles, gloss on Book III, chapter 1, "Of the operations of the legislator in bringing the arts of Foreign Countries to his own," Rae 1834: xvi). Rae made a case for cautious and temporary support by bounties or tariffs of new home manufactures importing foreign technology and subsequently advancing beyond the imported techniques by invention.

## Conclusion

John Rae's *New Principles of Political Economy* holds a justly acclaimed place in the history of capital theory. Rae's cogent rationale for protection of infant industries and his analysis of the gains of trade, with its striking analogy between international exchange and technical progress (invention), also merit a place in the history of trade theory, where Rae has had less attention.

# 11

# JOHN RAE AND THE PROMOTION OF INFANT INDUSTRIES

*Andrea Maneschi*[1]

## Introduction

In his *Statement of Some New Principles on the Subject of Political Economy, Exposing the Fallacies of the System of Free Trade, and of Some Other Doctrines Maintained in the "Wealth of Nations,"* John Rae (1834) made two fundamental contributions which came to the attention of John Stuart Mill through Nassau Senior: his pioneering formulation of capital theory, and his argument in favor of the promotion of infant industries.[2] Mill quoted passages from Rae's book at some length in chapter 11 ("Of the Law of the Increase of Capital") of Book 1 of his *Principles of Political Economy*, and placed Rae's analysis of the forces leading to the accumulation of capital on a level with Malthus's principle of population growth (Mill [1871] 1920: 165).[3]

The formulation of capital theory found in Rae's *New Principles* anticipated the much later ones of Eugen Böhm-Bawerk and Irving Fisher. In articulating the important role of invention and of the growth of knowledge in a country's economic development, Rae noted that these can be more easily transferred by the efforts of legislators to a country which lacks them rather than through "the violent operation of foreign wars, and intestine commotions" (Rae 1834: 50), as had usually occurred in the past. Rae's rationale for the promotion of new industries inspired Mill to write his well-known paragraph justifying infant-industry protection under carefully prescribed circumstances in Book 5 (entitled "On the Influence of Government") of his *Principles of Political Economy*. Thanks to Mill's cogent defense, this argument entered into mainstream economics.[4] After tracing its history and comparing Rae's formulation to previous such attempts, Lionel Robbins (1968: 113) concluded that, "if we are looking for pure excellence of intellectual analysis, the palm must clearly go to John Rae."

It is no coincidence that two of Rae's contributions noted by Mill, capital theory and the analysis of infant industries, involve the passage of time.

Time is required both for capital instruments to yield a return and for an industry to grow to maturity, so it can compete with current imports. Looking first at the theory of capital, Rae constructed it by fashioning two building blocks: the speed with which capital instruments yield a return, and the community's "effective desire of accumulation," a term corresponding to Irving Fisher's (1930) "rate of time preference," or "degree of impatience." The latter is in part determined by altruistic feelings towards future generations, which Rae referred to as the "social and benevolent affections." He defined the "order" of an instrument by the period of time it takes for a given outlay to yield a return double in value. The shorter this period, the "quicker" this return, that is, the higher the instrument's productivity or rate of return.[5] Rae represented the more quickly returning orders by the letters A, B, C, . . ., and the more slowly returning ones by Z, a, b, c, . . . The interaction between a community's effective desire of accumulation, the materials available to it, its power of invention, and its rate of wages determine the order of return to which these instruments are carried (Rae 1834: 109).

While Rae formulated his capital theory in Book Two of the *New Principles*, the circumstances surrounding infant industries are mainly analyzed in Book One, which is devoted to a critique of Adam Smith's *Wealth of Nations*, while the related policy implications for the transfer of technology from abroad are outlined in Book Three. Rae's articulation of the infant-industry argument built and improved on previous such efforts.[6] It is not clear that he was acquainted with (or would have been much enlightened by) the numerous mercantilist arguments of this type, such as those from the seventeenth and eighteenth centuries quoted by Viner (1937: 71–72). But a quotation in the *New Principles* (1834: 365–6) from the *Report on the Subject of Manufactures* by Alexander Hamilton ([1791] 1966) shows that Rae was familiar with it. This *Report* was the last of four major reports on the American economy which Hamilton, Secretary of the Treasury to George Washington, submitted to Congress on December 5, 1791. There are many similarities, as well as some notable differences, between this *Report* and Rae's *New Principles* that will be remarked on in this chapter. The first and foremost similarity is their authors' advocacy of the introduction of manufactures in what Mill would later describe as "a young and rising nation" ([1871] 1920: 922). However, Rae's critique of Smith's *Wealth of Nations* was much more profound than Hamilton's, in part because it was presented at book length rather than in a government document. It is clear that both Hamilton and Rae had carefully studied the *Wealth of Nations*. While they were deeply influenced by the philosophy underlying it, they differed from it in certain fundamental respects. Curiously enough, Smith is never mentioned by name in Hamilton's *Report*, even though parts of it paraphrase the *Wealth of Nations*, at times using Smith's very words and expressions.[7] Rae, on the other hand, was more than willing to quote passages from the *Wealth of Nations* in order to rebut some of its arguments. His critique, unlike Hamilton's, was enhanced by his capital-theoretic frame of reference, and his consequent alertness to the needs of futurity in the formulation of public policy.

## Infant-industry promotion: Rae's critique of Smith

The passages which Rae quoted and criticized in Book One of the *New Principles* were to a large extent drawn from Book 4 of the *Wealth of Nations*, which contains the principal elements of Smith's foreign trade theory. After contending that it pays tailors, shoemakers, and farmers to specialize in their trade and buy other commodities from other tradesmen, Smith had argued by analogy that:

> what is prudence in the conduct of every private family, can scarce be folly in that of a great kingdom. If a foreign country can supply us with a commodity cheaper than we ourselves can make it, better buy it off them with some part of the produce of our own industry, employed in a way in which we have some advantage.
>
> (Smith [1776] 1976: 457)

Rae argued that Smith had postulated a series of "axioms" in the *Wealth of Nations*, such as that wealth can increase only via capital accumulation, and that the latter depends on saving out of current revenue. Since he presumed that government regulations turn industry to a less advantageous direction, Smith deduced that they must also reduce income, and hence saving, capital accumulation, and future welfare:

> By means of such regulations, indeed, a particular manufacture may sometimes be acquired sooner than it could have been otherwise, and after a certain time may be made at home as cheap or cheaper than in the foreign country. But though the industry of the society may be thus carried with advantage into a particular channel sooner than it could have been otherwise, it will by no means follow that the sum total, either of its industry, or of its revenue, can ever be augmented by any such regulation. The industry of the society can augment only in proportion as its capital augments, and its capital can augment only in proportion to what can be gradually saved out of its revenue. But the immediate effect of every such regulation is to diminish its revenue, and what diminishes its revenue, is certainly not very likely to augment its capital faster than it would have augmented of its own accord, had both capital and industry been left to find out their natural employments.
>
> (Smith [1776] 1976: 458)

Rae believed that Smith's "axiom" about wealth creation was unwarranted since the latter depends primarily on knowledge and skills, which can often be transferred from other countries through legislative efforts.[8] Rae took exception to Smith's contentions that "the natural advantages which one country has over another in producing particular commodities are sometimes so great, that it is acknowledged by all the world to be in vain to struggle with them," and that "whether the advantages which one country has over another, be natural or acquired, is in this respect of no consequence" (Smith [1776] 1976: 458). Rae argued that:

> on the contrary, in my opinion, it is of the greatest consequence. Now natural advantages cannot be procured by any expenditure of revenue or capital. But one country can often with ease, and at a trifling expense, acquire the practical skill and the knowledge of particular arts and manufactures which another possesses, and, by doing so, gain the advantage of procuring for itself the products of this skill and knowledge at home, instead of having to go abroad for them.
>
> (Rae 1834: 71–2)

He criticized those who characterize a country's "actual productions" as its "natural productions":

> The products of different regions are spoken of by political economists, as bestowed on them by nature, are termed natural productions, and the attempt to transfer them to other sites, is held to be a procedure in opposition to the designs of providence, whose intentions, it is asserted, in giving them these productions, were, that the inhabitants of different countries should exchange the products of their several territories with one another. Because one country alone now produces particular commodities, we are by no means warranted to conclude that nature intended they should be produced only there. On the contrary . . . these arts [of production] should be advanced from their first rough simplicity, and carried to greater and greater excellence, by passing from one region and people to another.
>
> (Rae 1834: 257–8)

To underline the changeable nature of a country's specialization, Rae noted perceptively that the occurrence of technical progress in a country can hurt its trading partner:

> As there are no limits to the inventive faculty, so no community can assure itself that any commodity which it now produces and exports to some other community, may not come to be produced

> in that community, and so be no longer exported there. . . . But while in the society B, the effects of the progress of invention would be thus beneficial, in A they might operate prejudicially.
>
> (Rae 1834: 304–5)

Import-biased growth in B can lead to a deterioration of A's terms of trade, and to a decline in its rate of capital formation. The facility with which technology can be transferred prompted Rae to ask the rhetorical question: "who can positively say what fifty years hence will be the productions of any country?" (Rae 1834: 258).[9]

To buttress his case for the promotion of new industries, Rae (1834: 44) pointed out that Adam Smith himself had insisted that, "the revenue of a trading and manufacturing country must, other things being equal, always be much greater than that of one without trade or manufactures" (Smith [1776] 1976: 677), since manufactures can advantageously exchange for the "rude produce" of other countries.[10]

## Infant-industry promotion and benefit–cost analysis

The transfer of a manufacturing process from abroad is a difficult and expensive operation which risk-averse individuals are reluctant to undertake. Since it partakes of the nature of a public good, "the necessary first cost of the scheme should be borne by the whole community" (Rae 1834: 53), and therefore requires the direct assistance of policymakers:[11]

> The difficulty is, to discover a method of inducing an individual to incur an unavoidable outlay, the returns from which, although very beneficial to the whole society, are no more so to him who lays out a great deal, than to others who lay out nothing. The whole society, or rather the legislator, the power acting for the whole society, might do so, and in similar cases has done so, and, to judge of the measure by the events consequent on it, with the happiest success. Why, then, should he not?
>
> (Rae 1834: 55–6)

Like Hamilton, Rae based his argument for the promotion of infant industries on the desirability of a manufacturing base for a country's economic development and the difficulties faced by entrepreneurs intent on establishing them. Rae described such difficulties in much more detail than Hamilton, including such factors as the cost of importing special machinery or attracting specialized workmen from abroad, the large financial outlay initially required, the need to modify the technology in the face of differences in climate, materials, and factor prices in the host country, and the trial and error process inevitably associated with a new venture (Rae 1834: 46–56).

Both Rae and Hamilton advocated caution in recommending candidates for promotion as infant industries.[12] Decision-makers were urged by Rae to establish "rules determining when the passage of any art is practicable, and when the benefits derived from it will exceed, or fall short of the necessary expense of effecting the passage." The criterion for success was that "the commodity, the product of the art in question, comes to be made at the same cost in the country to which its manufacture is transferred, as in that from which it comes, or at less cost than there" (Rae 1834: 364). Since J.S. Mill, following Rae, adopted the same criterion for infant industry protection, it has become known as the "Mill test."[13] Rae expressed it as follows: "[the legislator] is never justifiable in attempting to transfer arts yielding utilities from foreign countries to his own, unless he have sufficient reason to conclude that they will ultimately lessen the cost of the commodities they produce" (Rae 1834: 367). Although the term "ultimately" implies no specific time frame, it is clear that Rae believed that protection should be granted only on a temporary basis.[14]

It was subsequently pointed out by Bastable (1903: 140) that the Mill test, while necessary, is not sufficient. As Kemp (1960: 65) has put it:

> the ultimate saving in costs should compensate the community for the high costs of the protected learning period. It is necessary that, when a suitable discount is applied to the early excess costs and to the eventual cost savings, the commodity still should be worth producing.

That Rae came very close to formulating the Bastable test can be gleaned from a passage in which he intimates that the calculation to be made by policymakers in selecting an industry for promotion should coincide with that made by individuals who appraise an investment project:

> We know indeed that we must expend something, but we think that in the long run we shall be better repaid for this expenditure, by this undertaking, than by any other in which we could employ our funds. The question to be determined in every such case, would then be similar to that which an individual determines when deliberating on any scheme for the augmentation of his private capital, and would resolve itself into an inquiry, whether or not the probable returns from the proposed measure, be likely to be a sufficient remuneration for the expense of carrying it into effect.
>
> (Rae 1834: 60, 67)

This calculation includes not only the direct benefits and costs of the project, but the saving of transport costs and a benefit much harder to quantify, namely, the assurance that supply would not be interrupted in the case of wars or other disturbances. Rae was thus sketching a rudimentary benefit–cost appraisal which takes into account risk factors as well as more conventional economic outputs and inputs. It is unfortunate that the above passage (and other similar ones) appeared in Book 1 of the *New Principles*, so that Rae could not express the criterion for acceptance of candidates for promotion more precisely by using the capital-theoretic tools he developed in Book II. Clearly it would have been helpful to condition the acceptance of such an "undertaking" on the community's effective desire of accumulation. Its benefits could then have been expressed in present value terms, or (to use Rae's preferred expression) in terms of the "capacity" (or productivity) of instruments and of the "absolute capital" they embody, where the latter represents "a mode of expressing in present days' labor the whole capacity of the instruments owned by any society" (Rae 1834: 172).

Book III of the *New Principles* would have been a logical place to combine the capital-theoretic framework of Book II with the advocacy of infant promotion found in Book I, but Rae decided to devote it to the policy implications for legislators. If the transfer of a technology is desirable, the latter can effect it "by premiums for successful individual imitations of the foreign article" in order to ascertain the viability of the transfer of technology. If encouragement is warranted, these should be followed "by general bounties on the home manufacture; or by duties on that imported from abroad" (Rae 1834: 368). These are some of the same protective measures advocated by Hamilton, but Rae (whose book was addressed to a different audience) did not elaborate on them in the detail which Hamilton thought appropriate for his *Report*.

## Free trade and infant-industry protection: competitive or complementary?

Rae's powerful advocacy of the promotion of infant industries, and the full title of his book, might suggest that he was opposed to free trade. But chapter 12 of Book II of the *New Principles*, "Of Exchanges between Different Communities," describes in glowing terms the benefits resulting from such exchanges. Like most economists of the classical period, Rae focused more on the benefits of foreign trade than on the sources of comparative advantage. This is even more understandable in his case because of the fluid nature which he envisaged specialization to have in a developing economy. To appraise the gains from trade, Rae classified commodities into "utilities" and "luxuries" using the following criterion:

> In so far as any commodity, when compared with another, excels it only in the gratification it affords to vanity, it is to be considered a luxury, in so far as it compares with others in the capacity

> which its physical qualities give it to gratify real wants, it is considered as a utility.
>
> (Rae 1834: xv)

He argued that trade in utilities lowers the amount of labor needed to provide a community with these commodities and carries its capital instruments to more quickly returning orders, thus stimulating capital formation. His view of the gains from trade was inspired by his capital-theoretic framework, and thus differed from that of other classical writers or of the neoclassical economists who followed them. According to Rae, trade produces not only the static gain of the saving of resources involved in the indirect production of imports via exports, but a dynamic one similar to that resulting from an invention or "improvement".

> The revolution effected might nearly compare to an improvement in both societies. . . . Like other improvements, they would not be confined in their operation to the particular branches of industry in which they had place, but would be diffused equally over both societies, carrying the whole instruments in each towards the more quickly returning orders. Profits would rise equally in all employments. The absolute capital of both communities would be increased in proportion to the augmented provision made for their future wants.
>
> (Rae 1834: 303)

Just as free trade yields dynamic benefits, trade restrictions imply a less dynamic economy:

> The fewer obstructions, therefore, that stood in the way of such transfers [of commodities between different societies], the farther, in these cases, would the stock of instruments in those societies be carried towards the order A, as any obstruction that might occur would, on the contrary, have the effect of checking the progress towards the more quickly returning orders, and keeping them nearer the order Z.
>
> (Rae 1834: 304)

The quickening of the orders of the society's entire range of capital instruments and the consequent rise in the profit rate stimulated by trade were the same conclusions that Rae had derived in the case of an improvement in the art of bread baking in a previous chapter of his book. In the context of trade, it is the fall in the price of utilities which increases the ratio between the "capacity" of all instruments and their cost, carrying them to more quickly returning orders. It is unfortunate that trade theorists have neglected to follow up on, and formalize, the dynamic gains described by Rae.

We are now in a position to examine the question of whether Rae was consistent in simultaneously supporting free trade and the promotion of infant industries by various means, including duties.[15] His capital theory is the key to clarifying what on the surface may appear to be an inconsistency. Both policies have the potential for raising a society's profit rate by carrying its capital instruments to an order of quicker return, since they raise the ratio of the "capacity" or productivity of instruments to their cost. By focusing on situations involving changes in technical knowledge or learning by doing, where the time required for a new technique of production to become established is an integral part of the analysis, the infant-industry argument pertains to the realm of capital theory rather than that of trade theory. As has been many times remarked (see e.g., James 1965c: 158–9), this argument is not inconsistent with a free-trade philosophy. Its appeal rests on the fact that after an infant industry has been successfully launched, there is improvement in the world allocation of resources.

## Conclusion

According to the mainstream theory of international trade, free trade is optimal if certain static assumptions are satisfied, such as a given technology, given factors of production and a frictionless and timeless movement along a given production possibility surface. These assumptions are not relevant to an analysis of infant industries, which focuses on the introduction of a new technology and the accompanying benefits and costs. The establishment of infant industries implies a change in the nature of a country's comparative advantage, and its successful implementation may well require government promotion.[16] Rae was confident that the manufacturing sector offered many instances of industries which can be successfully transferred to a developing economy from abroad. As this transfer occurs, the technology is actually "carried to greater and greater excellence, by passing from one region and people to another" (Rae 1834: 258). Conversely, if a technique of production is confined to a particular community, the presumption is that it is still in its infancy, and that it will advance towards maturity only if it becomes diffused to other countries. In analyzing the changeable nature of specialization in different countries, none of which can claim any commodity as one of its "natural productions," Rae became a remarkable forerunner of recent theorizing on the creation of comparative advantage.

## Notes

1 Vanderbilt University.

2 Mill ([1871] 1920: 869) was also impressed with Rae's views on the desirability of taxing luxuries, which he advocated in his *Principles of Political Economy*, citing both Rae and Sismondi in support.

3 It is unfortunate that Mill was apparently not struck by, because he never mentioned, Rae's treatment in Book II of the *New Principles* of the power of invention as the mainspring of economic development.

4 In discussing the infant industry argument, many authors have quoted in whole or in part Mill's paragraph. Even though it contains the statement that, "it is a just remark of Mr. Rae, that nothing has a greater tendency to promote improvements in any branch of production than its trial under a new set of conditions" (Mill [1871] 1920: 922), it is disconcerting to note that these authors, instead of following up on Rae's work, often ignore it.

5 James (1965b: 149) has concisely expressed this relation by means of the formula $(1 + r)^x = 2$, where $x$ is the order of the instrument in terms of years and $r$ is the internal rate of return.

6 Dimand has pointed out in this volume (pp. 177–84) that Rae's first analysis of infant industries appeared in an unsigned article ([1825] 1965) which James has attributed to him and, according to Dimand, "closely prefigured aspects of Rae's *New Principles*."

7 The *Report on Manufactures* even contained a citation (devoid of attribution) from the *Wealth of Nations*. For comparisons between these two publications, see Bourne (1894) and Rabbeno (1895). Bourne presented lists of related passages from both sources in parallel columns. He noted that: "Hamilton nowhere in the report mentions Adam Smith's name. Why should he have concealed the source of such valuable elements in his report? The answer, I think, is a simple one, – political expediency. The citation of an English writer on Political Economy would have weakened rather than strengthened his case" (Bourne 1894: 329).

8 Rae (1834: 12) noted that the process of growing rich differs between individuals and nations, since, "as individuals seem generally to grow rich by grasping a larger and larger portion of the wealth already in existence, nations do so by the production of wealth that did not previously exist. The two processes differ in this, that the one is an acquisition, the other a creation."

9 As Goodwin (1961: 126, 202) has pointed out: "Rae listed cases in which the transfer between countries of productive modes had altered comparative cost relationships. . . . John Rae, writing in Canada but unappreciated, was the only contemporary theorist who explained clearly the distinction and the possible conflict between short run optimum allocation and long run growth."

10 Hamilton had made a similar point, though without mentioning Smith.

11 Brewer (1990: 289–90) has stressed that Rae viewed knowledge as a public good and that he required the existence of some form of market failure in order to make a case for the promotion of infant industries.

12 Hollander in this volume (see pp. 199–221) provides "a series of qualifications that rule out any charge of irresponsible interventionism against [Rae]" (p. 200).

13 Mill's ([1871] 1920: 922) formulation was that: "it is essential that the protection should be confined to cases in which there is good ground of assurance that the industry which it fosters will after a time be able to dispense with it; nor should the domestic producers ever be allowed to expect that it will be continued to them beyond the time necessary for a fair trial of what they are capable of accomplishing." The terms "Mill test" and "Bastable test" were

coined by Kemp (1960: 65; 1964: 186), who combined them into the "Mill-Bastable dogma."

14 The desirability that protection for infant industries be time-limited is well brought out in Rae ([1825] 1965: 200, 202), as quoted by Dimand (see p. 181).

15 Maneschi (1998) examines this issue in greater detail.

16 For recent models which highlight policy-induced changes in comparative advantage, see Krugman (1990) and Lucas (1993).

# Part IV

# THE DEVELOPMENT OF ECONOMIC IDEAS

# 12

# JOHN RAE AND ADAM SMITH

*Samuel Hollander*[1]

## Introduction

John Rae represented Smith as maintaining an unconditional laissez faire stance regarding economic development. Sometimes he attributed the view that "legislative interference [is] necessarily and essentially evil" to "the followers of Adam Smith,"[2] but Smith himself is also held responsible (Rae 1834: 76–7). His concern was to show to the contrary "that the legislator may operate with advantage to the community, 1st. in the transfer of foreign arts to his own country; 2d, in applying to useful purposes funds which would otherwise be dissipated in luxury" (Rae 1834: 362). The primary purpose of this chapter is to demonstrate how close – despite appearances – Smith and Rae were *in practice*, considering not only Smith's significant allowances for government intervention, but also Rae's own profound caution.

In the second section we establish the broad lines of Rae's critique of Smith, particularly a charge against him of ruinous inconsistency, considering (1) Smith's own recognition of foreign sources of new technology, and even of the possibility that, by way of intervention, some industries might be established sooner than otherwise; and also (2) Smith's own case against luxury consumption. These concessions should have led Smith to recommend intervention. The third section elaborates on Smith's presumptive case for unregulated development, and shows that Rae misrepresented Smith by attributing to him the notion that the pattern of world trade is fixed by Providence, and by failing to convey the richness of Smith's technical case for the operation of the free market in the development context. Thereafter, we show that while Rae was correct to point out Smith's own recognition of international transfers of technology and his objections to "luxury," he at the same time failed to realize that Smith had in fact followed through by recommending a degree of intervention. Thus, in the fourth section, we demonstrate Smith's allowance for state intervention, where problems relating to knowledge, skill, or risk are encountered in the development process. That his hostile attitude towards luxury consumption also justified for him a degree of intervention is shown in the fifth section. The details of Rae's own case for the protection of infant industries are examined in the final section, particularly a series of qualifications that rule out any charge of irresponsible interventionism against him.[3] On these grounds, I am led to conclude that there is no sharp divide on development policy between Smith and Rae, a notion unfortunately encouraged by Rae himself in his famous preface (Rae 1834: xiii).[4]

## Rae's critique

We will be concerned with two aspects of Rae's critique of Smith's supposedly unqualified laissez-faire recommendation regarding economic growth. Both reflect a broad complaint that Smith committed the so-called error of composition, that he applied "[t]erms, and so also, reasonings, fitly applied to the operation of individuals in the preservation, enjoyment, and increase of wealth . . . immediately to societies" (Rae 1834: 381).

The first relates to Smith's preoccupation with the role of capital accumulation in the growth process. Rae objected:

> that individuals, as well as nations, acquire wealth from other sources than mere saving from revenue; that skill is as necessary, and consequently as valuable, a cooperator with the industry of both, as either capital or parsimony and that therefore the expenditure which either may be called on to make to attain the requisite skill, is very well bestowed.
>
> (Rae 1834: 61)

The criticism allows that Smith's link between accumulation and the augmentation of national wealth entails the facilitation afforded division of labor and increased efficiency, and that this expansion of real income in turn adds to potential for accumulation and further extension of division of labor. The problem though remained – namely that, according to Smith:

> the augmentation of the industry of the society is produced by an augmentation of its capital, and in no other manner, and its capital augmented by saving from revenue and nothing else, and that, from the action and reaction of these principles on each other, the whole phenomena of the growth of national capital are deducible.
>
> (Rae 1834: 67–8)

While "interference," Rae admitted, would indeed probably reduce the rate of accumulation in the short run and thus reduce the capital stock below what it would otherwise be – it might yet raise the *efficacy* of the capital stock (a contrast between so-called relative and absolute capital), and finally increase its magnitude (Rae 1834: 381–2). Adam Smith and his followers thus neglected a potential role for the state in the generation of knowledge. The sort of intervention Rae himself countenanced is formally described as "whatever promotes invention; 1. By advancing the progress of science and art within the community; 2. By the transfer from other communities of the sciences and arts there generated" (Rae 1834: 362).

Alexander Hamilton – American Secretary to the Treasury – in his *Report on Manufactures* (1791) to the Congress had long since supported infant-industry protection and various forms of subsidy, offering "very cogent reasons" against the position that "manufactures, without the aid of government, will grow up as soon and as fast as the natural state of things and the interest of the community may require" (Hamilton [1791]: 203). Those reasons:

> have relation to the strong influence of habit and the spirit of imitation; the fear of want of success in untried enterprises; the intrinsic difficulties incident to first essays towards a competition with those who have previously attained to perfection in the business to be attempted: the bounties, premiums, and other artificial encouragements with which foreign nations second the exertions of their own citizens, in the branches in which they are to be rivaled.[5]

Strangely, Rae did not formally refer to this case, but in expatiating on the "large indirect effect" of intervention – in his terminology "carrying instruments to orders of quicker return, by stimulating invention, and diminishing the propensity to servile imitation" – he did recognize Hamilton's proposition that:

> [e]very useful art is so connected with many, or with all others, that whatever renders its products more easily attainable, facilitates the operations of a whole circle of arts, and introduces change – the great agent in producing improvements – under the most favourable form.
>
> (Rae 1834: 365)

The specific citation from Hamilton makes out the case even with respect to "things in themselves not positively advantageous" since these "sometimes become so, by their tendency to provoke exertion. Every new scene which is opened to the busy nature of man, to rouse and exert himself, is the addition of a new energy to the general stock of effort" (Hamilton [1791] 1957: 196).[6] Though at this juncture Rae deliberately limits himself to "commodities, not luxuries" in his discussion of indirect effects, there is a certain ambivalence about his position in this regard.[7]

A further objection emerges in a reaction to Smith's remark that "whether the advantages which one country has over another be natural or acquired, is in this respect [the case for international specialization] of no consequence" (Smith [1776] 1937: 425). It mattered greatly, Rae observed quite rightly, if:

> a country can often with ease, and at trifling expense, acquire the practical skill and the knowledge of particular arts and manufactures which another possesses, and, by doing so, gain the advantage of procuring for itself the products of this skill and knowledge at home, instead of having to go abroad for them.
>
> (Rae 1834, 71–2)

And in justifying intervention to assist with set-up costs too high for individuals to meet – the case for infant-industry protection – Rae objected to Smith's famous remark regarding the technical possibility of growing grapes in Scotland; for Smith, while he recognized the actual phenomenon of "acquired" advantages, neglected to explore the true rationale for such acquisition in the first place. In fact, Rae subsequently goes so far as to attribute to Smith the notion of a more-or-less permanently fixed pattern of trade:

> the products of different regions are spoken of by political economists, as bestowed on them by nature, are termed natural productions, and the attempt to transfer them to other sites, is held to be a procedure in opposition to the designs of providence, whose intentions, it is asserted, in giving them these productions, were, that the inhabitants of different countries should exchange the products of their several territories with one another . . . [But] because one country alone now produces particular commodities, we are by no means warranted to conclude that nature intended they should be produced only there.
>
> (Rae 1834: 257–8)

The second aspect of Rae's case against Smith that concerns us relates to Smith's purported objection to any intervention that raises the cost of commodities, including "luxuries."[8] From Rae's perspective:

> if there be any class of commodities, the estimation of which depends wholly, or in part, on their power to mark the possession of a certain relative superiority, or a command greater or less of the labor of other men, then the generally diminished cost of such commodities, lessening their power to mark the desired distinction, and taking thus in a like degree from that for which they

> were altogether, or in part, esteemed, either makes no change in the general revenue, or a smaller change than that indicated by the amount of the diminution.
>
> (Rae 1834: 383)

In these terms, Rae made out a case for the taxation of goods characterized by a sort of conspicuous consumption, "giving a revenue to the legislator, and taking nothing from the society" (Rae 1834: 372).[9]

This second class of legitimate intervention involving "whatever prevents the dissipation in luxury, of any portion of the funds of the community," is in a sense the reverse of the first, since knowledge applied in the luxury sector entails positive social waste: "The labor expended in the formation of luxuries, is so much direct loss to the community, one man's superiority being here equivalent to anothers inferiority" (Rae 1834: xix). Any benefits flowing from "invention" and "improvement" when applied to luxuries, would be at most "indirect" and "accidental"; the "direct operation is always to dissipate a part of the national funds proportioned to its strength" (Rae 1834: 292).[10] Throughout it is implied that "direct" effects normally exceed "indirect" effects, but the case against luxuries is obviously diminished by the allowance for some positive indirect effects or spillovers emanating therefrom (see also Rae 1834: 290–1).

Rae represented Smith's formal position as one excluding all sources of new knowledge bar those relating to internal expansion.[11] Yet he points out that Smith had *himself* acknowledged international transfers of technology, thereby undermining his own position:

> Arts and manufactures, the great sources of increase to the productive powers of labor, do, *it is granted*, pass from country to country.[12] It would appear then, that the gradual increase which the accumulation of capital produces on the productive powers of any society, is not alone sufficient to call forth all the resources which that society possesses. [emphasis added]
>
> (Rae 1834: 68)

The damage was yet greater since Smith had also admitted "that a manufacture may be introduced by government intervention by the operations of the legislator, sooner than it could otherwise be, and thus come to be made at home as cheap, or cheaper, than abroad" (Rae 1834: 69).[13]

As for the charge against Smith regarding the matter of "luxury," it is not that he neglected to allow for intervention in a minor range of cases. The neglect was all but incomprehensible, since Smith who had himself so clearly recognized the luxury phenomenon and its extensiveness,[14] had yet "not thought it necessary to adduce any reasons to show that the operations of the legislator, on such commodities, may not have the beneficial effects indicated in [Rae's] text" (Rae 1834: 383 n.).

## Smith's presumptive case for "unregulated" development

Rae's assertion that Smith considered "attempt[s] to transfer" industries to conflict with "the designs of providence" is unjustified.[15] Smith's presumption in favour of unregulated development rests on a firmer foundation than Rae apparently imagined, a foundation entailing a concept of national "advantage" in terms of relative factor endowment, as I have shown elsewhere with particular reference to his analysis of the colonies (Smith [1776] 1937: 547–9 as treated in Hollander 1987: ch. 7). Smith's analysis of development can scarcely be appreciated apart from the processes of competitive resource allocation in an international context.

Now, though international trade divorced the domestic growth process from strict dependence on domestic agriculture, an economy which happened to enjoy extensive agricultural resources possessed advantages over the economy which lacked them, so that "landed nations" were ill-advised to industrialize by artificial means. Ultimately, when conditions were suitable in terms of resource endowment, manufactures would be set up "naturally" in the agricultural economy. And these would be able to compete against those of already well-established manufacturing economy – initially in the domestic market only, but subsequently even in the foreign markets – for Smith was convinced (though he provided no grounds for this conviction) that *any initial disadvantage in skills would be temporary only and, in any event, counterbalanced by the presumed availability of cheap domestic raw materials and food supplies*:

> The continual increase of the surplus produce of their land, would, in due time, create a greater capital than what could be employed with the ordinary rate of profit in the improvement and cultivation of land; and the surplus part of it would naturally turn itself to the employment of artificers and manufacturers at home. But those artificers and manufacturers, *finding at home both the materials of their work and the fund of their subsistence, might immediately, even with much less art and skill, be able to work as cheap as the like artificers and manufacturers of such mercantile states. who had both to bring from a great distance* . . . The cheapness of the manufactures of those landed nations, *in consequence of the gradual improvements of art and skill*, would in due time, extend their sale beyond the home market, and carry them to many foreign markets, from which they would in the same manner gradually jostle out many of the manufactures of such mercantile nations. [emphasis added]
>
> (Smith [1776] 1937: 635)[16]

Thus *all* economies in the "natural" course of development would initially devote their growing capital and labor resources to agriculture alone, and subsequently introduce and extend manufactures. *But the more substantial and productive the agricultural base, the sounder will be the ability to proceed ultimately to the successful development of a manufacturing sector.*

## Smith and the infant-industry problem

Smith's case for unregulated development turns on the assumption that no special problems are to be expected regarding the acquisition of knowledge – on this he is explicit in the foregoing passage. It is also implied that no other impediments, such as unusual riskiness, attach to novel ventures. What, though, if these assumptions cannot be sustained? We turn next to this matter.

Jacob Viner cited early formulations of the argument for the temporary protection of young industries by various seventeenth- and eighteenth-century writers – Yarranton, Wood, Dobbs, Bindon, Steuart, and Tucker – and without elaborating he described Smith's reaction as "somewhat over-critical" (Viner 1937: 712). Smith allowed that by intervention it "may sometimes" be possible to stimulate the earlier development of a particular industry; but any such stimulation would involve the diversion of capital from other activities and reduce national income below the level it would otherwise attain, and thus (probably) reduce the surplus and consequently the rate of capital accumulation:

> By means of such regulations, indeed, a particular manufacture may sometimes be acquired sooner than it could have been otherwise, and after a certain time may be made at home as cheap or cheaper than in the foreign country. But though the industry of the society may be thus carried with advantage into a particular channel sooner than it could have been otherwise, it will by no means follow that the sum total, either of its industry, or of its revenue, can ever be augmented by any such regulation.
>
> (Smith [1776] 1937: 425)[17]

In this statement against intervention, the protected industry would, after the withdrawal of support, stand on its own feet, though it is presumed that it would *ultimately* have been able to do so even without protection – it is only a matter of its *earlier* development by artificial means. This latter presumption finds analytical support in the technical argument referred to in the third section, that the optimal pattern of investment adopted at any stage of a country's development depends on circumstances, and, in particular, on quantitative differentials in factor endowment between countries and changes therein over time. Smith's case is far stronger than Rae imagined. But Smith extended his position against protection to instances where the industry in question would *not* be established in the absence of support, and gives the expected response – that in such an event nothing is necessarily lost:

> Though for want of such regulations the society should never acquire the proposed manufacture, it would not, upon that account, necessarily be the poorer in any one period of its duration. In every period of its duration its whole capital and industry might still have been employed, though upon different objects, *in the manner that was most advantageous at the time*. In every period its revenue might have been the greatest which its capital could afford, and both capital and revenue might have been augmented with the greatest possible rapidity. [emphasis added]
>
> (Smith [1776] 1937: 425)

Now the question arises whether by "never acquire" was intended, never acquire because the industry in question was inappropriate for that country, or because of costly (or risky) set-up costs. The allusion to the pattern of activity "most advantageous *at the time*" suggests that Smith intended the first situation. That he had nothing to say about the second seems to justify Viner's estimate that he had been "overcritical" in taking his skeptical position regarding intervention, since it neglects the most interesting issue – the case for support of industries that would be self-supporting *provided transitional difficulties can be overcome*. There are tangential references to the problem but it is not properly dealt with:

> Whether the advantages which one country has over another, be natural *or acquired*, is . . . of no consequence. As long as one country has those advantages, and the other wants them, it will always be more advantageous for the latter, rather to buy the former than to make it. It is an acquired advantage only which the artificer has over his neighbour, who exercises another trade; and yet they both find it more advantageous to buy of one another, than to make what does not belong to their particular trades. [emphasis added]
>
> (Smith [1776] 1937: 425–6)

But *how* and *why* "acquired"? – These are the issues Smith failed to address in this context, and Rae's charges seem to be confirmed.[18]

When, however, we look further afield the picture clears somewhat, and provides some indication of how Smith might have responded to Hamilton's case for intervention to counter the "fear of want of success in untried enterprises."[19] The fact is that *on his own terms* he would have been hard pressed to reject that position out of hand. We shall address in turn the problem

(1) of risk relating to the *adoption of new technology* and (2) of *skill*, demonstrating Smith's allowances for government intervention where such problems are encountered.

Certainly, there is much to be said for Spengler's view of Smith's undertaker as a "prudent, cautious, not overly imaginative fellow, who adjusts to circumstances rather than brings about their modification," and of Smithian technical progress as "primarily the product of a vast number of minor changes introduced by a multitude of comparatively small undertakers," rather than "the result of activity on the part of a minority of creative leaders" (Spengler 1959a: 8–9; also 1975: 398–400, 411). Yet this is far from the full picture. Novel techniques available to the firm may also derive from developments occurring in other industries, particularly with suppliers of equipment and with full-time inventors, though it is true that these sources of knowledge turn on the growing opportunities for specialization created by expansion of the industry and of the economy as a whole (Smith [1776] 1937: 86, 10). *And there is also the recognition of foreign sources of new technology deriving from commercial contact.*[20] Though this phenomenon too reflects a widening of the dimensions of the economy, it extends far beyond increased opportunities for "division of labor" with scale in a strict and narrow sense of the term.

But there is more.[21] Smith did recognize innovative activity *unrelated to scale as such* and appreciated the *risk* attached to it; his objection to bank-financing of long-term and capital-intensive industrial and agricultural projects does not mean that such projects were entirely neglected (Smith [1776] 1937: 279 ff.). Costly innovatory investment undertaken with the prospect of extraordinary returns in the face of risk is discussed explicitly thus:

> The establishment of any new manufacture, of any new branch of commerce, or of any new practice in agriculture, is always a speculation, from which the projector promises himself extraordinary profits. These profits sometimes are very great, and sometimes, more frequently, perhaps, they are quite otherwise; but in general they bear no regular proportion to those of other old trades in the neighbourhood. If the project succeeds, they are commonly at first very high. When the trade or practice becomes thoroughly established and well known, the competition reduces them to the level of other trades.
>
> (Smith [1776] 1937: 115)[22]

Indeed, Smith qualified his well-known minimization – on grounds of typical negligence of management divorced from control by the owners – of the potentialities of the joint-stock company as a profit-making organization. Thus if the undertaking required particularly heavy conscription of capital (as with banks, insurance companies, canals, and water-works) there might be a legitimate argument for the establishment of a joint-stock organization (Smith [1776] 1937: 714). *And it is also conceded that a joint stock trading company might justifiably be formed in the case of a new, risky, and expensive venture which, if successful, might even be accorded a temporary monopoly*. These were the same grounds that justified patent and copyright protection:

> When a company of merchants undertake, at their own risk and expense, to establish a new trade with some remote and barbarous nation, it may not be unreasonable to incorporate them into a joint-stock company, and to grant them, in case of their success, a monopoly of the trade for a certain number of years. *It is the easiest and most natural way in which the state can recompense them for hazarding a dangerous and expensive experiment, of which the public is afterwards to reap the benefit*. A temporary monopoly of this kind may be vindicated upon the same principles upon which a like monopoly of a new machine is granted to its inventor, and that of a new book to its author. [emphasis added]
>
> (Smith [1776] 1937: 712)

Here is a nice instance of legitimate intervention to assure a social return otherwise unattainable.

As for agriculture, Smith recommended that care be taken to choose those forms of land taxation least likely to affect the profits yielded by improvement. For example, increased land values due to improvements should be exempt from taxation for a fixed term of several years (Smith [1776] 1937: 784).[23] In the same context, he also recognized the expense and risk attached to inventive activity; it is only the wealthy landlord who can afford to undertake risky experiments relating to land improvements. Here, Smith had in mind the new commercial landowners who had all the personal qualities necessary for successful improvement. And elsewhere he speaks of them as "bold undertakers" willing to make large innovatory expenditures (ibid. 384–5).

It is fair to conclude that in Smith's view a certain range of inventive and innovative activity does require costly investment and entail a significant element of risk, considerations which justify some degree of government intervention to assure that the potential social return is captured. *The argument can be applied in principle to support those "infant industries" constrained by transitional difficulties, though Smith himself did not do so*. It is noteworthy, however, that Smith's allowance for a monopoly to be accorded new trading ventures turned on "*their success*."[24] Such caution, as we shall see, characterizes Rae, who suggested a practical means of satisfying this condition.[25]

We turn next to the treatment of skill. Apart from institutional impediments to the process by which wages in different occupations were kept in line, Smith was apparently confident that the market process could be relied upon to generate appropriate supplies of skilled labor (Smith [1776] 1937: 437); on these grounds he condemned contemporary practices relating to apprenticeship (ibid. 134–5; also 123).[26] In fact, the degree of skill required in manufacturing was less than that in agriculture, where the system of apprenticeship was not applied (ibid. 101, 126–7). Nonetheless, it is allowed that "[the] first invention of such beautiful machines [clocks and watches] . . . and even that of the some of the instruments employed in making them, must, no doubt have been the work of deep thought and long time" (ibid. 123); it is only "when both have been fairly invented and are well understood" that the skills required in both application and construction of the appropriate instruments and machinery can be easily and rapidly attained. This allowance is no mere aside. It emerges again as the exception to the usual coincidence of private and social returns to skill in a citation from David Hume:

> Most of the arts and professions in a state, are of such a nature, that while they promote the interests of the society, they are also useful and agreeable to some individuals; and in that case, the constant rule of the magistrate, *except, perhaps, on the first introduction of any art*, is, to leave the profession to itself, and trust its encouragement to the individuals who reap the benefit of it. [emphasis added]
>
> (Smith [1776] 1937: 742)

The allowance that government aid might be called for "on the first introduction of any art" is of obvious importance in our context. Smith opposed government aid to *specific* types of skill, arguing that in the absence of institutional restrictions and (as we shall see) *with the extension of elementary education*, monopoly returns would be competed away. Accordingly, the consequence of intervention would be to drive the returns to skilled trades below the competitive level and thereby generate "inadequate" wage differentials (Smith [1776] 1937: 129–30). But this case does not, it is clear, apply to *new* skills, entailing as they do a disequilibrium situation.

Smith's case for intervention extends beyond the issue of new skills. He allowed that workers could not afford a costly education (ibid. 737). And he accordingly justified government support of elementary education on grounds of a divergence between social and private returns.[27] A modernized curriculum was recommended extending to "geometry and mechanics" (ibid. 737–8). Thus, though the emphasis is formally upon *elementary* education, the case for public aid relates not only to beneficial "social" effects of a general kind resulting from literacy, but also to specifically economic advantages with an eye to productivity.

The economic advantages are implied not only in the curriculum recommended. It is also the case that amongst the stultifying effects of specialization – which could be neutralized by education – Smith included the danger that the industrial worker would find it ultimately impossible to operate "in any other employment than that to which he has been bred" (ibid. 735). We conclude that Smith's optimism, regarding the high degree of mobility upon which was based his confidence in the operation of the free market in the provision of skills, was contingent upon a necessary minimum degree of elementary training, *towards which government was advised to contribute*.

From all this we conclude that Smith recognized the extraordinary costs attached to novel ventures – both regarding risk and skill – and, to this extent, allowed for some state intervention. Now his formal argument against the support of infant industries, we found,[28] left open his reaction in the case of industries with high potential but whose set-up costs relating to risk and acquisition of skilled labor precluded their initial establishment. The evidence we have accumulated suggests that Smith could not, as a matter of principle, have ruled out of court Hamilton's argument for intervention in such cases. Indeed, a *formal* place for such an allowance exists under Smith's class of "public works" – projects "of the highest degree advantageous to a great society [but] of such a nature that the profit could never repay the expense to any individual or small number of individuals, and which it therefore cannot be expected, that any individual or small number of individuals should erect or maintain" (Smith [1776] 1937: 681) – especially since infant-industry protection would be *temporary*.

Brewer (1990: 289) has, in fact, called attention to Rae's representation of knowledge as a public good (1834: 217, 222), the production of which is subject to market failure (Rae 1834: 51–2). It falls precisely into the Smithian category. And for the reasons just given, I am not convinced that Smith would *necessarily as a matter of principle* have objected. Certainly, he would have insisted on some minimum assurance of the ultimate success of the protected infant;[29] but we shall presently see that this was also a major concern of Rae, and one for which he offered a practical solution.[30]

We must, however, register a caution. Smith's justification of the going usury laws (to which we turn in the next section) puts "projectors" on a par with "prodigals," seemingly portraying the former (as Bentham complained) as "all such persons as, in the pursuit of wealth, strike out into any new channel, and more especially into any new channel of invention," for "in the nature of things, no new trade, no trade carried on in any new channel, can afford a security equal to that which may be afforded by a trade carried on in any of the old ones" (Bentham [1787] 1952, 1: 168, 170).[31] And there is something to Bentham's objection, since Smith at one point identifies the antisocial effect of "projection" and of "misconduct," here alluding to "[e]very injudicious and unsuccessful project in agriculture, mines, fisheries, trade or manufactures," which leads on to bankruptcy (Smith [1776] 1937: 325). There is no hint here that bankruptcy might reflect failure that cannot reasonably be termed "misconduct." Against this, we have encountered a more tolerant position in Smith (ibid. 115, cited above, p. 207). We are obliged to say that though Smith did not neglect true innovation, as we have argued, he certainly did not *consistently emphasize it*.[32]

## Smith and luxury

Notwithstanding Smith's presumptive case for nonintervention based *inter alia* on the "natural right" of individuals not to be interfered with and the technical case for the market, intervention in the interest of expansion was not rejected out of hand. Smith, we have seen, made the extraordinary concession that since most investors were unable to use their funds prudently and safely, the maintenance of the maximum interest rate imposed by the usury laws was necessary to prevent "prodigals and projectors" from cornering the supply of loans ([1776] 1937: 339–40).[33]

This and various other instances of legitimate intervention[34] are designed to encourage effective *investment* at the expense of purely speculative ventures and "prodigal" uses. And they reflect, or at least are consistent with, Smith's disapproval of excessive ("luxury") consumption.[35] The notion of "luxury" as entailing a form of conspicuous consumption is clarified in a contrast between "true" utility and "status-oriented" utility. For any given degree of the former, desirability rises with expense:

> With the greater part of rich people, the chief enjoyment of riches consists in the parade of riches, which in their eye is never so complete as when they appear to possess those decisive marks of opulence which nobody can possess but themselves. [In their eyes], the merit of an object which is in any degree either useful or beautiful, is greatly enhanced by its scarcity, or by the great labour which it requires to collect any considerable quantity of it, a labour which nobody can afford to pay but themselves. Such objects they are willing to purchase at a higher price than things much more beautiful and useful, but more common.
>
> (Smith [1776] 1937: 172)[36]

The same notion emerges in the essay 'Of the Imitative Arts' (1980: 182–83) – undated, but probably "the product of a mature understanding."[37]

Though Smith made no formal application of the principle to the taxation of luxuries (unlike Rae or Sismondi or J.S. Mill, see above, p. 203), the later welfare application is a direct deduction from the Smithian perspective – it is only that Smith did not hit upon it. More important, the allowances for tax abatements of various sorts to encourage investment by landlords and the legitimization of an interest-rate maximum all point, as mentioned, to the generation of capital accumulation at the expense of what otherwise would be wasted in "prodigality," that is, in luxury consumption. It may be added that he also recommended higher tolls on the luxury carriages of the rich than upon freight, whereby "the indolence and vanity of the rich is made to contribute in a very easy manner to the relief of the poor, by rendering cheaper the transportation of heavy goods to all the different parts of the country" ([1776] 1937: 683).

Smith's denigration of excessive consumption extended even to the labouring class, though the definition of the term "luxury" differed considerably ([1776] 1937: 821–2).[38] However, the possibility that productive workers might choose to enjoy any increase in real wages by expenditure on "luxury" goods plays havoc, potentially, with the automatic population response usually envisaged. And indeed, Smith suggested the use of excise taxes to alter the pattern of working-class consumption as a device to assure population expansion, by directing consumption away from "luxuries" and towards more healthful categories (ibid. 823).

## Rae's program in practice

Rae's presumptive case was in favour of intervention just as Smith's was opposed (1834: 360). And the normal course of events had, in fact, involved progress fueled by international transfers of knowledge (Rae 1834: 363). That is taken for granted. Fortunately, Rae turns to a more specific and responsible statement of rules for intervention:

> The question . . . resolves itself into particulars and the investigation of the political economist, would seem to be confined to tracing out, from the principles of his science, rules determining when the passage of any art is practicable, and when the benefits derived from it will exceed, or fall short of the necessary expense of effecting the passage. It is not my intention to attempt a full discussion of these various particulars. It will be sufficient for the object in view, to enumerate the general advantages which such transfers produce, and to state some of the chief circumstances, favourable, and some of the others adverse to their success.
>
> (Rae 1834: 364)

The striking feature of Rae's position which emerges when he does descend to specifics, is the *minimization of the broad case for intervention based on spillover effects*.[39] Thus a "completely successful" protective measure would be one such that "the commodity, the product of the art in question, comes to be made at the same cost in the country to which its manufacture is transferred, as in that from which it comes, or at less cost than there" (ibid.), and:

> while the legislator is called on to act, he is also called on to act cautiously, and to regulate his proceedings by an attentive consideration of the progress of events. He is never justifiable in attempting to transfer arts yielding utilities from foreign countries to his own, unless he have sufficient reason to conclude that they will ultimately lessen the cost of the commodities they produce, or are of such a nature, that the risk of waste to the stock of the community, from a sudden interruption to their importation from abroad, is sufficiently great to warrant the probable expense, both of the transfer and of maintaining the manufacture at home. It is his business first to ascertain these points, and to regulate his proceedings accordingly.
>
> (ibid. 367)

Rae went to some lengths to indicate tests to assure the avoidance of irresponsible intervention. The first relates to an assurance that "the effective desire of accumulation" does not fall short of that ruling abroad:

> When there are circumstances particularly unfavourable to the practice of the art, and no countervailing circumstances particularly favourable to it, the first introduction of it must always cost the society high, and the subsequent maintaining of it will in all probability be a burden on the common industry and stock. *Among unfavourable circumstances may be noted a strength of the effective desire of accumulation, less than that of a foreign country*, and instruments consequently remaining at orders of quicker return. This is a circumstance lying beyond the reach of the legislator, and which he cannot hope to change. If then there are no other counteracting favorable circumstances, the art cannot be transferred and preserved, but at great and continual expense. [emphasis added]
>
> (ibid.)[40]

This rule, in effect, precludes intervention in industrial development otherwise excluded by a relatively high interest rate, the consequence of a low willingness or ability to save. There is no point in artificially stimulating long-winded projects since such support would have to be permanent. It emerges, then, that Rae's support of protection applies only to those industries whose time has come, but which, presumably because of friction of various sorts, are not introduced by private initiative.[41] *We are, in practice, close to Smith.*

A second condition relates to the appropriate agricultural base:

> Among circumstances particularly favourable to the transfer of a foreign art, may be noted the raw materials of the manufacture existing within the territory of the society in abundance. The acquisition of the art in this case saves the expense of a double transport. On this account, bringing the woollen manufacture to England was a very happy measure.
>
> (ibid. 368)

*But strangely it is Smith who had specified, in making his case against forced industrialization, that a sound agricultural base contributes to the successful development of industry.*[42]

Rae's extraordinarily cautious stance is reflected in his specific recommendation for an experimental testing of the waters before any full-fledged commitment is made to support an industry. The statement in question fully confirms that his concern was to assure the establishment of domestic industries that are *appropriate*, given the circumstances, but precluded because of "the difficulties attending new undertakings, the want of skilled labor, and a sufficiently accurate knowledge of the properties of the materials to be employed," that is, are precluded because of *friction*:

> The legislator effects his purposes by premiums for successful individual imitations of the foreign article; by general bounties on the home manufacture; or by duties on that imported from abroad. Of these, premiums take so little out of the common funds, that their amount forms an item too small to enter into the calculation, in questions of national policy. *They are useful as testing the practicability of the transfer*. That having been done, it having been made sufficiently apparent that nothing prevents the branch of industry in question being established, but the difficulties attending new undertakings, the want of skilled labor, and a sufficiently accurate knowledge of the properties of the materials to be employed in the formation of the new instruments, it is then proper to proceed to direct and general encouragements by bounties or duties. In this way real capital, and healthy enterprise are directed to the art, the difficulties attending its introduction overcome in the shortest possible space, and the commodities yielded by it are produced at less outlay, and afforded at a less price than that, at which they were before imported. [emphasis added]
>
> (Rae 1834: 368)

What has happened in all this to the case for intervention turning on spillover effects? That case covers support of industries even – to use

Hamilton's terminology – "in themselves not positively advantageous," and as we know, Rae had cited Hamilton favourably in formulating his *general* position against Smith.[43] It does not completely disappear in Rae's Book Three ("Of the Operations of the Legislator on National Stock") with which we are now concerned. Thus allusion is made to savings of transport costs:

> The advantages hence resulting to the parts of the country where the new art fixes itself, may be estimated by observing the great rise in the value and rent of land which follows it. We have also a good measure of them [the advantages], in the difference between these [value and rent] in the neighbourhood of manufacturing towns and villages, and in places distant from them.
>
> (ibid. 365)[44]

A case of this sort might suggest a program of *autarchy*. But this is not Rae's position in the present applied context. Here, the transport savings are represented merely as one of "the advantages which the community derives" from "*completely successful*" interventions, as defined above – namely, support of industries that will ultimately stand on their own feet.[45]

A second spillover involves:

> a large indirect effect in carrying instruments to orders of quicker returns, by stimulating invention, and diminishing the propensity to servile imitation. Every useful art is so connected with many, or with all others, that whatever renders its products more easily attainable, facilitates the operations of a whole circle of art, and introduces change – the great agent in producing improvements – under the most favorable form.
>
> (ibid.)

Hamilton is cited, as we have seen. Again for Rae, however, the spillover effects do not alone justify intervention; such effects are treated as desirable by-products of "successful" intervention which, as we have shown, *must be justified for each case on its own terms*.[46]

There is one further consideration. Unlike Smith[47] at no point does Rae justify an interest-rate maximum to counter "prodigals and projectors" despite his hostility towards both categories: "We may . . . assume the rate of interest as a fair measure of the real average rate of profits" (Rae 1834: 196). It is Smith who, surprisingly, is the more interventionist in that regard.

## Conclusion

The contrast between Rae and Smith on the role of government in development is greatly exaggerated by Rae. This is apparent in Rae's extreme caution in practice – notwithstanding his embarrassing panegyric regarding American protectionism, his specific infant-industry case is muted indeed (see the devices suggested to avoid granting *premature* protection) and might well have served to answer some of Smith's likely objections (see also James 1965b: 1:158–9). It is apparent also in Smith's allowances for a degree of legitimate intervention where the axioms of the model on which he based his case for a freely operating development process are not satisfied.

This latter consideration diminishes the strength of Rae's charge against Smithian "system building." His complaint relates to the irresponsible adoption of axioms and their being carried out to "their extreme consequences" – the Ricardian Vice no less. Though there was a legitimate place for general systems (but not a means of "discovery"), the case:

> is completely altered, when the loose and popular principles on which such a system proceeds, are adopted as demonstrative axioms, the discoveries of real science, and are carried out to their extreme consequences. Their original purpose is then altogether changed, and instead of serving to bring before the mind a collection of facts, they lead it farther and farther away from truth and reality, into the barren and wearisome regions of mere verbal abstractions.
> (Rae 1834: 351)

This propensity prevented Smith from recognizing a role for government, notwithstanding his own "informal" allowances regarding foreign sources of technology and recognition that industry might be established by intervention "sooner than it could otherwise be" (Rae 1834: 68, 69, 76–77). Smith's denigration of "luxury" and the case allowed for intervention in the capital market similarly undermine Rae's complaint. It is to Smith's credit,[48] considering that the charge does seem to apply against certain conspicuous instances of irresponsible application by Smith,[49] and this despite the latter's own repeated warnings against excessive attachment to system as by the Physiocrats ([1759] 1976: 233; [1776] 1937: 638; [1795] 1980: 77).

## Notes

1 Department of Economics, University of Toronto. Phone: (416) 978–5105. Fax: (416) 978–6713. I am indebted to Robert Dimand, Betsey Price, and Masazumi Wakatabe for helpful comments.

2 E.g., Rae (1834: 380), where he seems to have had in mind Storch and Say.

3 In the original paper given at Aberdeen, I also considered further the legitimacy of various complaints against Smith by Rae of a methodological nature and the charge against Smith of "inconsistency" over matters of policy.

4 In a "Postscript" to the "Preface," Rae explained that he had no need to expound at length on the American "policy of the protective system" in a book prepared for the American market: "The doctrines which Adam Smith maintained with

so much ability, never took so deep [a] hold in this country as in England, and they have been more strongly opposed. There is, hence, a very considerable difference between the state of public sentiment in Great Britain and America, concerning the most interesting practical questions of political economy. This is especially the case with regard to the policy of the protective system. The practical bearings of that system on the condition of things in this republic, have been discussed so often, and with so much ability, that probably few new arguments or facts concerning it can be brought forward by any one, least of all can they be expected from a foreigner. Although, therefore, *I look on the effects of the policy pursued by the legislature of the United States, as affording the best practical illustration hitherto existing of the correctness of some of the principles I maintain*, I have scarcely at all referred to them for that purpose, but have contented myself with showing how the benefits resulting from the operations of the legislature, in this and in other similar cases, are to be accounted for" (emphasis added) (Rae 1834: xiii).

It is not absolutely clear what Rae had in mind by his panegyric. A new, stringent tariff, the so-called Tariff of Abominations, had been introduced in 1828. This was the "culminating point of the first period of the American policy" (Smart 1910, 2: 461), and was replaced in 1830 and 1832 by "a more moderate application of the protective principle," in concessions to opposition from the Southern states (Taussig [1931] 1964: 102–3).

The Postscript dated 1834 was added to the Preface dated 1833 the year that the book was completed. Though Rae had planned to publish in England, he was persuaded by Alexander Everett (publisher of the *North American Review*) to publish in Boston as part of his protectionist campaign (Dorfman 1946: 780).

5 Hamilton had earlier stated that in the absence of *foreign* interventions which undermined the "system of perfect liberty," any case for *domestic* intervention would be far weaker; indeed, "the option ought, perhaps, always be in favour of leaving industry to its own direction" (Hamilton [1791] 1957: 201). Semmel (1970: 177–78) describes Hamilton as one of the "national economists," a group including Daniel Raymond, Friedrich List, and Henry Carey, contributing to a "Mercantilist revival."

6 Cf. Rae's emphasis on positive spillover or external effects generated by the acquisition of skill – e.g., the greater "durability" of national than individual skill since it extends beyond a simple lifetime – creating an excess of social over private return (Rae 1834: 61).

7 See below, pp. 202–3.

8 The appellation "luxury" applies "[i]n so far as any commodity, when compared with another, excels it only in the gratification it affords to vanity . . . [;] in so far as it compares with others in the capacity which its physical qualities give it to gratify real wants, it is to be considered as a utility" (Rae 1834: xix). It is admitted that "[t]here are few commodities . . . in which utility, as well as vanity, has not a considerable share" (Rae 1834: 286).

9 J.S. Mill cited and elaborated upon Rae's argument in support of the taxation of luxuries, attributing it also to Sismondi (Mill [1848] 1965, 3: 869). For a comparison of Veblen with Rae emphasizing similarities – though Veblen avoided specific policy prescriptions – see Edgell and Tilman (1991).

10 In fact, the contrasting impact of invention provided a means of distinguishing the two categories of true *utilities* and *luxuries*.
11 See above, p. 201.
12 Cf. also: "It [is] acknowledged by every one, even by yourself, that the improvements of the productive powers of labor thus effected by the continued spread of the arts of civilized life from country to country, are among the chief causes of the progress of national wealth and property" (Rae 1834: 68). On Smith's allowances for foreign transfers of technology, see above, p. 207.
13 On this matter, see above, p. 204.
14 For the main statement by Smith, see [1776] 1937: 172. See also above, p. 211.
15 See above, p. 202.
16 Cf. also (Smith [1776] 1937: 393) where Britain's bright prospect is partly related to the "natural fertility of the soil" as well as excellent means of transport.
17 Also: "No regulation of commerce can increase the quantity of industry in any society beyond what its capital can maintain. It can only divert a part of it into a direction into which it might not otherwise have gone; and it is by no means certain that this artificial direction is likely to be more advantageous to the society than that into which it would have gone on its own accord" (Smith [1776] 1937: 421).
18 See above, p. 202. Only two cases for intervention are allowed, the first of which – the case for protection of defense industries – applies even if the industry would *not* be able to stand on its feet after the withdrawal of protection (Smith [1776] 1937: 429–30). The second case relates to equalizing taxes (Smith [1776] 1937: 431–32).
19 See above, pp. 201–2.
20 See above, pp. 202–3. Regarding China, Europe and the colonies, for example, see Smith [1776] 1937: 645, 242, and 532.
21 I base myself on Hollander 1987: 166–70. See also Elmslie 1994.
22 It appears from the text that Smith seems to have had in mind particularly the new Birmingham trades (Hollander 1973: 105).
23 Similarly, the church tithe is condemned because it reduces the motive for "expensive improvements" (Smith [1776] 1937: 789). Cf. ibid. 879–80 for further warning against introducing changes in the system of taxation which might threaten the return on landlord's investments.
24 See above, pp. 207–8.
25 See above, p. 214.
26 This may have been an error of judgement. It was partly because the Carron ironworks could not supply the skilled artisans whose help was essential that Watt's experiments on the steam engine could not be easily completed (Ashton 1966: 68).
27 The government would establish parish schools. The teachers would be paid in part from public funds. Fees would also be charged to assure against the "dereliction of his duty."
28 See above, p. 206.
29 See above, p. 208.

30 I do not, however, wish to go overboard. There remains a quite legitimate objection that is at least hinted at in Smith ([1776] 1937: 425; see above, p. 205) and well formulated in modern development texts. E.g., infant-industry protection "alone is an ineffective means of promoting economic growth" if it "overlooks the problem of capital supply. This is the task of creation, of finding the sources, open or concealed, available for accumulation, and of devising the ways and means of moulding them into productive forms . . . Tariff protection of infant industries has failed because it has done little or nothing to create the capital needed for industrial development" (Nurkse 1967: 105).

31 On Smith's use of the term "projector," see Pesciarelli 1989.

32 Koebner (1959: 389 f.) argues that Smith did not see the contributions of the "projectors" as very important for economic progress, an error of judgement in part reflecting the circumstance that Smith's major concern was to attack the merchants and manufacturers for distorting the pattern of activity. On balance, the negative effects of their influence-peddling outweighed their contributions to innovation.

33 The maximum would be "somewhat above the lowest market price, or the price which is commonly paid for the use of money by those who can give the most undoubted security" – our prime commercial rate – but "not . . . much above the lowest market rate" (Smith [1776] 1937: 339). In 'Defense of Usury, Bentham strongly objected to Smith's justification of such controls "which attempt to direct individuals in their private concerns" ([1787] 1952, 1: 128, also 176).

34 For example, to encourage agricultural investment and experimentation, Smith recommended tax abatements for those landlords who cultivated part of their own land at some risk ([1776] 1937: 784). He approved too of British colonial practice which had restrained the engrossing of uncultivated land by obliging proprietors to improve and cultivate a certain proportion of their property within a limited time (ibid. 539).

35 Formally, Smith contrasted "parsimony" with "prodigality" which refers to consumption actually encroaching upon capital ([1776] 1937: 322); but he appears to disapprove of excessive consumption as such, as, for example, in the dictum that "in public, as well as in private expenses, great wealth may, perhaps, frequently be admitted as an apology for great folly" (ibid. 489; added to the third edition of 1784). There is too his view that excessively high profits are likely to have a *depressing* effect upon savings: "The high rate of profits seems everywhere to destroy that parsimony which in other circumstances is natural to the character of the merchant. When profits are high, that sober virtue seems to be superfluous, and expensive luxury to suit better the affluence of his situation" (ibid. 578).

36 Rae cites this passage (1834: 270) and also an extension involving vanity reflected in the "multitude and variety" of dress, in cases where cheapness applies: "when by the improvements in the productive powers of manufacturing art and industry, the expense of any one dress comes to be very moderate, the variety will naturally be very great. The rich not being able to distinguish themselves by the expense of any one dress, will naturally endeavour to do so by the multitude and variety of their dresses" (Smith [1776] 1937: 649).

37 Wightman, Bryce and Ross, in Smith (1980: 175).

38 In the *Theory of Moral Sentiments*, Smith objected to Mandeville for whom "every thing is luxury which exceeds what is absolutely necessary for the support of human nature, so that there is vice even in the use of a clean shirt, or of a convenient habitation" ([1759] 1966: 456–57).

39 See above, pp. 200–4.

40 For a helpful historical instance of inappropriate intervention that clarifies the condition, see Rae (1834: 367–68). By contrast: "Great strength of the accumulative principle, is . . . [a] particularly favourable circumstance. This rendered the efforts of the English in the beginning of last century, to acquire many foreign manufactures, prudent and successful" (ibid. 368).

41 Moreover, in an earlier paper of 1825, Rae had clarified that his case for protection relates to *temporary* measures: "While England was gradually raising up that astonishing fabric of manufactures which now exists, various expedients of a temporary and subsidiary nature were adopted, serving the purpose of ladders, frames and scaffolding, which she can now with safety and advantage throw down and project" (Rae 1825: 202). He added: "But the memory of such regulations remains for the instruction of other nations in the commencement of their manufacturing career" (ibid.).

42 See above, pp. 204–5.

43 See above, p. 201.

44 This is discussed in greater detail in Book II, chapter 11.

45 Earlier Rae (1834: 74–5) stated the case for a saving of transport costs without qualification.

46 A complexity is created by the fact that positive spillovers are sometimes said to attach also to *luxuries*, albeit indirectly (see above, p. 203), thus reducing the case against that category of commodities. Hume, who detested "vicious" luxury – "a gratification is only vicious, when it engrosses all a man's expense, and leaves no ability for such acts of duty and generosity as are required by his situation and fortune" – had also allowed that such luxury could be advantageous to economic growth ([1752] 1955: 30–2). Rae, however, does not refer to Hume on luxury.

47 See above, p. 211.

48 Cf. Viner ([1937] 1965: 137): "It is to [Smith's] credit that when there was a sharp conflict between his generalization and his data, he usually abandoned his generalization."

49 For example, on the basis of the result that "the money price of corn regulates that of all other home-made commodities," Smith concluded that "the nature of things has stamped upon corn a real value which cannot be altered by merely altering its money price. No bounty upon exportation, no monopoly of the home market can raise that value" (Smith [1776] 1937: 482). To deny the possibility of raising the relative profitability of agriculture by appropriate intervention is to neglect the fact that every model is necessarily a simplification of reality, requiring appropriate qualification in application. Even if we accept the basic reasoning of the model – and Ricardo brought to light the logical defects – there is the neglect of frictions; there will be at least a period during which agriculture can be stimulated (Malthus 1803: 458 ff.).

A second instance of irresponsible application is alluded to by Thomas Pownall ([1776] 1967: 44–5), who complained of Smith's treatment of government interference with the colony trade based upon a blood-circulation analogy (Smith [1776] 1937: 571). The implications to be drawn from the apparent refutation of the model's predictions, Pownall further objected, were ignored by Smith who, after the event, apologetically sought out the disturbing causes which must have been at play.

13

# RAE AS MONETARY ECONOMIST

## Another Scottish tradition in a Canadian setting

*Masazumi Wakatabe*[1]

### Introduction

In the recent literature on John Rae,[2] there is a certain tension about how to characterize his economic thought. On the one hand, there is an argument that Rae belongs to the so-called Scottish tradition,[3] on the other hand Rae is considered one of the best Canadian economists (or the best).[4] One of the problems of a concept such as the "Scottish Tradition" is its ambiguity. Dow (1987: 342) summarizes the characteristics of the "Scottish political economy tradition" under eight categories:

1 An acceptance of the limitation of theory.
2 A recognition of the sociological and psychological aspects of theory appraisal.
3 A concern with practical issues.
4 A consequent preference for breadth of understanding of the background to these issues, over depth of isolated aspects.
5 A preference for drawing on several disciplines in an integrated manner to provide that depth.
6 A preference for arguing from first principles.
7 A preference for approaching a subject's first principles by discussing their historical development.
8 A specification of first principles in terms of a non-individualistic representation of human nature, with a consequent emphasis on conventional behaviour.

These categories are so broad that scarcely any great economist can escape such a categorization. The same is also true for what constitutes "Canadian" elements.

One clue to this problem rests on how to interpret the relationship between Adam Smith and John Rae. It is well known that Rae is one of the fiercest critics of Adam Smith, as is shown from the subtitle of his one and only economics book, *Statement of Some New Principles on the Subject of Political Economy, Exposing the Fallacies of the System of Free Trade, and of Some Other Doctrines Maintained in the "Wealth of Nations,"* published in 1834. On the other hand, no proponent of the "Scottish tradition" would deny that Smith should be included within that tradition.[5] Therefore, it is essential to examine the relationship between the two economists in order to settle this problem.

However, studies that analyze and compare theoretically the economic thought of both economists are strikingly few.[6] Thus it is still unclear what the real differences between Rae and Smith are. The purpose of this paper is to examine the economic thought of John Rae compared with that of Adam Smith, and to ascertain similarities and differences, in particular with regard to monetary economics. There are two reasons why the monetary aspect of his economic thought is chosen. First, this is the most neglected part of the economic thought of the "most unjustly neglected book" (Robbins 1968: 50). Though Rae devoted many pages to money and banking, and became increasingly interested in the issue,[7] the monetary aspect of the *New Principles* has received rare, and at best, only brief recognition.[8] Secondly, a strong interest in monetary issues is common to the Scottish writers, so that in this respect, we may legitimately claim a "Scottish tradition" providing us with a better point of reference.[9] Thirdly, monetary economics has always developed in a manner closely related to the contemporary issues of the day. It is necessary to have a good knowledge of contemporary financial institutions to be a good monetary economist. Thus Rae's writing on monetary issues will shed light on his understanding of contemporary economic situations.

The organization of this paper is as follows. The first section briefly reviews the historical background and characteristics of Rae's economic theory in general, paying attention to his microeconomic foundation of the theory of capital. The second section explores Rae's view on money. Like other classical economists, Rae considered money mainly as a medium of exchange, although he was aware of its function as a store of value. This aspect is argued in relation to uncertainty in foreseeing the exact amount of transaction. The third section discusses Rae's view on banking. He pointed out not only the benefits, but also the disadvantages of banking, one of which is his argument on panic. The conclusion reviews the main points of the paper on Rae's theoretical framework, and points out some remaining problems.

## Rae's framework

Before discussing Rae's views on money and banking, it will prove useful to review briefly the historical background, especially the development of money and banking in Canada until the 1830s, together with Rae's economic theory in general.

The history of money and banking in Canada until the time of the publication of the *New Principles* can be characterized as the formative period which laid down the basis of later development.[10] After several unsuccessful attempts by local merchants to establish banks, the Bank of Montreal was finally established in 1817 as a private corporation. The following year, two more banks were established, and in 1822 the three banks received a charter. At the same time, banking started in the Maritimes when the Bank of New Brunswick was chartered in 1820.

In relation to Rae, however, it suffices to point out three things. First, when Great Britain established its dominance in Canada in 1763, "the monetary system was in great disorder" (Goodwin 1961: 71). Canada lacked its own coinage, and therefore the shortage of a medium of exchange became a major problem. However, this shortage proved to be one of the most urgent of several forces that encouraged the formation of banking in Canada.[11] Second, before the establishment of banks, "the functions of banks had been assumed by merchants" (Neufeld 1972: 71). At the end of the eighteenth century:

> in Upper Canada the leading merchants in the rising towns performed practically all the functions of a bank except the issue of notes, although some of them provided an irregular issue of Bonds. In Western Canada particularly the larger merchants were both exporters and importers of practically every variety of goods required in the settlements. Nearly all exchanges were made through them; credits were both extended by them and orders for goods and money drawn upon them. . . . They received deposits of money and bills, made payments to order and advanced loans or credits, to be met later by produce bills or cash.
>
> (Shortt and Doughty 1914: 605)

At least in its early stage, the development of Canadian banking is the product of a long time process of spontaneous responses by economic agents. Thirdly, the Scottish banking system played a significant role in forming the Canadian system. Many of the first bankers were immigrants from Scotland who had been trained before they left the old country. Other Scottish characteristics – the small number of the banks with large capitals, the branch banking system, the competitive issue of notes, and the payment of interest on deposits – were also those of the Canadian banking system (Breckenridge 1894: 12–16, 27–8).[12]

Rae's theory of capital has been recognized as his highest achievement,[13] but it should be noted that his theoretical system as a whole is a theory of economic development composed of the theory of capital accumulation, "accumulative principle," and also the theory of technological change, "inventive principle."[14] He assumes that the return to capital, or profit,[15] would fall if "invention" is absent, while it would rise if "invention" occurs. In his own words, Rae's theory is summarized as follows:

> 1. Accumulation of stock or capital, is the addition made to these, through the operation of the accumulative principle.
> 2. Augmentation of stock or capital, is the addition made to them, through the operation of the principle of invention.
> 3. Increase of stock or capital, is the addition made to them, by the conjoined operation of both principles.
>
> Accumulation of stock diminishes profits: augmentation of stock increases profits: increase of stock neither increases nor diminishes profits.
>
> (Rae 1834: 264)

It is important to appreciate that Rae developed his theory on what we would now call microfoundations. He clearly recognizes the wants-satisfying nature and time element of economic activity. According to Rae, what distinguishes man from other animals is his "provident forethought":

> the capacity for perceiving, and retaining in his mind, the course of events and the connexion [*sic*] of one with another, that leads man to perceive what advancing *futurity* is to bring forth, and enables to provide for its wants. [emphasis added]
>
> (Rae 1834: 81)

Having viewed man as a foreseeing animal, he emphasized two things: end–means relationship in human activity, and time element. He used the word "instruments" to define "any means for the attainment of some ends" (Rae 1834: 86). This concept is so broad that it appears to be confusing, but it reflects his particular recognition of the end–means relationship.[16]

The main argument of the *New Principles* evolves around the question of how these "instruments" are formed, under what circumstances, and by what forces. Of the four determinants of the amount of instruments, the most important is the "strength of the *effective desire of accumulation*."[17] He defined it as the "determination to sacrifice a certain amount of present good, to obtain another greater amount of good, at some future period" (Rae 1834: 119). This is what we would now call "time preference" and is no doubt an astonishing accomplishment. He not only uses the term like "present goods" and "future goods," but also relates this effective desire of accumulation to the formation of instruments. He starts his theory of capital with individual behaviour, comparing "present goods" and "future goods," and concludes that if "the production of that future greater good, be conceived to deserve the sacrifice of this present smaller good, the instrument will be formed, if not, it will not be formed" (Rae 1834: 118). In this sense, Rae self-consciously lays his theory on what we would now call a microeconomic foundation.[18] Moreover, uncertainty plays a major role in his "effective desire of accumulation." It is not always the same and constant, but varies across different societies and times, for it is intensified by the "strength of the intellectual powers," such as foresight, "the *social and benevolent affections*" (emphasis added) or altruism, and social stability, but weakened by myopia, improvidence, and uncertainty (Rae 1834: 124).[19]

The attention to the microeconomic foundations of his theory, the emphasis on uncertainty and its effects on capital accumulation constitute the basis of Rae's monetary economic thought, to which we will turn next.

## Rae on money

Rae discusses monetary issues mainly in Book II, chapter 8, "Of the Division of Employments and Other Phenomena Produced By Efforts to Accelerate the Exhaustion of Instruments," and in the long and most detailed "Note G." Following the tradition of classical monetary economics,[20] according to Rae, money is the "foundation of the mechanism of mercantile transactions," "the great medium of exchange" (Rae 1834: 176). Therefore his "explanatory comments on money and banking grew directly out of his theory of exchange" (Neill 1991: 69).

First, Rae explains the origin and use of money in the manner of Adam Smith. Like Smith (1776:bk. 1, ch. 4), he begins with commodity money, especially the precious metals (gold and silver) as money. Such precious metals are chosen as money because of "their beauty, their incorruptibility" and "the facility with which they may be transported from place to place" (Rae 1834: 176).[21] However, Rae's explanation of the uses of money differs from Smith's:

> In the very frequent revolutions and commotions that occur in the earlier ages of society, articles that do not decay, can be hid, or carried off without difficulty, and are always estimable, would naturally of all others be most coveted. They thus probably were first chiefly sought after, for the purpose of being retained, not for that of being exchanged; even yet in many countries, partly from old habits, and partly from still prevailing insecurity, they are chiefly prized as of all things, those best fit to be hoarded.
>
> (Rae 1834: 176)

This statement is particularly interesting, because, as we shall see later, he frequently emphasizes the uncertainty element when he discusses monetary issues, and this can be a major departure from Smith.[22] However, he does not explore the matter any further and returns to money as a medium of exchange:

> But, in whatever manner their use may have been introduced, or how much so ever in some countries it may be dependent on a feeling of insecurity, at present or formerly prevailing, and prompting their possessors to keep not to part with them, they are now more generally sought for, for the purpose of being immediately passed away, forming, in the shape of money, the great medium of exchange, and it is solely in the part they thus act, that we have here very briefly to consider them.
>
> (ibid.)

Rae goes on to explain the origin of money, providing the same division of labour argument as Smith's to the effect that as social division of labour extends ("men divide into different occupations"), men begin to exchange goods instead of making all the required goods by themselves. As a result of social division of labour, the "introduction, to a greater or less extent, of some sort of money, seems naturally to follow" (ibid.).

Relying on the example of butcher-baker exchange, which reminds us of Smith's argument, Rae distinguishes "two systems of cash, or credit":

> There are two modes by which the desired exchange may be effected. If the brewer and the baker have a commodity received by every one for all others, such as money is, they may each give the butcher a certain quantity of it for a quantity of meat, and when he requires their ale and bread, he may, in turn, send back to them also a quantity of money. Or, the butcher may be satisfied with the promise of the brewer and the baker, that at some future time, when he has occasion for it, they will give him a quantity of ale and bread, or of something else.
>
> (Rae 1834: 177)

Under the first system, in which "gold and silver forms the sole money," the quantity of money is regulated by the amount of commodity transacted, which in turn depends on the quantity of materials which are used to form "instruments," and on the progress of the division of labour. The causation runs from the number of instruments through the amount of exchanges to the quantity of money, and every economic agent tries to calculate the amount of exchanges and the number of instruments, in order to determine how much cash balance he should hold:

> In such a state of things as we suppose, could every man see exactly beforehand the whole series of the exchanges that would present

> themselves to him, every prudent man would so manage his exchanges, his purchases that is, and his sales, as to provide himself with the exact amount of money necessary to effect every exchange that he might deem it advisable to execute.
>
> (ibid.)

"But," Rae continues, "no man can with accuracy foresee what transactions may present themselves to him, or when they may do so," because the "amount of possible future exchanges that may offer to any man, and the time they may occur, are exceedingly uncertain." Among many things which are uncertain, there are "the operations of other individuals engaged in the formation of instruments, . . . the course of the winds and seasons, the fortune of war, the progress of treaties, and numberless other events" (ibid. 178).

Rae's theory of demand for money is important considering his broader theoretical framework; as we have seen before, he pays more attention to the time element in economic activity than Smith, which enabled him to point to an uncertainty element in exchange and demand for money. But the demand for money is also influenced by another circumstance, the rate of return, which is determined by the "principle of accumulation." Thus, as a result of uncertainty, an economic agent suffers two inconveniences, holding either too much or too little money. On the one hand, "if instruments are not far removed from the first orders," so that the rate of profit (interest) is still high, he would rather risk the inconveniences of having too little money by him, for he expects a higher return from employing his money. On the other hand, "if instruments are far removed from the first orders of our series," he would reserve a greater amount of money (ibid. 178).

Although, therefore, following the classical tradition, Rae considers money as a medium of exchange, by stressing the uncertainty element in the exchange process, he arrived at a version of the precautionary demand for money. The rate of return clearly enters into his demand function for money, and in a manner closely related to his theory of capital, though with a clearer view of the relationship between capital and the rate of return. Moreover, when he used such a word as "holding," he has an embryonic concept of money as a stock. In this sense, his argument is strikingly new.[23]

Rae's monetary theory led him to draw the empirical conclusion that:

> We should expect then to find, that, in countries where either the principle of accumulation is too weak to carry instruments on to the more slowly returning orders, or where it has not yet had time to do so, money would be scarce, and that, where this principle having had time to act, its strength has carried them to the farther orders, there money would be plenty.
>
> (Rae 1834: 179)

According to his diagnosis, "new settlements in America" including Canada belong to the country in which "from the superabundance of materials, instruments are of very quickly returning orders, the amount of coin to be found is exceedingly small."[24] Even though the amount of money thus determined is a kind of equilibrium cash holding, for a "man will never keep two hundred pounds in his chest, if he thinks it probable that one hundred will be sufficient, because he can always make something of the other hundred" (Rae 1834: 180), the real problem is the inability to calculate accurately the amount of cash holding due to uncertainty. Such miscalculation forces returns from instruments to be lower than they otherwise would be, with a resultant misallocation of resources.

Though commodity money constitutes a theoretical basis or starting point for monetary economy, the direct barter system, or the first system of cash economy, is not a reality; the "great bulk of transactions are carried on" (Rae 1834: 182) by the second system, that of credit. Using his example of the butcher, brewer, and baker, under the system of credit, they would not have to pay with commodity or the equivalent money at the same point of purchase and make transactions based on the promise of future payment. Moreover, "a transfer of obligations from hand to hand" (ibid.) would also be possible.

This system of credit is not flawless, because, by its nature, it depends on the complex interdependence of contracts: "its inherent complexedness and difficulty," and "liability of the contracting parties to fail in fulfilling their engagements, from dishonesty, miscalculation and accidents impossible to be foreseen" (Rae 1834: 183), are critical in implementing this system. Although, therefore the credit system – resulting from a product of spontaneous transacting process rather than design or planning[25] – reduces uncertainty in exchange, another uncertainty, namely, uncertainty in contracts, is persistent. This uncertainty arising from "dishonesty, or the imprudence and miscalculations of those who deal with him" imposes an extra cost on economic agents as a premium: "Aware of the risk he runs, he is obliged to balance it by charging an additional sum, over and above what he would otherwise demand, on all commodities that pass through his hands" (ibid. 184). Because of this transaction cost due to uncertainty in contracts, prices increase more than they otherwise would do, resulting in a diminution of transactions. Whether there is any institutional arrangement that mitigates this disadvantage of the system of credit is a question answered in his treatment of banking system.

## Rae on banking

Like Smith, Rae was also a great proponent of banking,[26] though both discussed the disadvantages as well as benefits of banking. Rae's position reflects the above mentioned basic tenet, specifically his emphasis on uncertainty inherent in the banking system.

### *"Benefits"*

Let us start with Rae's discussion of benefits. The essence of the banking system is summarized as follows: "The business of banking, seems to owe its foundation and extension, to its capacity for giving room for the development of the benefits, and for restraining and remedying the evils of the system of credit" (Rae 1834: 184). Under this system, the banker is conceived to be a kind of "instrument, through which the mass of the exchanges, taking place in the community, is performed."

The key function which the banker plays in this system is to provide appropriate information. In society, a person engages in a great deal of transactions, but:

> his circumstances can be known but to a few of them, nor is it possible for him to produce to each satisfactory evidence of his own capacity to discharge his engagements, or to give him the security of others for their performance, and even could he do this, it would be insufficient for the purchase of the greater part of them.
>
> (Rae 1834: 185)

In such a situation where information is asymmetric and costly to transmit, the banker acts as "the general lender, and receiver of the society" (ibid.) and enables people to lend or borrow money.

The banker derives advantages chiefly from the peculiar sort of money he lends:

> It is not specie, but merely an obligation to pay in specie. But as all who engage in business have to return cash to him, it is equally good to them [all who engage in business] as specie, and through them is equally well received among the other members of the community. Thus the money of the banker comes to make a great part, or nearly the whole, of the circulating medium.
>
> (ibid. 186–7)

Society derives the three following benefits. First, economic agents do not have to hold idle cash to meet "sudden emergencies": "When a man wants cash, he goes to the bank for it, when he has cash, he carries it to the bank. Money never lies idle". Secondly, the system of credit avoids deficiency in the circulating medium. Thirdly, it avoids the deficiencies of the credit system, in that the informed banker selects and screens those whom he deals with, so that the "dealings of men of prudence and character, are not so mixed up with those of improvident and suspicious persons" (ibid. 187).[27]

Rae emphasizes the effects of those three benefits on the real economy and incorporated his theory of banking into his broader theory of economic development. Banking would give a stimulus to the accumulative principle of the society, and thus an increase in the general stock of the society. At the same time, by the removal of "the obstruction to the additional exchanges," "division of employments" is also invigorated and new branches of business arise. These two effects combined, assure an increase in both the number and volume of exchanges.

As far as Smith's argument for social division of labour concerns, Rae relies on and thinks in terms of the Smithian framework. Yet he insists on differentiating his position from Smith's, and devotes some pages to contrast his argument with Smith's: "the view I have attempted to give of the whole subject of exchange, is quite opposed to that exhibited in the Wealth of Nations" (Rae 1834: 408). And "in my opinion the notion from which Adam Smith sets out, and which, since his time, has kept possession of all speculations on this subject, and been the foundation of many important practical measures, is essentially erroneous" (ibid. 411). Nevertheless, there are similarities between the two systems, and, as we shall see later, Rae himself sometimes seems to admit them.

First of all, both base their theories of banking mainly on the Scottish banking system of the day.[28] In many places, Rae expresses his highest praise for it: "No where has banking been productive of more acknowledged advantages, and no where have the evils occasionally attendant on it been fewer" (Rae 1834: 251).[29] In fact, "Note G," the longest and most detailed note to the text in the *New Principles*, is almost entirely devoted to the description and praise of the Scottish banking system.

Moreover, Rae often quotes from Smith in favour of his own argument, while he vigorously attacked the same Smith. For Rae, the most fundamental difference with Smith lies in the relationship between the division of labour and capital, or stock of instruments. Rae attributes to Smith the view that the causation runs from exchange to stock through the division of labour. In other words, if the amount of exchange transacted in a society remains the same as before, the amount of money or stock should remain the same. Rae believed that the causation should be reversed, that is, the increase of stock should come first, thus expanding the amount of exchange through the division of employments. This claim seems unfair and trivial, because Smith discusses the accumulation of capital as a necessary condition of the progress of the division of labour.[30] However, this emphasis of difference has the utmost importance for Rae, because he wanted to refute Smith's thesis that (in Rae's terms) "there is always a certain sum of money necessary to carry on the transactions of every society, the amount of which is proportioned to the transactions carried on" and its corollary that "the advantages of banking are limited to the substitution of paper for specie, and the creation to that amount of a fictitious capital" (Rae 1834: 411).

As we have already seen, Rae's purpose is to show how the introduction of credit, or a banking system, is beneficial: it reduces uncertainty and thus transaction costs. Rae agrees with Smith on this basic point:

> If the reader have still any doubts on the subject, he may, I conceive, satisfy himself of the accuracy of this view, by reference to the pages of the "Wealth of Nations" itself. Adam Smith, by no means, limits the advantages of banking as practiced in Scotland, to the substitution of paper for specie, and the direct fictitious capital thus created. On the contrary, he thinks that every person dealing with the banker, that is, every person engaged in business, derives individually very great advantages from the system.
>
> (Rae 1834: 409)

However, he differed on the problem as to what extent the banking system is beneficial:

> to effect the same transactions, it requires far less bankers money, whether that money be paper or specie, than was required of the money in existence before the establishments of banks, the celerity of motion making up for the deficiencies of quantity, . . . if the same number of transactions only takes place after the establishment of banks, as before their introduction, then much less money will be necessary, and if the same money be circulated, the fact indicates, that a great addition has been made to the business transacted, and still more if the money circulated exceeds that formerly circulated.
>
> (ibid.)

In this process, he also takes the role of velocity of money into consideration. Money, "where there are no banks, circulates slowly and after intervals of inactivity between dealer and dealer," while when "the bank forms the centre of circulation," money serves with "a more rapid circulation":

> in the same way, as when a road is much improved, though one horse may be sufficient to transport what three did before, yet the commodities transported so increase, that there are, notwithstanding, thrice the number of horses employed.
>
> (ibid.)

Finally, Rae incorporates his banking theory into the broader theory of economic development. According to him, the extent of the banking system depends on four factors:

> 1st. The amount of the science, skill, and population existing in the country, to work up the materials it affords, and the abundance of these materials.
>
> 2d. The strength of the accumulative principle, the opportunity it has had to operate, and consequent division of employments,

> approach of instruments to the more slowly returning orders, and accumulation of stock. . . .
>
> 3d. The general intelligence, sagacity, and integrity of the members of the community. A person greatly deficient in any of these respects, is one with whom a banker would not wish to deal. . . .
>
> 4th. The efficiency and security of the system of banking adopted.
>
> (Rae 1834: 188–9)

Among them, (1) and (2) determine the amount of exchange, and along with (3) and (4) constitute the stage in which the banking system operates. In this setting, the banking system itself is considered to be a sort of art: "The art which has most immediate connexion with the increase of wealth, the business of banking, is itself in some measure illustrative of the influence of change in producing improvements in all arts" (Rae 1834: 250). As we have seen, the banking system itself is an innovation mitigating uncertainty and reducing transaction cost by introducing the informed banker. Like all arts, this art can belong to "the inventive principle," which is limitless (see Spengler 1959: 401), therefore it seems to add optimistic overtone to his banking theory. However, we should recall that the banking system depends also on (3) and (4). What happens if (3) and (4) are shaken? The answers to this question add another nice example to the comparison between Smith and Rae.

### *"Evils"*

Rae is aware of various negative aspects of banking and points out two main "occasional evils resulting from the system of banking, diminishing its general utility" (Rae 1834: 187). His qualifications are important, for they show not only how Rae was influenced by Smith, but also how he went beyond Smith.

The first, which seems to reflect a fear shared with Smith, is expressed by Rae as "a great deficiency of real principle" (Rae 1834: 190): The "money which bankers circulate, must be the representative of real property. It must be exchangeable for some commodity, or commodities, equal to the amount at which is rated." By "real," Rae means convertibility for specie or some real commodity. "If it may be always exchanged for specie, or for some proportion of the general revenue abstracted for the purposes of government, it will be a representative of something real." Like Smith, Rae always assumes convertibility; in this respect, this is similar to Smith's version of the Real Bills Doctrine.[31] However, Rae's emphasis rests more on the loss of "confidence" when "bankers squander, or waste, the funds" (Rae 1834: 189) than does Smith's. It is also of note that Rae had the same dislike or fear of speculation as Smith.[32]

The second is more significant, as it relates to his basic vision of economic activity. It follows naturally from his emphasis on uncertainty that the "second evil arising from the practice of banking, has its origin, in the system of credit itself: and the shock which, as it is founded on prevailing opinion, it is liable to receive from whatever shakes public confidence" (Rae 1834: 190). What he explains here is his version of theory of panic, or "distress." By its nature, credit has an inherit vulnerability. The essence of credit lies in widening economic agents' constraints, which enables them to transact, but there is always a danger of "the non-performance of the engagements contracted." This would not be problematic if this happened only to "persons of really abundant capital." But, "it also happens to those, whose capitals have been reduced by misfortune or imprudence, and therefore, there are always many in every mercantile community, whose ability to discharge their obligations is more or less doubtful" (ibid. 191).

Rae considers that the credit system itself is inherently unstable because it depends heavily on chains of contracts, but the cause of "distress" was exogenous rather than endogenous to the system, or more properly, not specified. Though he was not clear about the cause of "distress," "any cause operating extensively, and prejudicially, on mercantile transactions" was considered to lead to a distress:

> it generally happens, that there arise cases of incapacity to meet engagements, and, as one man depends for the means of discharging his debts, on the debts others owe him, that embarrassment and distress spread throughout the whole mercantile body. The experience of the misfortunes attending this state of things, leads every one engaged in business, when he thinks there is reason to fear its approach, to endeavor to withdraw himself from the danger, by avoiding to contract obligations to pay. There is consequently a *general* diminution of purchases, and a *general temporary* fall in prices. [emphasis added]
>
> (Rae 1834: 191)

As is shown from the above-quoted passage, this distress is general, though temporary, which suggests that Rae believed that the economy would recover sooner or later.[33] Before recovering, however, this distress would be further accelerated and deepened by an asymmetry among people in terms of debt. On the one hand, "prudent" people are able to secure themselves from a danger of "the non-performance of the engagements contracted," they in turn would increase the difficulties of those who have contracts with "prudent" people and some of them would become incapable of obtaining the means of meeting their contracts, "their failure increases the general distress, and farther lessens the number inclined to purchase" (ibid.).

In this whole process, the banking system plays a crucial part. Because of the reduction of demand, there is less money required for transaction, and people need specie, "the most desirable of commodities":

> The situation of the banker becomes therefore at this crisis, very critical. He cannot, in justice to himself, grant all the requisite accommodation, and yet, his refraining from doing so must aggravate existing evils . . . If he be unable to meet these difficulties, his failure adds very much to the general mass of misfortune, and farther diminishes public confidence.
>
> (ibid. 192)

But, such distress would end naturally, because contracts and also debts are eventually diminished, although this "natural termination" would be retarded by two factors: one, by "the struggles of those whose real funds, in proportion to the extent of their business, are smallest, and whose motives to engage in fresh transactions, are chiefly the hopes of extricating themselves from the embarrassments in which present transactions have involved them"; and second, "more injuriously" by "the failure of those engaged in the business of banking" (ibid.).

As a whole, compared to Smith, Rae went further in pointing out this negative aspect of the credit system and analyzing the possible consequent distress. However, the essential vulnerability and insecurity of the banking system are already mentioned by Smith, therefore it can be said that Rae developed his theory in a framework not fundamentally different from Smith's.[34] Of course, his theory of panic is not flawless. Despite the "liability of the mercantile community to be largely affected by such sudden pressures" (ibid.),[35] he did not propose any concrete policy recommendation, and he lacked any argument about Central Banking and monetary policy. Although Rae emphasized the role of "confidence" in permeation of panic, he seemed to consider it as an "inherit" evil, and, unlike Henry Thornton, he did not see it as curable. It is also noted that his theory is not complete as a theory of business cycle, because he did not specify the turning points clearly.[36] Others, however, also remind us of Smith's failure to develop them. On the other hand, what made it possible for Rae to develop his theory of panic is the same key concept of his theory of demand for money and capital: persistence of uncertainty. Here we should find his true innovation, the true difference from Adam Smith and many others.

## Conclusion

As we have seen, in many respects, Rae's work does remind us of Smith's, though Rae insisted on their differences. In fact, Rae's economic thought becomes much closer to Smith's economic thought if we look at the monetary aspects of both economists. On money, both begin with exchange and treat money as a medium of exchange. On banking, they are both enthusiastic supporters of the banking system and emphasize the role of credit, and both learn much from the experience of the Scottish banking system.[37] In this sense, we could conclude that both belong to the "Scottish tradition," sharing a strong interest in money and banking.[38]

On the other hand, there certainly are differences with Smith. On money, unlike other classical economists, Rae argues precautionary demand for money explicitly. In fact, Rae goes further than Smith in emphasizing the effects of banking on the real economy. In addition to that, he has a clear grasp of the potential danger of the banking system.

These differences are not alien to his economic system as a whole. On the contrary, they are derived from his microeconomic foundation based on the wants-satisfying nature of economic activity and the time and uncertainty elements, and they constitute an integrated part of his theory of capital, or economic development. If we look for his innovation in monetary theory, there is much in common with his innovation in the theory of capital. His major contribution is to have tackled monetary issues on a microeconomic foundation.

However, it should be admitted that Rae's monetary economics lacks several vital components. First and foremost, there is no explicit theory of inflation, or the general level of price. Ironically, in this sense, he cannot be called an inflationist. While he tended to expound the Real Bills Doctrine, he always assumed convertibility. His emphasis of the beneficial effects of credit on the real economy is not related to the stimulus given by the increase of money supply, but to what we would now call the microeconomic stimulus of the accumulative principle. Second, he has no argument about a theory of Central Banking and national money supply. Curiously enough, this lessens the difference between Smith and Rae, because mainly based on the experience of the Scottish banking system and the new settlements in Upper Canada, he seems to believe in the spontaneous growth of the banking system. On this matter, he is not an interventionist.[39] Third, he does not take the international aspect of monetary economics into consideration. This is really one of the biggest deficiencies in his monetary economics, considering the fact that he does notice the existence of the problem.[40]

At the end of this chapter, it is fair to point out some remaining problems. First, this paper's scope is narrowly limited, since we focused on the Smith–Rae relationship. In order to evaluate Rae's monetary economics fully and fairly, we need an analysis of his relationship with contemporary monetary economic thought, especially that of the Banking School. While living in Canada, Rae was always keen on current economic issues in Great Britain. It seems highly suggestive that the only book he mentions in "Note G" other than the *Wealth of Nations* is Thomas Joplin.[41] Secondly, suppose that

Rae's theoretical innovation rests on his clear recognition of the wants-satisfying nature of economic activity and the emphasis on time and uncertainty, what is the source(s) of his innovation and its relationship with the "Scottish tradition" or Canadian content? In other words, does his innovation mean any break from Smith? In order to tackle this problem, it is necessary to explore the various possible theoretical influences.[42] Thirdly, the pursuit of a Canadian context is the weakest part of this paper. Rae often mentions Canadian examples, and it seems indeed true that his monetary economics corresponded to the actual course of development of money and banking in Canada, considering his emphasis of the shortage of medium of exchange in Canada, his view of the evolution of banking business as a spontaneous process, and his reliance on the Scottish banking system as a primary example of ideal banking. However, it requires further study to establish any firmer link between the contemporary economic situation of the day and his theory. This problem is complicated if we take the "Scottish influence upon the early banking system of Canada" (Goodwin 1961: 88)[43] into account.

Schumpeter once praised Rae and compared Rae's *New Principles* to Smith's great work: "We must see in his work: another *Wealth of Nations* or, more correctly, something that with ten additional years of quiet work, graced by an adequate income, could have grown into another – and more profound – *Wealth of Nations*" (Schumpeter 1954: 468). Indeed, these words seem to be more appropriate after reviewing both economists' monetary economics. Both have many similarities and also differences. To put it simply, Rae's *New Principles* is not the *Wealth of Nations*. It is something else, something which is very similar to Smith's great book in many points (in this sense, "Scottish tradition" could be useful), but different in many others. Whether the second adjective "more profound" is suitable or not is not easy to tell (in some points, for example, pointing out the inherent instability of the credit system could be profound), but the stress should be placed on the first adjective and the noun.

## Notes

1 University of Toronto and Waseda University. I am grateful to the International Council for Canadian Studies and Waseda University which made it possible for me to study at the University of Toronto. I would like to thank Professors Samuel Hollander and David Laidler for their helpful comments and criticism, although the remaining errors are solely mine.

2 He was born in Scotland in 1796, emigrated to Canada in 1822, lived there until 1849, and died in New York in 1872. For his colourful life and work in general, consult James (1965a, 1: pts 1 and 2). This is a masterful and scholarly work which has not yet been surpassed. James (1951) is more concise and still valuable. As revealed by James, Mixter's introduction to Rae (1905) turns out to contain factual errors, but it is also useful.

3 This term was originally coined by Macfie (1955). See also Dow (1987) and Mair (1990).

4 See James (1965a), Brewer (1991), and Neill (1991) with qualifications. In fact, Neill carefully conceded that, "The principal insight of his [Rae's] theory may have been fully developed before he left Scotland, or before he left continental Europe." But, "That makes no difference, because he was able to elaborate his theory with the experience of the Canadian frontier in full view" (Neill 1991: 57). Mair (1990) is more complicated and argues for the presence of another strand of "Scottish Tradition," "the 'bastard' line originating in Rae which, despite many vicissitudes, has survived to make a seminal infusion into the bloodstock of Institutionalist and post-Schumpeterian economics" (Mair 1990: 286).

5 This is not so obvious, since Smith is heavily influenced by French writers, such as the Physiocrats.

6 See Brewer (1991), Ahmad (1996a), and Hollander (this volume, Ch. 12). Brewer's paper lucidly reviews and compares the economic thoughts of both Smith and Rae, concluding that Rae is right in emphasizing differences with Smith. His procedure is correct in the sense that he compares the main system of economic thought of both economists, i.e., the relationship between the division of labour, capital accumulation, and technological change. Ahmad's paper was written as a critique to Brewer, questioning Brewer's understanding of Smith's system. Hollander takes up the issue by examining their attitudes toward government intervention, regarding especially the infant-industry problem and luxury, and concludes that Rae and Smith were closer than Rae wished to depict.

7 The "Note G," presumably written near the end of his writing, was the longest and most detailed one. Also, in his letter to J.S. Mill dated December 5, 1853, Rae revealed his plan to write "a treatise on Banking and Currency, the true principles regulating which I have long conceived can be clearly deduced from what I may venture to call my doctrines, and scarcely otherwise" (James 1965a, 2: 422).

8 Goodwin (1959) is rather brief but quite helpful. Goodwin (1961) also provides useful information about Canadian banking of the day. The topic is briefly mentioned in James (1965a, 1: 135), Dean and Dean (1972: 104), and Neill (1991: 69–70). Edmonson (1970) is valuable, but the perspective is limited to what we would now call the precautionary demand for money, and is too brief. Birchler, the most comprehensive study on Rae, only restates what is found in the above-mentioned writers (see Birchler 1980: 213–15).

9 It remains a mystery why the proponents of the "Scottish tradition" have not yet mentioned this quite impressive tradition ranging from Hume, Smith, and Francis Homer on the one side of monetary economics, to John Law and Sir James Steuart on the other side. Henry Thornton, the best monetary economist of the day, was not a Scot, but curiously enough, he and Rae had a similar background; Thornton's father made a fortune by Russian trade, while Rae was the son of a timber merchant and supposedly visited Norway in his youth. He also shows some knowledge about Scandinavian countries (Rae 1834: 316). For an interesting intellectual relationship between Sweden and England regarding the Bullionist Controversy, see Eagly (1968).

10 For a general overview, see McIvor (1958: chs 1–3), Neufeld (1972: chs 2 and 4). Goodwin (1961: ch. 3) discusses the relationship between the development of money and banking and contemporary opinions.

11 McIvor pointed out five factors at play: (1) the successful operation of the First Bank of the United States (1791); (2) the shortage of currency in the colony; (3) the variety of the currency, both as to origin and condition; (4) the nuisance created by promissory notes and merchants' "bons" issued without authority; and (5) the shortage of capital (McIvor 1958: 26–27). Among them, Neufeld named (2) as "the overwhelming economic impetus to the formation of the first Canadian banks" (Neufeld 1972: 36).

12 However, Shortt (1896) all but denied the influence of the Scottish banking system, insisting instead on the influence of American experience. Of course, the American influence should not be ignored, but Shortt tended to overlook or neglect other sources of influence.

13 The best praise for his contribution to the theory of capital is probably from J. S. Mill: "On the subject of population this valuable service has been rendered by the celebrated Essay of Mr. Malthus; and on the point which now occupies us I can refer with equal confidence to another, though a less known work, "New Principles of Political Economy," by Dr Rae. In no other book known to me is so much light thrown, both from principle and history, on the causes which determine the accumulation of capital" (Mill [1848] 1871: 162). Considering how much Mill praised Malthus and was influenced by him, it would be hard to find more suitable expression than this. On how much Mill was influenced by Rae, see Spengler (1960). As a next best praise, we could quote from Fisher, who dedicated his work to Rae: "My own theory is in some degree every one's theory. Every essential part of it was at least foreshadowed by John Rae in 1834" (Fisher 1930: ix). For other recent evaluations, see Schumpeter (1954: 469), Spiegel (1960: 95), and Niehans (1990: 85–86). The exception to this tradition of interpretation is Gray and Thompson (1980), which says that "indeed his work is largely a study of the place of invention in social development" (Gray and Thompson 1980: 186).

14 For an excellent summary of Rae's theory of economic development, see Spengler (1959). Goodwin (1961: 122–27), Dean and Dean (1972), Brewer (1991) and Neill (1991: ch. 4) are also useful.

15 Quoting from Adam Smith (1776: bk 1, ch. 9, para. 22) and following the habit of Classical economists, Rae "assumes the rate of interest as a fair measure of the real average rate of profits, in any country, and consequently of the order in our series, at which instruments are there arrived" (1834: 196). In this sense, as Niehans correctly puts it, "whereas Jevons, Böhm-Bawerk, and Fisher sought to determine the rate of interest, Rae was focusing on capital accumulation" (Niehans 1990: 86).

16 "Instruments" include not only "all tools and machines" (Rae 1834: 89) such as "the steam engine, or the cotton mill" but also "a field" (ibid. 87), or even consumption goods such as bread in terms of satisfying wants (ibid. 88). He uses the term deliberately being aware that his usage is unusual (ibid. 88–89). Like Smith, Rae classified instruments further into three components: "a stock reserved for immediate consumption", "fixed capital," and "circulating capital"

(ibid. 170–71), and in fact does not differentiate his theory of formation of "instruments" and that of capital.

17 The other three factors are: the progress of the inventive faculty; the quantity and quality of the materials owned by society; and the rate of wages (Rae 1834: 109). The place of the rate of wage in Rae's theory of capital accumulation is an interesting point relating to his understanding and digestion of Ricardian economics. He assumes fixed wages "for the sake of simplicity," but knows that "in a society making a steady and healthy progress, they should rather be continually increasing, the labourer as well as the capitalists, gaining something by the improvements which the progress of invention produces" (ibid. 327).

18 Rae did not ignore the productivity side of capital. He calculated the return to instruments in a very peculiar way. The "capacity of instruments" is defined as "their power to produce . . . events equivalent to a certain amount of labor", the instruments are ordered according to their capacity to yield returns over costs per time period. Under the simple assumption that "every instrument is constructed at one precise point of time, and exhausted at another" (Rae 1834: 100), Rae understood the orders by "the period of time at which instruments placed in them, issue, or would issue, if not before exhausted, in events equivalent to double the labor expended in forming them" (ibid. 100–101). Following Spengler's exposition, let $e = y/c$ stand for efficiency, where $y$ is the returns yielded by an instrument during the interval between its initial formation and its exhaustion, and $c$ is the initial cost of the instrument. Moreover, let $(1 + r)$ exp $n = k$, where $r$ is rate of return above cost yielded annually by instrument ($e = k = 2$), and $n$ is the order of an instrument, or the number of years required by it to yield double its cost. If $r$ = 100 percent, $n = 1$, and the instrument is said to be of order A; if $r$ is approximately 41percent, $n = 2$, and the order is B, and so on (see Spengler 1959: 396).

19 Irving Fisher later recapitulates Rae's argument under the heading of "The Personal Factor" (Fisher 1930: 80–89).

20 For the tradition of the classical monetary economics, "the orthodoxy of the 1870s," consult Laidler (1991: ch. 2).

21 In another place, he summarized uses of "gold and silver" into four characteristics: (1) the most precious, and easily preserved of all articles, (2) their capacity for being divided and re-united without injury, (3) convenience then to have rendered it expedient to have them formed into pieces of a certain weight, and fineness, (4) proper measures to give fixedness to those obligations to future delivery of things in exchange (Rae 1834: 193).

22 However, we should be careful about emphasizing the difference between Smith and Rae too much. Smith (1776: bk. 1, ch. 4, para. 2) could be interpreted as saying that he implicitly assumes uncertainty in exchange. Moreover, durability (and the function of money as a store of value only in this sense) is always a necessary condition required for money, which was never overlooked by classical economists (see Laidler 1991: 8).

23 Edmonson (1970) sees here an element of liquidity preference, while he, correctly, does not insist on any relationship between Rae's liquidity preference and others' such as Keynes's.

24 Two further examples are China and Holland, which are Smith's favourite examples of, respectively, a country in stationary state and a most advanced country.

25 Rae mentioned two systems: *viremens*, or transfers in Lyon and among London bankers; and cash account conducted among merchants "in many parts of North America, but more especially in new settlements in Upper Canada" (1834: 185). His argument of the evolution of money and credit is quite similar to Hicks (1989: esp. chs 5–7).

26 My understanding of Adam Smith as a great proponent of banking relies heavily on Laidler (1981).

27 Related to this matter, the banking system supports and facilitates entrepreneurship. Suppose on the one hand, a wealthy merchant dies with a large stock of instruments left, but "his widow, and young children" cannot use the legacy. On the other hand, "young men of ability" with little or no capital may use instruments efficiently and "yield more than the ordinary returns, and so, after paying for the usual profits, may leave a considerable surplus as the reward of their exertions" (Rae 1834: 399). The banking system transfers the fund held by the former to the latter, by the lending to individuals, discounting bills, or by bank credits.

28 On how deeply Smith's argument for banking is rooted in the oral tradition of the Scottish banking community of the day, consult Checkland (1975).

29 For another example, he described Scotland as "a country in which, to judge from the circumstances attending its introduction, and the practical benefits arising from its operation, it has probably arrived as near perfection as anywhere" (Rae 1834: 398).

30 "As the accumulation of stock must, in the nature of things, be previous to the division of labour, so labour can be more and more subdivided in proportion only as stock is previously more and more accumulated" (Smith 1776: bk. 2, introd., para. 3).

31 For Smith's version of the Real Bills Doctrine and its implications, consult Laidler (1981). Also see Hollander (1973: 205–7).

32 For Smith's concern with speculation, "prodigals and projectors," see Smith (1776: bk. 2, ch. 4, para. 15). Rae thought the "temptation to divert the fund . . . to speculations promising great gain, but sometimes producing great loss" was great in society at orders of quick return, concluding that banking "will consequently be in general safest, where capital is most largely accumulated" (Rae 1834: 190). Although Rae does share the same view of speculation with Smith, unlike Smith, he is against the interest rate maximum regulation (ibid. 196 n.).

33 Whether Rae held a Malthusian argument for "general glut" or not needs another separate analysis. Interestingly enough, Rae was influenced by both Lord Lauderdale and J.-B. Say. He also agreed with Ricardo on attacking Smith's theory of the falling rate of profit due to "competition of capital" (Rae 1834: 346). Gray and Thompson (1980) grouped Rae with Lauderdale and Sismondi into critics of Smith, but did not treat Rae as an "underconsumptionist." Nonetheless, there are several passages which can be considered to hold a Lauderdale-like, if not Malthusian, argument in Book I of *New Principles*.

34 For example, recall Smith's cautious words to banking such as "a sort of wagon-way through the air," or "the Daedalian wings of paper money" (Smith 1776: bk. 2, ch. 2, para. 86).

35 These are: (1) the peculiar circumstances of the country; (2) the nature of the employments and trades carried on in it; and (3) the system of banking. For the system of banking, he refers to its capacity: to furnish funds where there is real capital; to check unsafe and gambling transactions by withholding funds from those desirous of extending hazardous speculations, though deficient in capital; and to pursue its operations steadily and confidently notwithstanding any general embarrassment.

36 This is also true for classical economists (see Laidler 1991: 24).

37 Rae did mention about the Bank of England in Note G, in which he demonstrated his knowledge about the Bank of England as originally established for the payment and receipt of the revenue of the state. This seems mere repetition of exactly what Smith remarked on the Bank of England (Smith 1776: bk. 2, ch. 2, paras 79–85). Moreover, he was very cautious about this connection between the Bank of England and the state: "Indeed, I think there is reason to believe, that, from the great fluctuations thus introduced into what is called the money market, by the magnitude of the transactions of the state, the union of the two, when it takes place, operates injuriously on the general system of exchange of the country" (Rae 1834: 397). This explains in part why he could or did not develop the theory of Central Banking.

38 As a matter of fact, this field best fits into Dow's several characteristics of the "Scottish Tradition."

39 His interventionist element, especially his protectionist stance in international trade, has been most often asserted in the literature, and Rae has often been grouped into protectionists such as List or early American economists. However, this element should also be carefully analyzed against the background of Smith, who more than often argued for intervention. On this matter, see Hollander (this volume, ch. 12).

40 Rae briefly mentioned on the matter of "the exchange of the precious metals between different countries." He was even aware of the possible link of business fluctuations through international market: "Banks, as the great dealers in these metals, are necessarily exposed to the inconvenience of having to provide a supply for the demands occasioned by fluctuations in the business of different countries" (Rae 1834: 397–8). However, like Smith, he did not explicitly refer to Humean price-specie-flow mechanism.

41 Other than "Joplin on Currency," he did not name the full title of the book; we should therefore conjecture from the contents, referring to the relationship between the state of trade and the interest rate (Rae 1834: 403). With the help of the splendid work by O'Brien (1993), until now my best guess is Joplin (1832). If he actually read Joplin (1832), he could have known Thornton's argument.

42 He read and quoted from quite a few economists such as Lord Lauderdale, Say, and Sismondi. Moreover, we should be careful not to ignore Smith and English classical economists, since the wants-satisfying nature is always there, for example, in a treatment of value in use.

43 James (1965b: 135) said that Rae must have known some of the members of the Constitutional Society of Lower Canada, a select group of ultra-loyal pamphleteers, including John Fleming, director and vice-president of the Bank of Montreal in the period 1826–30 and the fifth president from 1830–2.

# 14

# RAE AND THE TRADITION OF SCOTTISH POLITICAL ECONOMY

*Alexander Dow, Sheila Dow, Alan Hutton, and Michael Keaney*

## Introduction

Attention has been drawn in some recent writing to the concept of a Scottish tradition in political economy. Macfie (1955) first drew attention to what he saw as uniquely Scottish characteristics in the development of economic thought. This was picked up by Dow (1987) and Mair (1990) as something worthy of attention in considering the current crisis in economics. They suggest that the characteristics of the Scottish tradition hold much in common with modern nonorthodox economics. In seeking an alternative to modern orthodox economics, therefore, it was suggested that it would be productive to consider the Scottish tradition further. Such a consideration would be useful for its own sake, as a case study of an alternative body of thought. But further it is useful in that various strands of modern nonorthodox economics may be seen to have been directly influenced by the Scottish tradition. For example, Skinner (1990: 163) notes elements in common between the Scottish tradition on the one hand, and the German historical school and American institutionalism on the other, while Prychitko (1995: 13) finds Scottish roots in Austrian economics. Mair (1990) makes the point about Scottish ancestry explicitly with respect to Rae, pointing to his (sometimes) acknowledged influence on Austrian economics, American institutionalism, and Schumpeterian economics (see also Elliott 1983; Edgell and Tilman 1991).

It is our purpose in this chapter to consider the particular issue of whether or not Rae should (as Macfie and Mair attest) be regarded as representative of the Scottish tradition. The first step is to consider what is meant by the concept of tradition itself. In the following section we shall consider why we might expect Rae to conform to the Scottish tradition (particularly given his emigration from Scotland). Then we shall look in some detail at the

Scottish tradition in political economy, and Rae's work in relation to it. Since Smith is often taken (e.g., by Dow 1987) as archetypal of the Scottish tradition, and yet Rae is often seen as counterposing himself to Smith, particular attention is paid to a comparison between Rae and Smith. It will be argued that Rae may indeed be treated as representative of the tradition in many respects, particularly with reference to his practice of economics. But it will be argued that he was not representative in the way in which he professed his methodology.

## The concept of tradition

The concept of intellectual tradition is not altogether straightforward. An attempt has been made in Dow et al. (1995) to specify what is meant by it, in particular distinguishing the notion of tradition from other classifications of thought. Other possibilities include "schools of thought," "paradigms" and "research programmes." While all of these modes of classification, including tradition, entail some overlap, there are features of the concept of tradition that make it most satisfactory for capturing the characteristics of Scottish thought which were evident in the early Scottish economists and which can be identified in those influenced by them.

A "school of thought" is generally used to refer to a collection of economists who are roughly contemporaries, as in the German historical school. This contemporaneity in turn entails direct communication among the participants. Given technological advance in communications, schools may now be more geographically dispersed than in Rae's time, when a school would tend to be identified with a particular geographical area. While it is clearly a matter of degree, *the concept of tradition refers rather to a lengthy period of time, where ideas are passed on from one generation to the next through a variety of means, of which direct communication is only one.*

Thus the concept of tradition is more diffuse than the concept of a school, referring to the conditions which lead economists in one generation to be subject to intellectual influences similar to those of their predecessors, and to absorb the ideas developed by their predecessors. *The concept of tradition thus entails the notion of continuity in the influences which nurture the tradition.* These influences include the educational, philosophical, and cultural environment. This emphasis on a nurturing environment is evident in all of Macfie, Dow, and Mair's discussions of the Scottish tradition. Further, continuities over the centuries in the cultural, religious, intellectual, and educational environment in Scotland may serve to explain the continuation of aspects of the tradition to the present day which are identified by all three authors.

Where individuals carry the tradition elsewhere, as in Rae's case, there must be sufficient in the new environment in common with the old to nurture a continuation of the tradition. In considering Rae in relation to the Scottish tradition, therefore, we need to consider the scope of its influence before he left Scotland, and the degree to which the new environment in which he found himself nurtured the tradition. First, Rae was brought up in Scotland and therefore absorbed the style of reasoning, and types of concerns, which characterized all aspects of life in Scotland. A philosophical approach to questions addressing practical and moral concerns was most evident in the Scottish system of higher education. A Scottish Arts degree, such as Rae took at Marischal College in 1815 is described by Davie as follows:

> If we look more closely at the Scottish Arts course . . . its really distinctive factor, its unique peculiarity as compared with courses not merely in England but on the Continent would seem to be that, while classics and the exact sciences were taught in addition to philosophy, the standard attained in the philosophical side of the course was considerably higher than in the other two parts of it. This was the result of an arrangement whereby the student regularly got a double dose, each from a different point of view, of the central problems of the Theory of Knowledge, such as Perception, Universals and Causality. The student was first taken through this very difficult subject by the Professor of Logic, and then again the following year by the Professor of Moral Philosophy.
>
> (Davie 1964: 11)

Further, as Davie demonstrates, the prominence of this approach to philosophy in the curriculum was reflected in the style and content of other disciplines. Thus, while Rae proceeded to study medicine at Edinburgh, medicine itself had a philosophical focus, and one which encouraged argument from first principles in order to address practical issues. Thus, for example, the major figure in Scottish medicine, Cullen, was primarily interested "in finding a general theory of disease which would connect up with speculation about the nature of life, and its relations to mind and matter" (Davie, 1964: 23–24). The social sciences too emerged under the influence of the Scottish philosophical tradition that had been institutionalized in the Scottish higher education tradition.

This was the set of influences which Rae carried with him when he emigrated from Scotland. It is evident from his prominent role in attempting to promote Scottish values in Canada that Rae was strongly conscious of the distinctiveness of his Scottish upbringing. Further, there was sufficient in common between the educational, religious, and cultural environment in Canada and that of Scotland (not least because of the influence of Scottish immigrants in a wide variety of fields) that Rae would have found a significant degree of continuity. Nevertheless, it is likely that his infrequent contact with other scholars must have allowed the influence of the Scottish tradition to dim somewhat.

A tradition is distinctive in a third important aspect. In particular, it differs from a paradigm or research programme in that these entail some fundamental agreement on foundations. In the case of a paradigm, there is agreement on worldview and choice of methods of enquiry (see Kuhn 1974), such that normal science (representative of the paradigm) consists of addressing puzzles within the agreed framework. In the case of a research programme, there is agreement on a hard-core set of assumptions, and on a negative and positive heuristic to direct lines of enquiry (see Lakatos 1970). Again there is overlap with the concept of tradition in that a tradition entails some shared methodological principles. But a tradition is a looser concept than paradigm or research programme, allowing for disagreements which spawn different theories based on different assumptions. Thus, for example, both Marxian and neo-Austrian economics can be seen to have had roots in the Scottish tradition.

This embracing of theoretical differences is important for any discussion of the Scottish political economy tradition, in that there were unquestionably differences among key figures in the tradition who were contemporaries, and even more so among those who were not. Certainly, the content of Rae's economics differed from that of Smith, although it can be argued that Rae exaggerated these differences, and that there was a significant amount of content in common (see Hollander in this volume). We will consider in more detail below the particular differences between Rae and Smith on methodology, since it is at that level that a tradition is defined. It is important therefore to identify those elements that define the tradition in order to identify those differences which are compatible with the tradition and those which are not. In the next section, we consider in turn the various features which identify the Scottish tradition. Rae's work is considered in relation to each of these features.

## The Scottish political economy tradition

The Scottish political economy tradition can be identified in terms of a range of features (as outlined in Dow 1987).

### 1 *A concern with practical issues*

Macfie regards this predilection as the result of the influence of an emphasis on Roman culture in Scottish classical education, rather than Greek culture. But it is, in fact, hard to disentangle cause from effect; all fields of Scottish life were approached in this manner (from religion to mathematics), which in turn must have encouraged the interest in Roman culture. Indeed, the necessities of a poor nation must have forced a concern with practical issues. A consequence of particular interest was the development of Common Sense philosophy. Philosophy in turn, and especially moral philosophy, coloured the approach taken to all other disciplines, through the higher education system.

Rae clearly conforms to this feature in his evident concern with the practical issues posed by survival in the Canadian wilderness in particular, and of innovation and economic development in general.

2 *A consequent preference for breadth of understanding of the background to these issues, over depth of understanding of isolated aspects of issues*

The theory of knowledge most closely associated with the Scottish tradition arising from the Enlightenment period is represented in Thomas Reid's Philosophy of Common Sense. As Davie puts it:

> Common sense knowledge . . . is knowledge of bodies which we could not get from the senses when they are in isolation from one another but which can be got from the senses when they are employed in co-operation so as to enable us to compare them together. The importance of this common sense knowledge is that it gives us a knowledge of aspects of things which in a genuine way transcends the senses and which thus is rightly called intellectual knowledge.
>
> (Davie 1986: 187)

The emphasis then is on knowledge arising from a combination of sources, rather than linearly from single sources. As Macfie puts it:

> [T]he Scottish method is more concerned with giving a broad well balanced comprehensive picture seen from different points of view than with logical rigour. In fact, Smith was . . . a philosophic writer. . . . His aim was to present all the relevant facts critically. Modern writers start from a totally different angle. They found on the law of non-contradiction. they aim at isolating one aspect of experience and breaking it down by analysis into its logical components.
>
> (Macfie 1955: 84)

Rae's work conforms to this approach. In chapter 14 of the *New Principles of Political Economy*, Rae (1834: 320) provides a summary account "of the combined operation of the causes investigated in the preceding chapters" with respect to the determination of "the nature and production of stock." The causes are classified according to whether they are material, not material, and partly material, partly not material. Thus the nature of man is investigated as well as the nature, level, and productivity of factors of production. Further, Rae is explicit that social science, in taking account of the nature of man, must reflect the complexity of the interactions between causal forces. Referring, therefore, to his analysis of the causes of economic development, Rae points out:

> We have considered them separately, but they never appear so, always acting in combination. This circumstance would not of itself affect any conclusions concerning them, for it applies to phenomena of all sorts, the causes influencing every one being compound. But the peculiar nature of the human mind, rather excited to action by motives, than passively operated on by them, and moulding, therefore, its energies to suit the course it adopts, occasions a difference between phenomena influenced by it and all others. Hence, according to the preponderating motive, and the course of action followed, the same powers and principles take opposite directions, and the will is able to draw to its purposes and make allies of those which would seem naturally opposed to it.
>
> (Rae 1834: 323)

3 *A preference for drawing on several disciplines in an integrated manner to provide that breadth*

This approach to knowledge was embodied in the breadth of the education system. There was further, however, a cross-fertilization between disciplines that may be explained in large part by their common philosophical underpinnings. Indeed, the social sciences emerged first as teaching applications of logic and moral philosophy. In turn, since this knowledge was being applied to practical issues, the scope for isolating aspects of these issues was limited if the results were to be at all useful. Since the chain of reasoning was not allowed to diverge too much from the question at hand, the importance of understanding context was of great importance, as was the need to take account of the complexity of influences on that context.

Again, Rae conforms to this characterization. He was concerned with questions which required attention to a wide range of disciplines. Thus, for example, he had planned at one stage to develop a natural history of man built on a philosophical conception of human society (see James 1951: 143). In his work on innovation, Rae quite deliberately took into account a much wider range of factors than the strictly economic, drawing in particular on history and sociology. Indeed it was his innovative development of the sociological approach to economics which was emphasized in the retitling of his *New Principles* by Mixter as *The Sociological Theory of Capital* when the book was reissued in 1905, and which inspired Irving Fisher's admiration (see James 1951).

4 *A preference for arguing from first principles*

In addressing practical issues, Scottish Enlightenment thought was addressing the challenge of new practical problems, requiring innovative chains of reasoning. While this required the creative combining of different approaches to knowledge as outlined in sections 2 and 3 above, some principles were required to provide a starting-point. In the social sciences these principles referred to the nature of man and of society. Yet the nature of man and of society were understood to be complex, and nondeterministic, reflecting the origin of the social sciences as applications of moral philosophy. Hence, for example, Smith's use of the concept of self-interest was built on his understanding of man's social nature, as represented in his development of the concept of sympathy in the *Theory of Moral Sentiments*. The first principles of the Scottish tradition should therefore not be confused with the axioms of conventional modern economics, which provide a deterministic, reductionist account of man.

Rae again fits well into this aspect of the Scottish tradition. He explicitly sets out in *The New Principles of Political Economy* to develop his own set of first principles. In the process, he questions Smith's principle of the division of labour. He carefully builds up his principles from an enquiry into the nature of man, the nature of capital and the nature of wealth. As the quotation in section 3 above makes clear, however, his analysis of human behaviour is of something creative, proactive, and nondeterministic, allowing a range of chains of reasoning from his principles. Indeed, Rae (1834: 96) explicitly refers to man as "an organic being," precluding the atomistic representation of economic man, as he was later represented by orthodox economics. Rae thus also embodied another important feature of the Scottish tradition, namely:

5 *A specification of first principles in terms of a nonindividualistic representation of human nature, with a consequent emphasis on social or conventional behaviour*

6 *A preference for approaching a subject's first principles by discussing their historical development*

This feature of the Scottish tradition again derives from the system of higher education and from its philosophical foundations. Because knowledge was not seen as an axiomatic system which could be parcelled up into discrete disciplines, each discipline was presented as an evolution of ideas drawing on a range of influences. The predominant teaching method was thus to impart first principles by means of teaching the historical evolution of the discipline through a variety of contexts. Mathematics, for example, was taught in this way, rather than as a closed axiomatic system. As Davie puts it:

> The Professors of Mathematics found, for example, that the best way to render their task of imparting the elements of geometry, algebra and arithmetic interesting to themselves and to their youthful pupils was to concentrate on the philosophy and the history of the branches of mathematics in question, and to treat the mathematics class as a cultural course, concerned with the relations of the subject to social life and to the plain man.
>
> (Davie 1961: 11)

This approach is clearly evident in the extensive historical reference in *The Wealth of Nations*. It is also manifest in Rae's *New Principles*. In the chapter concerned with "the causes of the progress of invention, and of the effects arising from it" (1834: bk. II, ch.10), Rae displays an extensive knowledge of a wide range of ancient societies in order to develop its principles.

7 *An acceptance of the limitations of theory*

8 *A recognition of the sociological and psychological aspects of theory appraisal*

While the Enlightenment project in political economy can be understood as an attempt to specify a socioeconomic system, along the lines of the systems being developed in the natural sciences, it was a particular feature of the Scottish Enlightenment that no claim was made as to the absolute truth value of the system. In particular, in the *History of Astronomy*, Smith ([1795] 1980) outlined a psychological theory of the development of knowledge which suggested that knowledge progressed by means of providing psychological satisfaction rather than by demonstrably approaching absolute truth.

Rae, on the other hand, does appear to see his task as establishing absolute truth. He was concerned about limitations to knowledge in terms of the difficulty of prediction (given the problem of induction) and the difficulty in identifying true causes as opposed to surface appearances of cause (see Hamouda in this volume). But Rae (1834: 328; see also 331–2) explicitly challenges Smith's view of science as being opposed to the principle of induction:

> Now, I apprehend, that the spirit of the philosophy of the author of the Wealth of Nations was completely opposed to the inductive philosophy – the philosophy of Bacon, and that he never intended that that work should be received as if established on it.

Rae then argues instead for the Baconian approach of induction as the best means for discovering truth; theory appraisal then proceeds according to the principle of falsification. Rae here would appear to be at odds with the Scottish tradition.

Since these (sections 7 and 8) are the two areas in which Rae appears to be at odds with the Scottish tradition, we shall make this the focus of attention of the next section. There we explore in more detail these last two aspects of the Scottish tradition, and Rae's stance on them. Since Rae expressed his views on methodology in direct opposition to those of Smith, we will use this apparent opposition as a basis for discussing how far Rae did in fact depart from the Scottish tradition in these two aspects.

## Rae's methodological critique of Smith

In order better to understand the philosophical background to Smith and to Rae, Coleman's (1996) analysis of Enlightenment rationalism is helpful. There he discusses the tensions between the rationalists, who see uniformity in nature (including human nature), and the antirationalists, who see diversity in nature. The former are drawn towards deductivism based on self-evident axioms; the latter are drawn towards empirical work in an attempt to identify regularities. Coleman, however, argues that the two may come together in theorizing, where the former build theories on self-evident truths and the latter on empirically established axioms. He further maintains that the Scottish Enlightenment represented a complex combination of rationalism and antirationalism. Indeed, Hume ([1751] 1975) denied the validity of the distinction between a priori axioms and observed regularities on the grounds that ultimately the former were based on observation. Thus, in Stewart (1866), we find an emphasis on the importance of general principles, along with inductivism; this was justified on the grounds that the general principles arose from experience.

But both Stewart and Reid, whom he greatly influenced, explicitly objected to the instrumentalist aspect of Smith's ([1795] 1980) epistemology evident in the *History of Astronomy*, where he argued that speculative hypotheses may help us to identify underlying causes which mere observation cannot reveal. Certainly Smith pointed out that only those principles which accorded with already-understood knowledge would gain acceptance, in accordance with the philosophy of common sense. But his greater willingness to contemplate hypothetical knowledge raises the question as to whether he is in fact atypical of the Scottish tradition. This is of importance if we are to regard Smith as the archetypal Scottish political economist. It is also significant in understanding the subsequent, deductivist, developments in economics. Our concern here is to consider Rae's methodological position, expressed as it is in counterpoint to Smith.

Coleman's schema, employing the traditional dualistic categories of deduction and induction, rationalism, and antirationalism, is useful here because Rae himself expressed his methodology dualistically, and dualism was certainly a feature of the Enlightenment period in general. Nonetheless, the problem in applying this schema to the Scottish tradition, even in arguing that the Scottish approach entailed a combination of opposites, is that that tradition is nondualistic. The moral philosophical foundations of knowledge, the openness to different disciplines, the consciousness of the importance of history and context, and, above all, the social conception of human nature, embracing creativity and active agency, and the driving force of addressing practical problems, all preclude a focus on duals (see Dow 1990). The rationalism of the Scottish Enlightenment was not the rationalism of the English Enlightenment. Undoubtedly, Smith was a system builder, which requires a belief in some underlying order. That system was not deterministic, however, given his (typically Scottish) conception of human nature. Certainly, Smith introduced the notion of a psychological theory of the development of knowledge, but that did not mean that he saw theory as developing independently of observation; a glance through *The Wealth of Nations* is sufficient to establish that argument.

For all Reid's own objections to Smith, we would argue that his Philosophy of Common Sense represents the balance struck within the Scottish theory of knowledge between observation and theory. Observation is necessary, but intellectual knowledge, based on wide-ranging observation, has its own legitimacy (see Davie 1986: ch. 10). Reid's argument with Smith is an argument over the source of intellectual knowledge. But the Scottish philosophic tradition grounds intellectual knowledge in observation while giving it its own legitimacy. Smith had gone further by probing the motivation for and process of generating intellectual knowledge, which in no way undermines realist philosophy unless it involves a dualistic dichotomization between observation and theory. Both Reid and Smith had a (rationalist) belief in the existence of underlying forces which generated an ordered system. Observation of surface phenomena could be misleading. Yet the order was not a deterministic order, so that a retreat into deductivism with the aid of some universal self-evident axioms was not feasible. For Smith, the division of labour and the operation of self-interest were governing principles, but what these actually meant in practice required detailed observation of the social, political, historical, etc., context, so that theory could never depart significantly from observation if it were to be useful in addressing practical questions.

Rae presented his *New Principles* as a critique of Smith, at the level of content (notably with respect to the distinction between individual and national wealth), but also at the level of methodology. In Book II, chapter 15, of the *New Principles*, Rae challenges the understanding of Smith as engaging in induction, arguing rather that he engages in "explanation." The difference in content is purported by Rae to follow from the difference in method; he criticizes Smith for confusing effects with causes. He suggests that Smith has taken phenomena to be principles, rather than investigating further in order to find the real principles; thus he adopts the common man's confusion between individual wealth and national wealth, presuming rather than investigating the causal relations between the two. On the face of it, it would seem that Rae took a quite different approach to Smith and thus cannot be thought to be representative of the Scottish tradition.

Rae's methodological argument with Smith concerns the source of intellectual knowledge. Like Smith, Rae too seeks to identify underlying forces which are not apparent from simple observation. By criticizing Smith for relying unduly on surface appearances – that is, on popular common sense knowledge – Rae is arguing that Smith is not trying hard enough to develop intellectual knowledge of the underlying system. What Smith identifies as cause (the division of labor), Rae identifies as the effect of innovation. Rae's argument therefore seems to be that Smith is not taking a particular methodology far enough, not that he is employing a different (less-preferred) methodology. Their differences over general principles may then be treated as differences in theoretical content, rather than methodological differences.

Rae ventures further, however, in arguing that Smith does not go far enough because he does not employ the method of induction:

> To me it appears that [Smith's] philosophy is that of explanation and system, and that his speculations are not to be considered as inductive investigations and expositions of the real principles guiding the successions of phenomena, but as successful efforts to arrange with regularity, according to common and preconceived notions, a multiplicity of known facts.
>
> (Rae 1834: 331)

Following Francis Bacon, Rae sets out the position of falsification as the means for establishing true knowledge:

> The whole inductive philosophy may, indeed, be said to rest on the impossibility of the occurrence of exceptions to real laws. Hence the extensive use of *negative instances*, determining, at last, what is a principle by pointing out what is not.
>
> (ibid. 344)

He proceeds to illustrate the principle by pointing out counterexamples to Smith's argument that the wealth of nations is promoted by the seeking of individual wealth. (His reference here to gamblers is apposite to modern discussions about the activities of financial markets.)

The impression is created by Rae that Smith is deductivist and Rae inductivist. This impression is created partly by Rae's imposition of the dualistic categories (deduction and induction) employed by Bacon. This dualistic approach is uncharacteristic of the Scottish epistemological tradition, reflecting more diverse influences on Rae. It belies the complex interrelationship between observation and theory intrinsic to the Scottish approach. In particular, while Smith may have focused more than most on the role of conjecture in theory-building, the driving force behind theory-building for him was, in fact, falsificationism. In the *History of Astronomy*, Smith provided an account of theorizing which centered theory development on the response to surprise, i.e., to contrary observations. The dualistic approach also belies both Smith and Rae's actual methodological practice. Both, consistent with the Scottish tradition, intertwine extensive observation with an attempt to build up intellectual knowledge of underlying forces; they intertwine in the sense that observation provides the material for conjecture, and also the test of conjecture. The *New Principles* is best understood as setting out a system of economic development based on the principle of innovation, just as the *Wealth of Nations* is best seen as a system of economic development based on the principle of the division of labour. It is important to bear in mind, however, that, in line with the Scottish tradition, these systems are open systems, and cannot therefore be thought of in deductivist terms.

As far as the limitations to theory are concerned, both Smith and Rae had been influenced by Hume's scepticism about inductive knowledge, and were therefore conscious of the limitations on the scope for establishing arguments. This skepticism was reinforced by their understanding of the necessary openness of theorizing about evolving social systems; while it might be possible to agree on general principles, the meaning and applicability of those principles in particular contexts required detailed observation and exercise of judgement. Nevertheless, the goal was to identify underlying forces: for all the limitations to theory, there was a belief in the existence of real forces which it was the purpose of science to identify.

The conclusion emerges that Smith and Rae were much closer than Rae's statement of their methodological differences would imply. Indeed, Rae later acknowledges that his criticisms are directed more at Smith's followers than Smith himself:

> I shall conclude these remarks, by observing, that in my opinion the disciples and followers of Smith, in claiming for the speculations contained in the *Wealth of Nations*, and for the doctrines they have founded on them, the rank of an experimental science, the conclusions of which are entitled to the same credence with other experimental sciences act injudiciously, and by insisting on pretensions which are unfounded, injure the cause of that philosopher and conceal his real merits.
>
> (Rae 1834: 350)

But the *History of Astronomy* remains as a potential bone of contention, constituting as it did the focus of expressions of methodological differences between Smith and other key figures in the Scottish tradition. We devote the next section to a consideration of the *History of Astronomy* in relation to the *New Principles*, and again find much in common between the two.

## A missed connection between Rae and Smith

The *History of Astronomy* was concerned with understanding the sentiments "surprise," "wonder" and "admiration" which provide the stimulus for the development of knowledge:

> It is the design of this Essay to consider particularly the nature and causes of each of these sentiments, whose influence is of far wider extent than we should be apt upon a careless view to imagine.
> (Smith [1795] 1980: 34)

Philosophers are motivated in their theorizing by the need to dispel the sense of wonder, or discomfort, caused by surprising observations– that is, those observations which do not accord with currently held theories – and by the admiration inspired by new theories which accommodate these observations:

> Wonder, therefore, and not any expectation of advantage from its discoveries, is the first principle which prompts mankind to the study of Philosophy, of that science which pretends to lay open the concealed connections which unite the various appearances of nature; and they pursue this study for its own sake, as an original pleasure or good in itself, without regarding its tendency to procure them the means of many other pleasures.
> (ibid. 51)

There are interesting parallels between the *History of Astronomy* and Book II, chapter 10, of the *New Principles*, where Rae investigates 'the causes of the progress of invention' (as well as its effects). Rae too distinguishes between inventors and other members of society, and seeks to explain what motivates them. Inventors are not motivated by the prospect of gaining wealth, since the outcomes of invention are subject to considerable uncertainty, and thus do not attract certain reward. Indeed, Rae goes to some length to outline the hardships and lack of recognition which are the customary lot of inventors:

> We in vain search for any sufficient motive exciting to this course of action, unless the good arising from communicating good, and

> the consequent desire to be a benefactor in the most extended possible manner.
>
> (Rae 1834: 210)

It is notable for our purposes that Rae explicitly refers to Bacon's parallel argument about the motivation for the advance of science (Rae 1834: 216–17). Indeed the conflation of Rae's use of the concept "invention" with the concept of "science" is encouraged, not only by his reference in both contexts to "men of genius," but also by the reader's perception that Rae's account of the lot of the inventor arises from his perceptions of his own situation as someone developing knowledge about the role of invention in economic development.

Rae's account of the "man of genius" does not accord well with a purist inductivist position. Referring to the isolation of men of genius from society, Rae continues:

> Abstract and scientific truth can only be discovered, by deep and absorbing meditation; imperfectly at first discerned, through the medium of its dull capacities, the intellect slowly, and cautiously, not without much of doubt, and many unsuccessful essays, succeeds in lifting the veil that hides it.
>
> (ibid. 213–14)

He identifies the motive of accumulation (the selfish motive of practical men) as encouraging invention along with the (selfless) motivation of the inventor to discovery. But the two motivations may act contrarily when the social order is disrupted, for example by war. While such disturbances make the prospect of accumulation subject to greater uncertainty, thus weakening the accumulation motive, they actively encourage the inventive faculty. In making this argument, Rae comes close to the Smith of the *History of Astronomy*:

> Whatever, therefore, breaks the wonted order of events, and exposes the necessity, or the possibility, of connecting them by some other means, strongly stimulates invention.
>
> (ibid. 223)

However, Rae does not give any sign of recognizing common ground between himself and Smith in this regard. Although all the discussion of the motivation for invention appears to apply equally to knowledge in general as well as to solutions to practical problems, the extensive examples of invention refer exclusively to the latter. Further, the emphasis in the examples is on the accumulation motive, with inventions being stimulated by resource shortages, requiring new technology applied to existing resources, or the development of alternative resources. The connection is not taken further between the practical man wishing to overcome constraints and the man of genius who invents the mechanism for doing so from the much wider range of knowledge he has developed, being uncertain of the outcome of his enquiries.

It seems unfortunate that Rae, having himself been so innovative in developing the concept of invention, made, by omission, a strong distinction between his discussion of invention and his discussion of scientific methodology. His use of the word "speculation" to describe the activities of the inventor holds echoes of Smith's discussion of scientific enquiry; there are strong parallels in the motivations of pursuing knowledge for its own sake, and seeking connecting principles from discordant observations. It was left to the neo-Austrians to develop in tandem the nature and origins of knowledge in economic theory and of knowledge in the economy.

## Conclusion

We have defined the concept of tradition as referring to a continuity over generations in epistemological and methodological approach, allowing for accommodation of theoretical differences. Moreover, we have argued that Rae conforms to most aspects of the Scottish political economy tradition.

The two areas of potential conflict are differences over perceptions of the limitations of theory, and a recognition of the sociological and psychological aspects of theory development. Rae pits himself against Smith by taking an avowedly purist inductivist position, following Bacon. The dualistic way in which he expresses this position is at odds with the Scottish tradition; it seems also to entail an understanding of science as revealing truth. But the practice of Rae's enquiries are in the mainstream of Scottish methodology, emphasizing the importance of general principles, which have their origin in experience, but which have their own legitimacy as intellectual knowledge. Further, these principles are developed and applied in the full consciousness of the importance of context, so that their discussion never departs far from detailed contextual accounts. His principles are different from Smith's, and thus have important differences of implications. The methodology, however, is very similar.

Rae joins with others in rejecting Smith's psychological account of theory development, as if it were counterposed to the principle of induction. Nonetheless, Rae's own account of the motivation for science is very similar to Smith's. In fact, he could have benefited considerably from paying more attention to the *History of Astronomy*, since contrary evidence (or falsification) is a primary motive for Smith in theory development. It is unfortunate that Rae seems to have conflated his opposition to the content of Smith's economics with an opposition to his philosophy of science, when in fact the latter was not too far away from that of Rae. Indeed, given the centrality of knowledge to Rae's economics, it is unfortunate that he did not use Smith's ideas for his own purposes.

How, then, does Rae stand in relation to the Scottish tradition as we have defined it? Mair (1991) distinguishes between "legitimate" and "bastard" lines in the tradition running from Smith, where Rae is identified with the bastard tradition. On the other hand, Pesciarelli (1994) argues that the diversity represented by Smith and Rae is compatible with a single tradition. Clearly, there are differences; it is a matter of judgement how much importance is given to these differences. In our judgement, if we ignore Rae's statement of his methodology and focus rather on his practice, he sits squarely in the Scottish political economy tradition.

# 15

# RAE AS AN EARLY POST-KEYNESIAN

*Douglas Mair and Anthony J. Laramie*

## Introduction

Although it may be sometimes misleading to label an individual as being the founder of a particular school of thought, John Rae undoubtedly had a major influence on the development of Austrian and Institutionalist economics. As Ahmad (Chapter 6) and Rymes (Chapter 8) report in this volume on Rae's capital theory, Rae had fully anticipated by at least fifty years the subsequent development by Böhm-Bawerk of Austrian capital theory. Drakopoulos in Chapter 2 also discusses the similarities between Rae and Menger in their use of the concepts of orders of instruments and orders of goods. Although Veblen never explicitly acknowledged his indebtedness to Rae, as Mason points out in Chapter 4, Rae's ideas on conspicuous consumption were clearly extended and developed by Veblen (1899) in his *Theory of the Leisure Class*. W.C. Mitchell is more explicit in recognizing Rae as "the founding father of American Institutionalism" (Mair, 1990). To the extent that Schumpeter is recognized as an important figure in the development of evolutionary economics, Rae may also be given credit through his influence on Schumpeter's early thinking, particularly in the latter's *Theory of Economic Development*. Our purpose in this chapter is to argue that in certain of the ideas which Rae set out in *New Principles* can also be seen as antecedents of post-Keynesian theorizing.

The outline of this chapter is as follows. (1) We record Macfie's (1955) assessment of Rae as an important figure in the Scottish political economy tradition. (2) We argue that it is quite legitimate to identify the method and content of modern post-Keynesian economics with the Scottish tradition. (3) We then assess the adequacy of contemporary tax theory to address issues of dynamics. (4) We go on to discuss Rae's views on the importance of the accumulative principle, on the role of the legislator, and on the use of taxation to control the consumption of luxuries. (5) Finally, we argue that Rae's ideas on taxation demonstrate close similarity to post-Keynesian ideas.

## Rae and the Scottish political economy tradition

The idea that there is a Scottish tradition in political economy was first proposed by Macfie (1955) and subsequently developed by Campbell (1976), Dow (1987) and Dow et al. (this volume, Chapter 14). Dow et al. define the concept of a tradition as referring to a continuity over generations in epistemological and methodological approach, allowing for accommodation of theoretical differences. On this basis, they argue that Rae conforms to most aspects of the Scottish political economy tradition. Although Rae set out to create the impression that he differed quite fundamentally from Smith on the issue of methodology – he being an inductivist and Smith a deductivist – this difference, according the Dow et al., turns out to be more apparent than real. Also, Hollander in this volume (Chapter 12) argues that the policy differences between Smith and Rae have been overstated. Thus we see no incongruity in regarding Rae and Smith as belonging to the same Scottish political economy tradition.

The essential feature of that tradition we wish to emphasize and which marks its fundamental difference from the nineteenth- and twentieth-century development of mainstream ideas is expressed by Macfie:

> It should not be laid to Smith's account that Benthamite Utilitarianism became the basis of orthodox economic thought. . . . It is in fact just an accident of history . . . that the method of static equilibrium originated in his [Smith's] Book I. The central assumptions of Benthamite Utilitarianism are themselves antithetic to the whole spirit of the Scottish social school. The main philosophic contrast is between a mechanistic psychology, which eliminates any truly moral theory and the optimistic forward-looking assumptions of the Scottish school; or again it is seen in the fact that the Scots saw the central fact as a *growing* society, a creature quite different from any mere individual, whereas to Bentham any society was merely an aggregate of individuals. This broad contrast is of central importance for modern economics simply because Marshall accepted as the basis of his positive economic theory the mechanistic "ethical" or psychological assumptions of Bentham. The static equilibrium theory of "normal" value is therefore itself inevitably mechanistic. It traces the run down, after disturbance, to a position of stable equilibrium. It has great heuristic value. But its practical inadequacey stands out; it is not equipped to deal with changes *away* from equilibrium. Yet these changes seem to dominate our economic fates. [emphasis in original]
>
> (Macfie 1955: 96)

The Scottish concern is, therefore, for a "growing society" and not the steady state which came to dominate English thinking. Macfie (1955) permits himself the indulgence of some speculation as to how economics might have developed had it gone down the route indicated by Rae instead of the route indicated by Bentham. Certainly, Macfie saw a Rae-inspired economics as a "better-balanced," "more realistic," and "more practical" science than it had developed by the mid-1950s.

> Suppose Benthamism had not captured the dynastic succession. It is possible that then the spirit and outlook of Lauderdale and Rae might have gained command? . . . they were both completely in the Scots manner and method. . . . They thought Smith's theory should give more weight to the importance of invention, novelty, new arrangements in history. Smith, of course, did much here, but to Lauderdale and Rae it is picked on as the core of economic growth and this is suggested as the central issue in theory and practice. . . . Enterprise is its most positive pole. . . . This is the drive behind economic growth. Had it grown [i.e. the emphasis in Lauderdale and Rae on invention and novelty] . . . our economic theory would certainly be a better balanced, a more realistic, more practical equipment than it is today.
>
> (Macfie 1955: 97)

## Post-Keynesian economics

There are two broad groups of post-Keynesians, one whose members see themselves as the only true disciples of Keynes and the other whose members draw their intellectual inspiration from Kalecki and, by extension, from Marx. The shared concern of all post-Keynesians is to offer an explanation of economic growth and income distribution, for both of which the key determinant is the rate of investment. However, where the two principal post-Keynesian camps diverge is over the direction of causation between investment and profits. For "Keynesian" post-Keynesians, profits are assumed to determine investment, whereas for "Kaleckian" post-Keynesians, investment determines profits. "capitalists may decide to . . . invest more in a given period than in a preceding one, but they cannot decide to earn more . . . therefore, their investment . . . decisions . . . determine profits . . . not vice versa" (Kalecki [1968] 1971: 78–9). Of this distinction, more below.

A second principal feature of post-Keynesian economics is its recognition that economies expand continuously, though unevenly, through time. This view of economic systems being in continuous motion stands in sharp contrast to neoclassical partial or general equilibrium models where it is assumed that systems will eventually come to rest after some disturbance.

Dow (1991) argues that in terms of methodology and content, both camps of post-Keynesians have their roots in classical political economy. The methodological groundwork was laid by Smith, particularly in *Theory of Moral Sentiments* and *History of Astronomy*. The content is to be found in the writings of Malthus, Ricardo and Marx. Malthus' views of the importance of effective demand lead on to Keynes and Kalecki; Ricardo and his subsequent influence on Sraffa lead to a rejection by post-Keynesians of neoclassical economics; and Marx's study of the laws of motion of capitalism, driven by the accumulative motive, leads to an explanation of the periodic crises of capitalism from which post-Keynesians of a Kaleckian persuasion derive inspiration.

We see in Macfie's rejection of the "mechanistic" and "static equilibrium" of Benthamism, many of the reasons for the emergence of post-Keynesianism. The issues which post-Keynesian economics considers important are the laws of motion of capitalism, economic growth, income distribution, unemployment, and the attendant role of the state. These we equate with the Scottish concern for the problems of a "growing society."

In general terms, we argue that in important respects post-Keynesian economics shares common concerns with the Scottish political economy tradition. Specifically, where we consider Rae's particular contribution to the development of post-Keynesian economics arises is in his treatment of taxation. At first sight, this may seem somewhat surprising because Rae's discussion of taxation is not a central theme of his *New Principles*, and until recently, post-Keynesian economics had not developed an explicit theory of taxation (Laramie and Mair, forthcoming). Yet, as we propose to show, Rae did identify a number of the essential conditions of a post-Keynesian approach to taxation.

## Problems of modern treatment of taxation

The apogee of Macfie's criticism of modern economics is its treatment of taxation. Much of the recent tax literature has focused on issues of tax optimality (Heady 1996). Smith's four canons of taxation of equality, certainty, convenience of payment, and economy in collection are recited as mantra from which an elaborate superstructure of theoretical welfare economics is erected to analyze the effects of taxation. We are tempted to accept Rothbard's (1995: 469) obloquy that public finance economists who have based their analyses on Smith's canons "have contributed little of interest to the subject of taxation."

The problem for mainstream comparative static theory of taxation has arisen because its microeconomic starting point is Paretian welfare economics and the recognition that lump-sum taxes and transfers are the only non-distorting instruments by which efficiency objectives can be achieved. This then allows public sector production decisions to be taken without jeopardizing the first-best conditions of the Paretian system. A great deal of the recent theory of optimal taxation has been an extension of first-best theory to situations where lump-sum taxes and transfers are not possible but where the other assumptions of first-best theory are retained. The macroeconomic starting point of the static theory of taxation is Harrod's (1939) warranted rate of growth equation, subsequently extended by Solow (1956) and Arrow (1962). In this family of orthodox growth theory models, the sole source of long-run growth in output per head is exogenous technical progress. But this is unsatisfactory from the point of view of understanding the determinants of growth and designing policies to influence it.

Orthodox public finance theory recognizes three economic functions of government: allocation, stabilization, and distribution (Musgrave 1959). With the emergence of monetarism and supply-side economics in recent years, the focus of attention has been on allocation, with little attention paid to stabilization and distribution. As a consequence of the preoccupation of orthodox theory with comparative statics, a fourth function of government activity – the growth function – has been completely neglected (Newland 1992).

To the extent that modern public finance theory has addressed the issue of tax dynamics, it has been through the medium of overlapping-generations models (Auerbach, Kotlikoff and Skinner 1983; Auerbach and Kotlikoff 1987). The entire focus of attention has been to establish the present and future sets of factor prices and factor supplies necessary to maintain the economy on its equilibrium growth path. Little thought has been given to consideration of the role of taxation in either stabilizing the economy or stimulating it onto a higher growth path.

There is now a belated recognition by mainstream public finance economists of the cul-de-sac into which they have manoeuvred themselves. Thus Kotlikoff and Summers (1987: 721) recognize:

> Much of the current tax incidence literature considers settings of certainty, perfect information and market clearing. As more sophisticated models relax these assumptions, the theory of tax incidence will be enriched and, with all probability, provide even more surprising and exciting insights.

More recently, Stern (1992: 293) has conceded: "The theory of optimal taxation has not had a great deal to say about dynamics and the theory of growth has been reticent on taxation," and Burgess and Stern (1993: 795) admit: "while the simple intuition developed in [static] theory has some usefulness, it may only have a limited role to play in the understanding of dynamic tax policy."

## Rae and the accumulative principle

So, let us reverse out of the cul-de-sac and set off down the road to Rae that Macfie so clearly signposted forty years ago. In his *New Principles*,

Rae produced a pioneering analysis of the roles of accumulation and invention. He argued that since capital accumulation is the result of fundamental human activities, one should not study it as a cause, as he suggests Smith did, but rather one should study those individual and collective activities which give rise to wealth. He attributed the generation of wealth, or the stock of capital or instruments, in any society to four specific elements, of which the two most relevant for our purposes in this paper are "the effective desire of accumulation" and the "inventive faculty."

The effective desire of accumulation, "is of different degrees of strength, not only in different societies . . . but also in the several individuals composing the same society" (Rae [1834] 1965: 130). The returns to instruments are increased by their exhaustion:

> by rapidly exhausting the capacity of any instrument, the returns yielded by it are not lessened but quickened. The powers it possesses to bestow enjoyment, or to aid in the formation of other instruments, are not diminished in quantity, but sooner brought into action, and it passes to an order of quicker return. When, therefore, the efforts of individuals, so divided, are successful, by placing the instruments operated on in more quickly returning orders, they stimulate the *accumulative principle* to give greater capacity to instruments of the sort, *and proportionally increase the capacity of the whole stock of instruments owned by the society*. [emphasis added]
>
> (ibid. 164)

Rae lists three positive and three negative circumstances which will affect the desire to accumulate. For our purposes in this chapter, the positive circumstances we identify are his second and third:

> 2. The extent of the intellectual powers . . . in the minds of the members of the society.
> 3. The stability of the affairs of the society, and the reign of law and order throughout it.
>
> (ibid. 124)

Here we interpret Rae as arguing that the accumulative principle, which is one of his two driving forces of economic growth, will depend on:

1 the intelligence of the members of society, that is, on their appreciation that there are positive measures which they can take to stimulate growth; and
2 on the role of the state in terms of its ability to maintain an orderly society.

## Rae and the role of the legislator

These circumstances lead us to an important point of difference between Rae and Smith. In Book Three of *New Principles*, Rae discusses the operations of the legislator on national stock or capital. He recognizes the need for representative democracy:

> When men unite in large societies, they cannot each take an active part in what concerns the common good. They are obliged to delegate their individual powers and rights to act, in things relating to it, to several or to one [who] may properly be termed the legislator.
>
> (Rae [1834] 1965: 358)

Though not quoting Smith and the *Wealth of Nations* directly, Rae then cites Dugald Stewart's ([1795] 1980) *Account of the Life and Writings of Dr. Smith* as evidence of Smith's hostile attitude to the state:

> Little else is required to carry a state to the highest degree of opulence from the lowest barbarism but peace, easy taxes and a tolerable administration of justice . . . All governments which thwart this natural course, which force things into a different channel, or which endeavour to arrest the progress of society at a particular point, are unnatural, and to support themselves are obliged to be oppressive and tyrannical.
>
> (Stewart [1795] 1980: 104; quoted in Rae [1834] 1965: 358)

Rae sees this hostile attitude to the state as an important feature of the subsequent development of Smith by his followers:

> The principle here set forth by Adam Smith, though not formally announced in the *Wealth of Nations*, runs, nevertheless, through the whole work and in its particular application to this science, *forms the most important of the conclusions to which his reasonings tend. It is very frequently, also, expressly brought forward by supporters of his opinions, as an argument against the interference of the legislator, and of all those they employ*. [emphasis added]
>
> (Rae [1884] 1965: 358)

On the other hand, Rae has a more positive attitude to the legislator. Drawing the distinction between things which happen by nature and those which happen by art, he argues:

> According to this view of the subject, it is the legislator alone, who can, of design, act with the view to advance the national

> opulence. It is held, however, that as this interference of the legislator disturbs the course which events would otherwise have taken, it acts in opposition to the course of nature, and, therefore, the presumption is that it will be injurious. *On the contrary, I hold, that a just analogy would rather lead us to infer that it will be beneficial.* [emphasis added]
>
> (ibid. 360)

He adopts a pragmatic, but generally pro-legislator, stance: "Is it then a thing to be assumed, *a priori*, as next to demonstrable, that art, the art of the legislator, cannot operate so as to advance the prosperity of nations?" (ibid. 361). Legislators, though not immune from error, are, nevertheless, concerned to promote the prosperity of the nation:

> That the result of a successful inquiry into the nature of wealth, would terminate in affording the means of exposing the errors that legislators had committed from not attending to all the circumstances connected with the growth of that wealth, whose progress it had been their aim to advance, and would so teach them, not that they ought to remain inactive, *but how they may act safely and advantageously*. [emphasis added]
>
> (ibid.)

Rae concludes in his chapter on the role of the legislator by restating the conditions he had earlier identified as necessary to promote the accumulative principle, namely, promoting the general intelligence of society and advancing the progress of science. The two specific policy prescriptions he recommends for the legislator to adopt are:

1. the inward transfer of foreign arts; and
2. the application to useful purposes of funds which would otherwise be dissipated in luxury.

## Rae, luxury, and taxation

One of Rae's enduring contributions to economics was to introduce the idea of conspicuous consumption. Again, Rae is at odds with Smith on this issue. Rae saw conspicuous consumption as something to be resisted. It fed off vanity, especially that of the capitalist class, and had no redeeming features. Luxury goods, deriving their value from their relative scarcity secured by high prices and limited availability, represented to Rae a loss to society by neither supplying real wants nor increasing overall well-being. He had two cures for conspicuous consumption. The first reflected the influence of Heinrich von Storch and advocated religious education as the means of tackling vanity, the root cause of the problem. The second, and more secular, approach was to tax the consumption of luxury goods.

Bearing in mind his generally pro-legislator stance, Rae argues in Book Three that the legislator *can increase the rate of growth of capital by the taxation of luxury goods*:

> It appears, therefore, that there are at least two modes by which the legislator *can effectively advance the general stock* . . . 2d By applying to useful purposes a portion of those funds, which in all societies, are otherwise dissipated in the production of mere luxuries . . . the legislator [is] as always endeavoring to act for the good the society, and capable of understanding what is for its good . . . it may be that he [the legislator] does not adopt judicious measures for the purposes, but if so, it is his judgment, not his will that is in fault. [emphasis added]
>
> (Rae [1834] 1965: 377)

Again, Rae emphasizes his difference with Smith over the issue of state intervention: "the doctrines of the followers of Adam Smith . . . hold up legislative interference as necessarily and essentially evil" (ibid. 380). He recognizes that in advocating the taxation of luxuries, he is laying himself open to the criticism that the rate of growth of capital will decline:

> It is said that capital can only augment by accumulation, and, as the interference of the legislator takes something from individual revenue, it must also take from the power to accumulate, and consequently, instead of augmenting, must tend to diminish the sum of the capitals of all the individuals in the society, that is the national capital or stock.
>
> (ibid. 381)

Interference by the legislator through the taxation of luxuries is justified by means of an argument which we consider to be extremely insightful:

> The answer to this objection is, that the proceedings of the legislator *may increase the absolute capital and stock of the society*, the provision, that is, for future wants embodied in the stock of instruments possessed by it . . . that is the amount of the absolute capital of the society, which is the proper measure of the wealth of the whole . . . and that whatever augments it not only directly, and of itself, advances national wealth, but ultimately, also, does so indirectly, *through the stimulus given to the accumulative principle* and the addition thence arising to relative capital. [emphasis added]
>
> (ibid. 381–82)

Rae ends this chapter with perhaps his most strongly worded criticism of Smith:

> The fundamental error on this subject of Adam Smith, and the present prevailing school of political economists in England, lies, in their assuming, that what is true concerning an individual is true, also, concerning a community, and maintaining, consequently, *that every impost is so much an absolute loss to the society and every diminution of it, so much gain.* Before this assumption can be made good, with regard to any particular impost, it is necessary that the three following questions concerning it should be determined.
>
> *1st. Will the duty so levied, by directly or indirectly effecting an improvement in the arts, increase the absolute capital of the society?* [emphasis added]
>
> (ibid. 384)

Here, Rae has, in our opinion, hit the problem of contemporary tax theory exactly on the head. Modern tax theory is preoccupied with defining the conditions under which the introduction of taxation will have a minimal effect on the Pareto optimal allocation of a given amount of resources. It has no means of addressing the issue of the scope for fiscal policy in affecting the growth performance of the economy.

It is of course a far cry to argue that because Rae had early identified the fallacy of composition, which still bedevils contemporary theory of taxation, and had recognized the possibility of an acceleration in the rate of growth of capital through the fiscal policy measures of enlightened legislators, he had worked out a fully articulated theory of taxation. Analysis of taxation did not occupy a central role in *New Principles* in the way that the principle of accumulation or the inventive faculty or the role of the banking system did. Rae's treatment of taxation appears almost as an afterthought in his discussion of conspicuous consumption. More importantly, though, Rae recognized that the effect of taxation introduced for the purpose of reducing the consumption of luxuries was not so much in reducing "individual utilities," but in its positive macroeconomic effects on the rate of growth of capital.

## Rae and post-Keynesian tax theory

As we have argued above, Rae and Smith can both be regarded as belonging to the Scottish political economy tradition and we see no incongruity in assessing Rae's ideas on taxation within the Kaleckian stream of post-Keynesianism.

Kalecki's aphorism, "Workers spend what they earn; capitalists earn what they spend," encapsulates two fundamental tenets of Kaleckian economic theory. The first is of differential savings propensities as between workers (whose savings propensity is assumed to be zero) and capitalists (who are the only source of savings). The second is that investment must preceed savings. Capitalists invest in the expectation of future profits, which finance their consumption and generate the savings for future investment.

Confirmation of Rae's view of the zero savings propensity of workers can be seen in a passage where he accuses workers of indulging in wine, women, and song:

> The laborer seeks preeminence in displaying his abilities to spend, and employs any spare funds he may possess in the purchase of fineries, in treating his companions at the alehouse, and in similar extravagancies.
>
> (Rae [1834] 1965: 326)

More generally, Rae's argument is that workers' purchases will be of instruments of the more quickly returning orders, that is, personal instruments," or what we would now call consumer durables. Thus there is clear evidence that Rae believed in differential savings propensities, with workers' "productive savings" propensity being zero.

Gootzeit's (this volume, Chapter 9) analysis of Rae's treatment of savings shows Rae also to be in close agreement with Kalecki's "capitalists earn what they spend" maxim. According to Gootzeit, Rae was certainly not part of the Smith–Mill–Marshall–Keynes tradition which focused on personal savings as productive. Instead, he was much more in the Senior–Cairns tradition which focused more on business savings as the chief force behind national expansion (Gootzeit 1995). Although Rae never used the term "productive savings," his ideas implied that business savings were more productive than personal savings. Because he believed that growth depended on the size of the nation's stock of capital, he tried throughout *New Principles* to identify the necessary types of "productive savings." He downplayed the role of personal savings and argued that business savings were the only type of savings that could lead to a nationally expanding stock of capital. In Rae's view, new capital instruments could only be formed from increased business profits or from direct business savings which would flow from invention.

Thus Rae has a completely different approach from the mainstream on the source of savings. The Keynesian tradition, which began in J.S. Mill and Marshall, holds that personal savings are the most important source of increases in a nation's capital stock. From a careful examination of Rae's concept of "augmentation of capital," Gootzeit (1997) argues it is clear that Rae saw business and not personal saving as being responsible for capital formation. This is also the view of Rae's biographer R. Warren James:

> [Rae] saw clearly that individuals might increase their wealth by saving but that the *formation of capital by societies* was influenced decisively by technical progress. He disputed vigorously Adam Smith's view that a country's wealth was determined by the willingness of its inhabitants to save. On these grounds, Rae saw a legitimate role for governments in stimulating invention encouraging capital formation. [emphasis added]
>
> (James 1951: 148)

Gootzeit therefore concludes that Rae's ideas on capital formation in the short period emphasized the risk-taking behavior of businessmen who saw invention as a bold new way to increase profits, which meant that after invention took place businesses would immediately desire to raise their rate of saving and invest in the new and improved capital goods. Business saving in the presence of technical progress would be identically equal to new investment in the current period. The nearly immediate conversion of business savings into investment was not unrealistic because financial intermediation was not necessary when firms used their own net returns for expansion or even when interbusiness lending occurred.

This discussion of Rae's views on "productive savings" confirms that if we are to seek to analyze Rae from a post-Keynesian perspective it must be from the standpoint of Kalecki and not of Keynes. Kalecki appreciated as early as 1937 that publication of Keynes' *General Theory* required a completely new approach to taxation. He wrote:

> Mr. Keynes' theory gives us a new basis for the enquiry into the problems of taxation. The analysis of the incidence of various types of taxes on effective demand leads, as we shall see, to quite unexpected results, which may be of practical importance.
>
> (Kalecki 1937: 444)

Central to Kalecki's whole theoretical schema is his theory of investment. Kalecki ([1968] 1971: 171) considered three determinants of new investment decisions: (1) entrepreneurial savings; (2) the prerequisites for the reinvestment of these savings; and (3) an innovations factor. These Kaleckian determinants, we argue, correspond to Rae's conditions for investment. Kalecki's "entrepreneurial savings" correspond to Rae's "business productive savings"; Kalecki's "prerequisites for the reinvestment of savings" correspond to Rae's "accumulative principle"; and Kalecki's "innovations factor" is Rae's "inventive faculty." Where Kalecki and Rae differ is in the emphasis they gave to these conditions. In his original formulation, Kalecki rather underplayed the role of his "innovations factor," while Rae gave pride of place to his "inventive faculty."

However, Gomulka, Ostaszewski and Davies (1990) have argued that Kakecki's growth theory did not give sufficient weight to the role of innovation. Kalecki focused almost exclusively on conditions of cautious capitalism, where either investors react slowly to changes in profitability, and/or the rate of innovation-induced investment is low, and/or it is possible for firms which do not innovate to survive. A balanced-growth theory, however, requires to accommodate conditions of rash capitalism when "animal spirits" are high. Gomulka et al. have reformulated Kalecki to take account of rash capitalism, and by so doing have brought Kalecki much closer to Schumpeter and further away from Marx. In the process, they have also brought Kalecki much closer to the Scottish concern with a growing economy.

Laramie and Mair (forthcoming) have developed a dynamic post-Keynesian theory of taxation from Kalecki by linking together his theories of taxation, income determination, income distribution, the business cycle, investment, and economic growth. We use this model to analyze the effects of balanced changes in wage and profit taxation on the amplitude of the business cycle and on the long-term trend rate of growth of the economy and its stability.

The key to Kalecki's theory is his treatment of investment. He distinguishes between the returns to new investment and the returns to older equipment. Innovation increases the productivity of new investment and increases the cost of producing from existing equipment, thus causing a transfer of production from existing to new investment. This reduces the real profits from existing equipment and increases the profits of new equipment.

The introduction of taxation of profits into Kalecki's investment theory has the effect of increasing the real tax bill associated with old equipment. By means of new investment, innovation has resulted in increases in productivity which result in lower prices. This increases the real costs and lowers the real profits associated with existing equipment. The decline in real profits to existing equipment accelerates its obsolescence, and this process is given a further impetus by the introduction of a tax on profits. We therefore argue that, in a Kaleckian model, one of the effects of introducing a tax on profits will be to increase the incentive for businessmen to invest in new equipment. There will be other macroeconomic effects going on at the same time, but these do not concern us here.

Through our dynamic Kaleckian tax model, we can identify the effects of balanced changes in taxation on the amplitude of the business cycle (Laramie and Mair 1996) and on the trend growth rate of the economy and its stability (Laramie and Mair 1995). The results we derive depend on certain key parameters and the assumptions we make about the extent of tax shifting which may take place. Suffice to say that we can identify circumstances under which changes in the structure of taxation can have beneficial effects on the dynamic performance of the economy by stimulating the rate of investment, with consequential positive effects on long-term growth and stability.

Essentially, we conclude that intervention in the economy through the introduction of appropriate fiscal policies by enlightened legislators can have beneficial long-term effects, operating through the combined effects of the "accumulative principle" and the "inventive faculty." It seems to us that Rae has gone a long way, and much further than the great majority of contemporary economists, in recognizing the potential for legislators to use fiscal policy for the purpose of increasing the growth performance of the economy. In so doing, Rae has identified a number of conditions which are central to post-Keynesian tax theory.

# BIBLIOGRAPHY


Aghion, P. and Howitt, P. (1994) "Endogenous Technical Change: The Schumpeterian Perspective," in L. Pasinetti and R. M. Solow (eds), *Economic Growth and the Structure of Long-Term Development*, London: Macmillan, 118–31.

Ahmad, S. (1991) *Capital in Economic Theory*, Aldershot: Edward Elgar.

——— (1993) "John Rae (1934), Schumpeter (1911), and Amsden (1989) on Technical Change and Economic Development," working paper, Department of Economics, McMaster University, Ontario, mimeo.

——— (1996a) "Smith's Division of Labour and Rae's 'Invention': A Study of the Second Dichotomy with an Evaluation of the First," *History of Political Economy* 28(3): 441--58.

——— (1996b) "On John Rae's Controversial Contributions to Economics," *Journal of History of Economic Thought*, 18: 207–28.

Alter, M. (1982) "Carl Menger and Homo Oeconomicus: Some Thoughts on Austrian Theory and Methodology," *Journal of Economic Issues* 16: 149–60.

——— (1990) "Carl Menger and his Legacy in Economics," in B. Caldwell (ed.), *Annual Supplement to the History of Political Economy* 22: 313–48.

Arrow, K. (1962) "The Implications of Learning by Doing," *Review of Economic Studies* 29: 155–73.

Ashton, T.S. (1966) *An Economic History of England: The 18th Century*, London: Methuen.

Auerbach, A.J. and Kotlikoff, J. (1987) *Dynamic Fiscal Policy*, Cambridge: Cambridge University Press.

Auerbach, A.J., Kotlikoff, J. and Skinner, J. (1983) "The Efficiency Gains from Dynamic Tax Reform," *International Economic Review* 24: 81–100.

Backhouse, R. (1985) *A History of Modern Economics*, Oxford: Blackwell.

Bacon, F. ([1620] 1813) *Novum Organum, sive. Indicia vera de interpretatione naturae*, Oxford: Clarendon Press.

——— ([1620] 1861) *The Works of Francis Bacon*, vol. 4, *New Organon*, London: Longman.

——— ([1640] 1975) *Advancement of Learning*, ed. William A. Armstrong, Athlone Renaissance Library Series, London: Athlone Press.

Barro, R.J. and Sala-I-Martin, X. (1995) *Economic Growth*, New York: McGraw-Hill.

Bastable, C.F. ([1887] 1903) *The Theory of International Trade*, 4th ed., London: Macmillan.

Bentham, J. ([1787] 1952) "Defense of Usury," in W. Stark (ed.) *Jeremy Bentham's Economic Writings*, vol. 1, London: George Allen & Unwin, 121–207.

Birchler, U.W. (1980) *John Rae (1796–1872): Seine Theorie der wirtschaftlichen Entwicklung*, Bern: Peter Lang.

Blanchard, O.J. and Fischer, S. (1989) *Lectures on Macroeconomics*, Cambridge, Mass.: MIT Press.

Blaug, M. (1976) "Kuhn versus Lakatos or Paradigms versus Research Programmes in the History of Economics," in S. Latsis (ed.), *Method and Appraisal In Economics*, Cambridge: Cambridge University Press.

——— (1978) *Economic Theory in Retrospect*, 3d ed., Cambridge: Cambridge University Press.

Bliss, C.J. (1975) *Capital Theory and the Distribution of Income*, New York: American Elsevier.

Böhm-Bawerk, E. von ([1884] 1900) *Capital and Interest*, vol. 1, *History and Critique of Interest Theories*, 2d. ed., trans. G.D. Huncke and H.F. Sennholz, South Holland, Ill.: Libertarian Press. 3rd edition (1921) and 4th edition (1959).

——— (1889; 1959) *Capital and Interest*, vol. 2, *Positive Theory of Capital*, trans. G.D. Huncke and H.F. Sennholz, South Holland, Ill.: Libertarian Press.

Bourne. E.G. (1894) "Alexander Hamilton and Adam Smith," *Quarterly Journal of Economics* **8**: 328–44.

Bowley, M. ([1937] 1967) *Nassau Senior and Classical Economics*, London: George Allen & Unwin, reprint.

Breckenridge, R.M. (1894) *The Canadian Banking System 1817–1890*, n.p.: Toronto.

Brewer, A. (1990) "John Rae's Theory of Capital and Economic Growth," in D. Mair (ed.), *The Scottish Contribution to Modern Economic Thought*, Aberdeen: Aberdeen University Press.

——— (1991) "Economic Growth and Technical Change: John Rae's Critique of Adam Smith," *History of Political Economy*, **23**(1): 1–11.

——— (forthcoming) "An Eighteenth-Century View of Economic Development: Hume and Stewart," *European Journal of the History of Economic Thought*.

Bronfenbrenner, M. (1971) "The 'Structure of Revolutions' in Economic Thought," *History of Political Economy* **3**: 136–51.

Burgess, R. and Stern, N. (1993) "Taxation and Development," *Journal of Economic Literature* **31**: 762–826.

Burgstaller, A. (1994) *Property and Prices: Towards a Unified Theory of Value*, Cambridge: Cambridge University Press.

Cairnes, J. ([1874] 1967) *Some Leading Principles of Political Economy*, New York: Kelley, reprint.

Campbell, R.H. (1976) 'Scottish Economic History,' *Scottish Journal of Political Economy*, **23**(2): 183–92.

p 274 724Cas, A. and Rymes, T.K. (1991) *On Concepts and Measures of Multifactor Productivity in Canada, 1961–80*, Cambridge: Cambridge University Press.

Checkland, S.G. (1975) "Adam Smith and the Bankers," in A.S. Skinner and T. Wilson (eds), *Essays on Adam Smith*, Oxford: Clarendon Press, 504–23.

Chipman, J.S. (1965–6) "A Survey of the Theory of International Trade," *Econometrica* **33**(3): 477–519; **33**(4): 685–760; **34**(1): 18–76.

Coats, A.W. (1969) "Is There a 'Structure of Scientific Revolutions' in Economics?", *Kyklos* 22: 289–96.

Coleman, W.O. (1996) "How Theory Came to English Classical Economics," *Scottish Journal of Political Economy* 43(2): 207–28.

Cournot, A. ([1838] 1960) *Recherches sur les principes mathematiques de la theorie des richesses* (Researches into the Mathematical Principles of the Theory of Wealth), tr. N.T. Bacon, London: Hafner.

Daumas, M. (ed.) (1968) *Histoire general des techniques*, vol. 3, *L'Expansion du machinisme*, Paris: Presses Universitaires de France.

Davie, G.E. (1964) *The Democratic Intellect*, Edinburgh: Edinburgh University Press.

——— (1986) *The Crisis of the Democratic Intellect*, Edinburgh: Polygon.

Deane, P. (1978) *The Evolution of Economic Ideas*, Cambridge: Cambridge University Press.

Dean, R.H. and Dean, J.S. (1972) "John Rae and the Problems of Economic Development," *Review of Social Economy*, 30: 97–111.

Dimand, R.W. (1988) *The Origins of the Keynesian Revolution*. Stanford, Calif.: Stanford University Press.

——— (1992) "Political Protest and Political Arithmetic on the Niagara Frontier: Robert Gourlay's *Statistical Account of Upper Canada*," *Brock Review* 1(1): 52–63.

——— (1995) "Ricardo and International Trade Theory," Discussion Paper no. 1995–1, Department of Economics, Brock University, Ontario.

Dorfman, J. (1946) *The Economic Mind in American Civilization, 1606–1865*, New York: Viking Press.

Dorfman, J. (ed.) (1973) *Thorstein Veblen: Essays, Reviews and Reports*, New Jersey: Kelley.

Dorfman, R. (1993) "Fisher's *The Rate of Interest*, and Böhm-Bawerk's *Positive Theory of Capital*," working paper, Department of Economics, Harvard University.

Dow, A.C., Dow, S.C., Hutton, A., and Keaney, M. (1995) "Traditions in Economics: The Case of Scottish Political Economy," Glasgow Caledonian University, mimeo.

Dow, S.C. (1987) "The Scottish Political Economy Tradition," *Scottish Journal of Political Economy* 34(4): 335–48.

——— (1990) 'Beyond Dualism', *Cambridge Journal of Economics* 14: 143–57.

——— (1991) "The Post-Keynesian School," in D. Mair and A.G. Miller (eds), *A Modern Guide to Economic Thought*, Aldershot: Edward Elgar.

Drakopoulos, S.A. (1991) *Values and Economic Theory*, Aldershot: Avebury.

Eagly, R.V. (1968) "Swedish and English Bullionist Controversies," in id. (ed.) *Events, Ideology and Economic Theory: The Determinants of Progress in the Development of Economic Analysis*, Detroit: Wayne State University Press, 13–31.

Edgell, S. and Tilman, R. (1991) "John Rae and Thorstein Veblen on Conspicuous Consumption: A Neglected Intellectual Relationship," *History of Political Economy* 23(4): 731–44.

Edmonson, N. (1970) "John Rae and Liquidity Preference," *History of Political Economy* 2(2): 432–40.

Eisenstein, E.L. ([1983] 1993) *The Printing Revolution in Early Modern Europe*, New York: Cambridge University Press, reprint.

Elliott, J.E. (1983) "Schumpeter and the Theory of Capitalist Economic Development," *Journal of Economic Behavior and Organisation* 4: 277–308.

Elmslie, B. (1994) "The Endogenous Nature of Technological Progress and Transfer in Adam Smith's Thought," *History of Political Economy* 26: 649–64.

Faulkner, R.K. (1993) *Francis Bacon and the Project of Progress*, Lanham, Md.: Rowman & Littlefield.

Ferguson, A. ([1767] 1967) *An Essay on the History of Civil Society*, ed. D. Forbes, Edinburgh: Edinburgh University Press.

Ferguson, E.S. (1968) *Bibliography of the History of Technology* Cambridge, Mass.: Society for the History of Technology/MIT Press

Ferrara, F. (1856) "Prefazione," in *Biblioteca dell economista*, ser. 3, vol. 11, *Raccolta delle piu pregiateopere moderne italiane e stranglere di economia polita: R. Torrens, S. Bailey, Whately, Ricardo, G. Rae*, Torino: C. Pomba.

Fisher, I. (1897) "Note," *Yale Review*, 6: 457.

——— (1907) *The Rate of Interest*, New York: Macmillan. Reprinted (1982), with introduction by Donald Dewey, Accountancy in Transition Series, New York: Garland.

——— (1930) *The Theory of Interest, as Determined by Impatience to Spend Income and Opportunity to Invest It*, New York: Macmillan. Reprinted (1970) New York: Kelley; and (1977) Philadelphia: Porcupine Press.

Gomulka, S., Ostaszewski, A. and Daview, R.O. (1990) "The Innovations Rate and Kalecki's Theory of the Trend, Unemployment and the Business Cycle," *Economica* 57: 525–40.

Goodwin, C.D.W. (1959) "John Rae: Undiscovered Exponent of Canadian Banking," *Canadian Banker* 66(3): 110–15.

——— (1961) *Canadian Economic Thought: The Political Economy of a Developing Nation 1814–1914*, Durham, NC: Duke University Press.

Gootzeit, M. (1992) "Senior's Abstinence Theory of the Supply of Business Savings," *Journal of the History of Economic Thought* 14: 244–56.

——— (1995) "The Evolution of the Savings Concept," *History of Economic Ideas* 3(1): 71–92.

Gourlay, Robert ([1822] 1966) *Statistical Account of Upper Canada*, 3 vols, East Ardsley, Yorks: S. R. Publishers; New York: Johnson Reprint Corporation.

Gray, A. and Thompson, A. (1980) *The Development of Economic Development: An Introductory Survey* 2nd ed., London: Longman.

Guccione, A. (1993) "Ferrara's Theory of Value and the Cost of Reproduction Principle," *History of Political Economy* 25(4): 677–96.

Haberler, Gottfried von ([1933] 1936) *The Theory of International Trade*, trans. Alfred Stonier and Frederic Benham. London: William Hodge.

Hamilton, A. ([1791] 1957) "Report on Manufactures," in S. Mckee (ed.) *Papers on Public Credit, Commerce and Finance*, New York: Bobbs-Merrill, 175–276. Reprinted (1966) in H.C. Syrett and J.E. Cooke (eds) *The Papers of Alexander Hamilton*, vol. 10, New York: Columbia University Press.

Harrod, R.F. (1939) "An Essay in Economic Theory," *Economic Journal* 49: 14–33.

Heady, C. (1996) "Optimal Taxation as a Guide to Tax Policy," in M. Devereux (ed.) *The Economics of Tax Policy*, Oxford: Oxford University Press.

Hennings, K. H. (1987) "Rae, John (1796–1872)," in John Eatwell, Murray Milgate and Peter Newman (eds), *The New Palgrave: A Dictionary of Economics*, vol. 4, London: Stockton Press, 39–40.

Hicks, J.R. (1965) *Capital and Growth*, Oxford: Clarendon Press.

——— (1973) *Capital and Time*, Oxford, Clarendon Press.

——— (1989) *A Market Theory of Money*, Oxford: Clarendon Press.

Hills, R.L. (1970) *Power in the Industrial Revolution*, Manchester: Manchester University Press.

Hollander, S. (1973) *The Economics of Adam Smith*, Toronto: University of Toronto Press.

——— (1979) *The Economics of David Ricardo*, Toronto: University of Toronto Press.

——— (1987) *Classical Economics*, Oxford: Blackwell.

Hume, David ([1752] 1955) "Of Refinement in the Arts," in E. Rotwein (ed.), *David Hume: Writings on Economics*, Edinburgh: Nelson, 19–32.

——— (1955) *Writings on Economics*, ed. E. Rotwein, Edinburgh: Nelson.

——— ([1748, 1751] 1975) *Enquiries Concerning Human Understanding and Concerning the Principles of Morals*, ed. L.A. Selby-Bigge and P.H. Nidditch, Oxford: Clarendon Press.

Jaffe, W. (1976) "Menger, Jevons and Walras De-Homogenized," *Economic Inquiry* 4: 511–24.

James, R.W. (1951) "The Life and Work of John Rae," *Canadian Journal of Economics and Political Science* 17(2): 141–65.

——— (1965a) *John Rae. Political Economist: An Account of his Life and a Compilation of his Main Writings*, 2 vols, Aylesbury, Toronto: University of Toronto Press.

——— (1965b) "Life and Miscellaneous Writing," in id., *John Rae, Political Economist*, vol. 1, Aylesbury, Toronto: University of Toronto Press, 3–192.

——— (1965c) "Rae on Political Economy," in id., *John Rae, Political Economist*, vol. 1, Aylesbury, Toronto: University of Toronto Press, ch. 11. Reprinted (1990) in D. Mair (ed.), *The Scottish Contribution to Modern Economic Thought*, Aberdeen: Aberdeen University Press.

Jevons, W.S. ([1871] 1879) *The Theory of Political Economy*, 2nd edn, New York: Macmillan. 5th edn (1957) and reprinted (1965), New York: Kelley.

Joplin, T. (1832) *An Analysis and History of the Currency Question*, London: Ridgway.

Kalecki, M. (1937) "A Theory of Commodity, Income and Capital Taxation," *Economic Journal* 47: 444–50; reprinted (1971), in id. (ed.), *Selected Essays on the Dynamics of the Capitalist Economy, 1933–1970*, Cambridge: Cambridge University Press, 35–42.

——— ([1968] 1971) "Trend and the Business Cycle," in id. (ed.), *Selected Essays on the Dynamics of the Capitalist Economy, 1933–1970*, Cambridge: Cambridge University Press.

Kemp, M.C. (1960) "The Mill–Bastable Infant-Industry Dogma," *Journal of Political Economy* **68**(1): 65–7.

——— (1964) *The Pure Theory of International Trade*, Englewood Cliffs, NJ: Prentice Hall.

Keynes, J.M. (1936) *The General Theory of Employment, Interest and Money*, London: Macmillan. Reprinted (1965) in Harbinger Book Series, New York: Harcourt, Brace.

Koebner, R. (1959) "Adam Smith and the Industrial Revolution," *Economic History Review* 11: 381–91.

Kotlikoff, J. and Summers, L. (1987)"Tax Incidence," in A.J. Auerbach and M. Feldstein (eds), *Handbook of Public Economics*, vol. 2, Amsterdam: North Holland.

Krugman, P.R. (1990) *Rethinking International Trade*, Cambridge, Mass.: MIT Press.

Kuhn, T.S. (1974) "Second Thoughts on Paradigms," in F. Suppe (ed.), *The Structure of Scientific Theories*, Urbana, Ill.: University of Illinois Press, 459–82.

Laidler, D. (1981) "Adam Smith as a Monetary Economist," *Canadian Journal of Economics*, 14(2): 185–200.

——— (1991) *The Golden Age of the Quantity Theory*, Princeton, NJ: Princeton University Press.

Lakatos, I. (1970) "Falsification and the Methodology of Scientific Research Programmes," in I. Lakatos and A. Musgrave (eds), *Criticism and the Growth of Knowledge*, Cambridge: Cambridge University Press, 91–196.

Laramie, A.J. and Mair, D. (1995) "A Note on Kalecki's Theory of the Trend, Unemployment and the Business Cycle: Implications for Tax Policy," Heriot-Watt University Discussion Paper in Economics 95/3.

——— (1996) "Taxation and Kalecki's Theory of the Business Cycle," *Cambridge Journal of Economics* 20(4): 451–64.

——— (forthcoming) "A Kaleckian Theory of Taxation," *International Papers in Political Economy*.

Lehmann, Helmut (1937) *John Raes Werk, seine Philosophischen und Methodologischen Grundlagen*, Dresden: M. Dittert.

List, Friedrich ([1841] 1974) *The National System of Political Economy*, New York: Garland.

Loasby, B. (1976) *Choice, Complexity and Ignorance*, Cambridge: Cambridge University Press.

Lucas, R.E. (1993) "Making a Miracle," *Econometrica* 23(1): 251–72.

Lutz, F. (1951) *Theory of Interest*, Princeton: Princeton University Press.

Macfie, A.L. (1955) "The Scottish Tradition in Economic Thought," *Scottish Journal of Political Economy* 1(2): 81–103.

Malthus, T.R. (1803) *An Essay on the Principle of Population*, 2nd edn, London: J. Johnson.

McIvor, R.C. (1958) *Canadian Monetary, Banking and Fiscal Development*, Toronto: Macmillan.

Mair, D. (1990) "John Rae: Ugly Duckling or Black Swan?," *Scottish Journal of Political Economy* 37(3): 275–87.

——— (1991a) "Introduction," in id. (ed.), *The Scottish Contribution to Modern Economic Thought*, Aberdeen: Aberdeen University Press.

——— (ed.) (1991b) *The Scottish Contribution to Modern Economic Thought*, Aberdeen: Aberdeen University Press.

Mandeville, B. de ([1714] 1924) *The Fable of the Bees: or Private Vices, Publick Benefits*, 2 vols plus Commentary, F.B. Kaye (ed.), Oxford: Oxford University Press.

Maneschi, A. (1995) "John Rae on Capital Theory, Inventions, Trade and Infant Industries," paper presented to History of Economics Society, Vanderbilt University, Notre Dame.

——— (1998) "John Rae on Trade, Inventions and Infant Industries: A Capital-Theoretic Perspective," *History of Political Economy*, Fall.

Marshall, A. (1890) *Principles of Economics*, London: Macmillan.

Marx, K. ([1890] 1962) *Complete Works*, vol. 3, *Capital*, translated from the 3rd edition of *Das Kapital* edited by Friederich Engels, Moscow: Foreign Languages Publishing House.

Mason, R. (1981) *Conspicuous Consumption: A Study of Exceptional Consumer Behaviour*, New York: St. Martin's Press.

Menger, C. ([1871] 1950) *Principles of Economics (Grundsätze der Volkswirthschaftslehre)*, tr. J. Dingwall and B. Hoselitz, Glencoe, Ill.: The Free Press.

——— ([1883] 1963) *Problems of Economics and Sociology (Untersuchungen über die Methode der Socialwissenschaften der politischen Oekonomie insbesondere)*, ed. L. Schneider and tr. F.J. Nock, Urbana, Ill.: University of Illinois Press.

Mitchell, W.C. (1934) "The Prospect of Economics," in R.G. Tugwell (ed.), *The Trend of Economics*, New York: Knopf.

Mill, J.S. ([1848] 1965) *Principles of Political Economy with Some of Their Applications to Social Philosophy*, in J.F. Robson (ed.), *The Collected Works of John Stuart Mill*, vols 2 and 3, with introduction by V.W. Bladen, Toronto: University of Toronto Press/Routledge. 5th edition (1864), reprinted (1909), ed. W. Ashley, and (1927), London: Longman, Green, and (1969), New York: Kelley. 7th edition (1871) [last edition edited by Mill personally], 2 vols, reprinted (1920), London: Longman, Green, Reader, and Dyer.

Mixter, C. (1897) "A Forerunner of Böhm-Bawerk", *Quarterly Journal of Economics* 11: 161–90.

——— (1902) "Böhm-Bawerk on Rae," *Quarterly Journal of Economics*, 16: 385–412.

——— (ed.) (1905) *John Rae: The Sociological Theory of Capital, being a Complete Reprint of the* New Principles of Political Economy *1834*, New York: Macmillan.

Musgrave, R. (1959) *The Theory of Public Finance*, New York: McGraw-Hill.

Neill, R. (1991) *A History of Canadian Economic Thought*, London: Routledge.

Neufeld, E.P. (1972) *The Financial System of Canada: Its Growth and Development*, New York: St. Martin's Press.

Newland, D. (1992) "A 'Europe of the Regions?' The Economic Functions of Regional Government in the European Community," *Current Politics and Economics of Europe* 2(3): 187–202.

Niehans, J. (1990) *A History of Economic Theory: Classic Contributions, 1720–1980*, Baltimore, Md.: Johns Hopkins University Press.

Nurkse, R. (1967) *Problems of Capital Formation in Underdeveloped Countries*, New York: Oxford University Press.

O'Brien, D.P. (1993) *Thomas Joplin and Classical Macroeconomics: A Reappraisal of Classical Monetary Thought*, Aldershot: Edward Elgar.

Perez-Ramos, A. (1988) *Francis Bacon's Idea of Science and the Maker's Knowledge Tradition*, Oxford: Clarendon Press.

Pesciarelli, E. (1989) "Smith, Bentham and the Development of Contrasting Ideas on Entrepreneurship," *History of Political Economy* 21: 521–36.

——— (1994) "Is There a Scottish Tradition in the Economics of Innovation?," in M. Albertone and A. Masoero (eds), *Political Economy and Natural Realities*, Torino: Fondazione Luigi Einaudi, 269–88.

Pevsner, Nikolaus ([1943] 1975) *An Outline of European Architecture*, Harmondsworth: Penguin Books.

Pigou, A.C. (1903) "Some Remarks on Utility," *Economic Journal* 13: 58–68.

——— (1910) "Producers' and Consumers' Surplus," *Economic Journal* 20: 358–70.

——— (1913) "The Interdependence of Different Sources of Demand and Supply in a Market," *Economic Journal* 23: 19–24.

Pilvin, H. (1953) "Full Capacity versus Full Employment Growth," *Quarterly Journal of Economics*, 67: 545–52.

Pownall, Thomas ([1776] 1967) *A Letter from Governor Pownell to Adam Smith*, New York: Kelley.

Price, B.B. (1992) "History," in O.F. Hamouda, *John R. Hicks: The Economist's Economist*, Oxford: Blackwell, 258–86.

——— (forthcoming) "Rae on the History of Technology," in id. *John Rae (1786–1872): At the Cusp of Modern Technological History* (MS in preparation).

Prychitko, D.L. (1995) "Methodological Individualism and the Austrian School," in id. (ed.), *Individuals, Institutions, Interpretations: Hermeneutics Applied to Economics*, Aldershot: Avebury.

Rabbeno, U. (1895) *The American Commercial Policy: Three Historical Essays*, Cleveland, Oh.: Arthur H. Clark.

[Rae, J.] (1825) "Sketches of the Origin and Progress of Manufactures and of the Policy which Has Regulated Their Legislative Encouragement in Great Britain and in Other Countries; – to which will be added An Enquiry into the expediency of establishing some new branches of industry in the Canadas, more particularly with a view to the employment of women and children in the cities of Quebec and Montreal," *Canadian Review and Literary and Historical Journal* 3. Reprinted (1965) in R.W. James (ed.), *John Rae, Political Economist*, vol. 1, Aylesbury, Toronto: University of Toronto Press, 195–206.

Rae, J. (1834) *Statement of Some New Principles on the Subject of Political Economy, Exposing the Fallacies of the System of Free Trade and of Some Other Doctrines Maintained in the "Wealth of Nations,"* Boston: Hilliard, Gray. Reprinted (1964), New York: Kelley; and (1965), in R.W. James (ed.), *John Rae, Political Economist*, vol. 2, Aylesbury, Toronto: University of Toronto Press.

——— ([1853] 1943) "John Rae and John Stuart Mill, A Correspondence," *Economica*, n.s., **10**(39): 253–55.

——— (1905) *The Sociological Theory of Capital; Being a Complete Reprint of the New Principles of Political Economy, 1834*, ed. C.W. Mixter, New York: Macmillan. This is a "considerable rearrangement," which gives precedence to Book Two of the original "on the subject of capital," but "the original work in its entirety is . . . made available" (editorial preface, p. xvi).

Rebelo, S. (1991) "Long Run Policy Analysis and Long Run Growth," *Journal of Political Economy* **99**(3): 500–21.

Ricardo, David ([1817] 1821) *The Principles of Political Economy and Taxation*, 3rd edn. Reprinted (1973) and (1978), with introduction by Donald Winch, London: Dent, and New York: Dutton, Everyman's Library.

Robbins, L.C. (1968) *The Theory of Economic Development in the History of Economic Thought*, London: Macmillan.

Robinson, J. (1953–4) "The Production Function and the Theory of Capital," *Review of Economics Studies*, **21**(2): 81–106.

——— (1962) *Essays in the Theory of Economic Growth*, London: Macmillan.

Roll, E. (1973) *A History of Economic Thought*, London: Faber.

Roscher, W. ([1854] 1878) *Principles of Political Economy*, tr. of 13th edn (1877) by J.J. Lalor, New York: Henry Holt.

Rothbard, M. (1995) *Economic Thought Before Adam Smith*, Cheltenham: Edward Elgar.

Rymes, T.K. (1989) "Technical Process, Research and Development," in G. Feiwel (ed.), *Joan Robinson and Modern Economic Theory*, London: Macmillan.

Samuelson, P. (1961) "A New Theorem on Non-Substitution," in H. Hegeland (ed.), *Money, Growth and Methodology, published in Honor of Johan Akerman*, Lund Social Science Studies, no. 20, Lund: Gleerup.

——— (1966) "A Summing Up," *Quarterly Journal of Economics* **80**: 568–83.

——— (1994) "Two Classics: Böhm-Bawerk's *Positive Theory* and Fisher's *Rate of Interest*, through Modern Prisms," *Journal of the History of Economic Thought* **16**(2): 20–8.

Schama, S. (1987) *The Embarrassment of Riches: An Interpretation of Dutch Culture in the Golden Age*, London: Collins.

Schumpeter, J.A. ([1911] 1934) *The Theory of Economic Development*, tr. R. Opie, Cambridge, Mass.: Harvard University Press. Reprinted (1961), New York: Oxford University Press.

——— (1954) *History of Economic Analysis*, London: Allen & Unwin, and New York: Oxford University Press.

Semmel, B. (1970) *The Rise of Free Trade Imperialism*, Cambridge: Cambridge University Press.

Senior, N. (1836) *Outline of the Science of Political Economy*, London: Clowes. 5th edition (1863), London: Charles Griffin. 7th edition ([1938] 1951), New York: Kelley.

Shortt, A. (1896) "The Early History of Canadian Banking," *Journal of the Canadian Bankers' Association*, 4(1): 1–19. Reprinted (1964) in E.P. Neufeld (ed.), *Money and Banking in Canada*, Toronto: McClelland & Stewart, 77–90.

Shortt, A. and Doughty, A.G. (eds) (1914) *Canada and its Provinces*, vol. 4, Toronto: Brook.

Sismondi, J.C.L. Simonde de ([1819] 1827) *Nouveaux Principes d'économie Politique*, Paris: Delaunay.

Skinner, A.S. (1990) "The Shaping of Political Economy in the Enlightenment," *Scottish Journal of Political Economy* 37(2): 145–65.

Smart, W. (1910) *Economic Annals of the Nineteenth Century, vol. 2, 1821–1830*, London: Macmillan.

Smith, A. ([1759] 1966) *The Theory of Moral Sentiments*, New York: Kelley. Reprinted (1976) in D.D. Raphael and A.L. Macfie (eds), *Adam Smith: The Theory of Moral Sentiment*, Oxford: Clarendon Press.

——— ([1763] 1964) *Lectures on Police, Justice, Revenue and Arms*, ed. E. Cannan, New York: Kelley.

——— ([1776] 1937) *An Inquiry into the Nature and Causes of the Wealth of Nations*, 5th edn, ed. E. Cannan, The Modern Library Series, New York: Random House. Reissued (1976), ed. W.B. Todd, R.H. Campbell and A.S. Skinner (gen. eds), *The Glasgow Edition of the Works and Correspondence of Adam Smith*, vol. 2, Oxford: Clarendon Press.

——— ([1795] 1967) "History of Astronomy," in J. R. Lindgren (ed.) *Early Writings of Adam Smith*, New York: Kelley, 53–108. Reprinted (1980), in D.D. Raphael and A.S. Skinner (gen. eds) *The Glasgow Edition of the Works and Correspondence of Adam Smith*, vol. 3, *Essays on Philosophical Subjects*, ed. W.P.D. Wightman and J.C. Bryce, Oxford: Clarendon Press.

——— ([1795] 1980) "Of the Imitative Arts," in D.D. Raphael and A.S. Skinner (gen. eds), *The Glasgow Edition of the Works and Correspondence of Adam Smith*, vol. 3, *Essays on Philosophical Subjects*, ed. W.P.D. Wightman and J.C. Bryce, Oxford: Clarendon Press.

Smith, J.H. (1905) *The Central High School Jubilee Re-union, August 1903*, Hamilton: n.p.

Solow, R. (1956) "A Contribution to the Theory of Growth," *Quarterly Journal of Economics* 70: 65–94.

Spengler, J.J. (1959a) "Adam Smith's Theory of Economic Growth – Part II," *Southern Economic Journal* 26: 1–12.

——— (1959b) "John Rae on Economic Development: A Note," *Quarterly Journal of Economics* 73: 393–406.

——— (1960) "John Stuart Mill on Economic Development," in B.F. Hoselitz (ed.), *Theories of Economic Growth*, New York: The Free Press, 113–54.

——— (1975) "Adam Smith and Society's Decision-makers," in A.S. Skinner and T. Wilson (eds) *Essays on Adam Smith*, Oxford: Clarendon Press, 390–414.

Spiegel, H.W. (ed.) (1960) *The Rise of American Economic Thought*, Philadelphia: Chilton.

Staley, C. (1989) *A History of Economic Thought: From Aristotle to Arrow*, Oxford: Blackwell.

Steedman, I. (1985) "On the 'Impossibility' of Hicks-Neutral Technical Change," *Economic Journal* 95: 746–58.

Stern, N.A. (1992) "From the Static to the Dynamic: Some Problems in the Theory of Taxation," *Journal of Public Economics* 47(2): 273–97.

Stewart, D. ([1792] 1866) *Elements of the Philosophy of the Human Mind*, 5th edn, ed. F. Bowen, Boston: W.H. Dennet.

——— ([1795] 1980) *Account of the Life and Writings of Dr. Smith*, repr. in A. Smith, *Essays on Philosophical Subjects*, ed. W.P.D. Wightman and J.C. Bryce, Oxford: Clarendon Press.

Storch, H. (1815) *Cours d'économie politique, ou exposition des principes qui determinent la prospérité des nations*, 6 vols, St Petersbourg: A. Pluchart. Microfilm reproduction (1980), Woodbridge, Conn.: Research Publications.

Taussig, F.W. ([1931] 1964) *The Tariff History of the United States*, 8th rev. edn, New York: Capricorn.

Tavlas, G. and Aschheim, J. (1985) "Alexander Del Mar, Irving Fisher, and Monetary Economics," *Canadian Journal of Economics* 18(2): 294–313.

Torrens, R. (1815) *An Essay on the External Corn Trade*, London: J. Hatchard.

Turgot, A.R.J. ([1770] 1911) *Reflections on the Formation and the Distribution of Riches*, Economic Classic Series, New York: Macmillan.

——— ([1788] 1973) "Philosophical Review of the Successive Advances of the Human Mind," in R. Meek (tr. and ed.), *Turgot on Progress, Sociology and Economics*, Cambridge: Cambridge University Press.

Veblen, T. (1899) *The Theory of the Leisure Class*, New York: Macmillan. Reprinted (1912) and (1967), New York: Viking Press.

——— (1909) "Fisher's Rate of Interest," *Political Science Quarterly* 24, June. Reprinted (1943) in L. Ardzrooni (ed.), *Essays in our Changing Order*, New York: Viking Press, 137–41.

Viner, J. ([1937] 1965) *Studies in the Theory of International Trade*, New York: Kelley.

Walras, L. ([1874], 1954) *Elements of Pure Economics*, London: Allen & Unwin.

Wicksell, K. (1893) *Uber Wert, Kapital und Rente nach den neueren nationalökonomischen Theorien*, Jena: G. Fischer. Reissued (1954) as *Value, Capital and Rent*, tr. S.H. Frowein, London: Macmillan.

West, E. (1826) *Price of Corn and Wages of Labour*, London: J. Hatchard.

Yeager, L. (1976) "Towards Understanding Some Paradoxes in Capital Theory," *Economic Inquiry*, 14(3): 313–46.

# INDEX